CW00467692

The Complete
IDIOT'S
Guide to
QuarkXPress

by Ted Alspach

a

alpha
books

A Division of Macmillan Computer Publishing
A Prentice Hall Macmillan Company
201 West 103rd Street, Indianapolis, Indiana 46290

Dedicated to Jen, my favorite trainee of all time.

©1994 Alpha Books

All rights reserved. No part of this book shall be reproduced, stored in a retrieval system, or transmitted by any means, electronic, mechanical, photocopying, recording, or otherwise, without written permission from the publisher. No patent liability is assumed with respect to the use of the information contained herein. Although every precaution has been taken in the preparation of this book, the publisher and author assume no responsibility for errors or omissions. Neither is any liability assumed for damages resulting from the use of the information contained herein. For information, address Alpha Books, 201 W. 103rd Street, Indianapolis, IN 46290.

International Standard Book Number:1-56761-519-8
Library of Congress Catalog Card Number: 94-72329

96 95 94   8 7 6 5 4 3 2 1

Interpretation of the printing code: the rightmost number of the first series of numbers is the year of the book's printing; the rightmost number of the second series of numbers is the number of the book's printing. For example, a printing code of 94-1 shows that the first printing of the book occurred in 1994.

Screen reproductions in this book were created by means of the program Collage Plus from Inner Media, Inc., Hollis, NH.

Printed in the United States of America

Publisher
Marie Butler-Knight

Managing Editor
Elizabeth Keaffaber

Acquisitions Manager
Barry Pruett

Product Development Manager
Faithe Wempen

Development Editor
Kelly Oliver

Production Editor
Mark Enochs

Manuscript Editor
Audra Gable

Cover Designer
Scott Cook

Designer
Barbara Webster

Illustrations
Steve Vanderbosch

Indexer
Greg Eldred

Production Team
*Gary Adair, Dan Caparo, Brad Chinn, Kim Cofer, Lisa Daugherty,
David Dean, Jennifer Eberhardt, Erika Millen, Angel Perez, Beth Rago,
Bobbi Satterfield, Carol Stamile, Karen Walsh, Robert Wolf*

Special thanks to Yvette Grimes for ensuring the technical accuracy of this book.

Contents at a Glance

Contents

8 Tooling Around in QuarkXPress   57

9 A Set of Discriminating Palettes   71

Introduction

"Uh, Boss, dese people stepping off de plane don't look like dey're ready for desktop publishing."

"Just because these people are not computer wizards, does not mean they cannot learn QuarkXPress."

"Well, I guess, so, Boss, if dat's dey're fantasy, huh?"

"It's more than just a fantasy, Tattoo. It's real life. Anyone can learn QuarkXPress, and we have 60 minutes to prove it."

A Little Background Music...

There are only three certainties in life: Death, taxes, and an endless glut of *Star Trek* spin-offs. Everything else will change, be altered, or cease to exist. In the case of desktop publishing, things change so fast you'd think there was a fashion show going on next door.

QuarkXPress is what computer people (go ahead, call them geeks) say is "the leader in desktop publishing." That means that it's considered to be the best page layout program out there. For years its chief rival, PageMaker, has had the reputation of being an easy-to-learn program, and QuarkXPress has had the stigma of just being too hard. Well, QuarkXPress does *seem* harder, but you'll find that with a few tips, it *is* scads easier to learn and use than PageMaker is.

If you've just started out with QuarkXPress, you'll feel right at home with this book. If you've had QuarkXPress for awhile and absolutely hate it because it seems so darn strange, welcome to reality. QuarkXPress is strange, but in a good way. This book will show you exactly how to tame the wild QuarkXPress beast, and you'll have a good time doing it—or my name isn't Alfred M. Pinkleswitch (check the front cover quickly).

A Note to Windows Users

Because QuarkXPress is most often used on the Macintosh, the screen shots and commands used in this book are all for the Macintosh versions. This doesn't mean that you can't use this book if you're running the Windows version of QuarkXPress. Just do a little substitution. Instead of the Command key (⌘), use the Ctrl key. Instead of Option, use the Alt key. Any major discrepancies between the two versions are noted in the text.

What You'll Find in This Book

This book is divided into six sumptuous parts, each of which is split into various numbers of carefully constructed chapters. Most of the organization makes sense (at least to me), so you should have no trouble finding the topic that interests you.

This book was written so that you can read it from front to back—although that method isn't particularly necessary. If you want to know how to print something, go to the printing part (Part V) and figure out which chapter there will be the most helpful. If you're totally befuddled, seek professional help or refer to the index at the back of the book.

Terms that you don't use in normal conversation (RAM, text box, pica, and so on) are defined or explained when they first appear. However, if you miss the definition, check out the glossary in the back, which is cleverly called "Speak Like a Geek: The Complete Archive."

The following sections give you a quick rundown of the six Parts and what they contain.

Part I: Opening the Box (and Other Basic Stuff)

This Part will help you become familiar with some of the rather rudimentary page layout concepts, and then rush you into installing Quark and setting up your first document. I'll also take you on a guided tour of the QuarkXPress screen, explaining what all the junk is that's cluttering up your view.

Part II: Beyond the Typewriter

QuarkXPress is not a substitute for a typewriter, and in this Part I'll explain why that's true. You'll learn about text boxes and text, how to tell the difference between characters and paragraphs, and how to make your text look like the award-winning prose I'm sure it is. There are so many neat things you can do with text that this is the largest Part in the book, containing ten chapters of (coincidentally) text.

Part III: Picture This!

Aside from the fact that this is a rude thing to say when you're being photographed, "Picture This!" tells you how QuarkXPress handles pictures. Better yet, it tells you how to handle QuarkXPress when working with pictures.

Part IV: Laying Out the Pages

This is the meat-and-potatoes part of the book, where you learn how to control everything that goes on your pages, where the pages go, and in what order those pages appear. Control freaks should love this section.

Part V: XPressing Yourself on Paper

This Part deals with what I consider the most frustrating and annoying thing in QuarkXPress: printing. Unfortunately, if you are unable to print, QuarkXPress is about as useful as that screen saver Joe-Bob put on your system that has crickets jumping all over your screen.

Part VI: XTra Goodies

This Part tells you about XTensions and troubleshooting, two topics that clearly fell within no other part—so they got one of their own.

About the Seedy ROM

My publisher wouldn't go for it, so instead we've included a CD-ROM that is stuffed full of tutorials, free XTensions, and XTension demos, as well as a few typefaces for your XPress pleasure. Just pop the CD-ROM in your CD-ROM player and open it. If you don't have a CD-ROM player for your computer, now is a good time to get one.

Running the Tutorials

Before you run the tutorials, make sure you have QuickTime installed and that you have a minimum of 5MB available. You don't need to run QuarkXPress to view the tutorials. Set your monitor to thousands or millions of colors if you can, and turn up the volume.

The tutorial program is fairly simple to use. The tutorials are organized like the book, and by clicking on the tutorial's title you access it. When the tutorial is running, remove the cursor from the center area or it will flicker annoyingly. You can always press **Esc** to end the tutorial instantly.

What Those Boxed Notes Mean

In the course of reading this book, you'll see several little gray boxes with all sorts of funky headings. They contain information that are side notes to the text. You can read them, ignore them, or go through the book page by page and color them in with a burnt sienna crayon. (I've already done that with my copy.)

These boxes contain information about areas where you might run into a pinch of trouble. Certain things happen in QuarkXPress that are obviously a conscious work of the devil. These boxes tell you how to deal with those things—as well as how to avoid them.

These boxes contain terms or concepts that only computer geeks (yuck) or Quarkheads (cool) need to know. At the end of the book, there is a compilation (called "Speak Like a Geek: The Complete Archive") of all the terms in these boxes and more.

These boxes contain keyboard shortcuts and show the quickest way to accomplish a task. The more of these you know, the more you'll like using QuarkXPress. I encourage you to read the E-Z boxes; they'll help speed you along in your quest to be a QuarkXPress guru.

TECHNO NERD TEACHES...

These boxes contain information on such high-brow topics as four-color vs. spot color trapping rules, how to use another program's auxiliary dictionary, and what Einstein really meant with all that silly relativity business. Only read these sections when your brain is up to it.

Also, anytime that you see two or more words separated by → (such as File→Quit), the first word is the menu that you should select, and the second word is the command or item within that menu that you should select.

Why Ted Alspach Wrote This Book...

...and *not* Alfred M. Pinkleswitch. Well, for starters, QuarkXPress is one of my three favorite programs of all time, both for Macintosh and Windows. Of course, I'm talking about productive programs, so that rules out the mild obsession I have with Prince of Persia (1 & 2), X-Wing, and F/A-18 Hornet. It may be hard to believe, but I actually enjoy using QuarkXPress (pause for gasps and mutters of disbelief). And once you master QuarkXPress (which shouldn't be too long from now, since you bought this book), you'll enjoy using it too.

I've spent the last several years training new users in QuarkXPress—the majority of whom really didn't want to learn it. And when you're forced to learn something, it makes learning a whole lot harder than it has to be. So I developed some different teaching techniques that I've incorporated here and in the tutorials on the CD-ROM that's in the back of this book (that's what that silver thing is!). Because this is only a book, I can't use the electroshock therapy I'm so familiar with, but I think the gist will come through anyway.

In my spare time I've been known to write books on other, lesser programs, as well as some noncomputer topics (gasp!). When I'm not spending my spare time writing, I'm busy running the Southwest's leading desktop publishing and training company.

How to Tell Me How Much You Love This Book

I eagerly await and reply to all correspondence from my readers, especially if it is sent via electronic mail through America Online or over the Internet. As far as being available for seminars, mall openings, and bar mitzvahs, write me and I'll check my schedule.

Here's the lowdown:

On America Online:
screen name "Toulouse"

via the Internet:
toulouse@aol.com

Acknowledgments

In writing a book like this one, I would have to be a complete idiot to imagine that I could do everything myself (yes, the working title of the book *was* "Ted's Guide to QuarkXPress"). That, of course, is not the case, and if it weren't for the assistance of several key persons, this book would still be sitting in my word processor, not in your greedy little paws.

The most important thanks go to Carol Garling, for providing the spark which lit the fire that got me moving on convincing the wonderful people at Alpha Books to publish this book. Without Carol's timely suggestion (or was it an order?), this book would have sat, unread, amidst unfinished screenplays and comic books, where it just wouldn't have the same effect that it does now.

Thanks go to Toulouse, Pyro, Lucy, and Linus, who all had to live with me through an incredible deaddot (it was too short to be a deadline), and resisted that ever-present urge to kill me. Thanks bunches, kids.

Special thanks and a nine club flash (okay, a five club flash) to Bill Giduz and the IJA for permitting me to use festival newsletter material for many of the examples you see in this book and on the CD-ROM. And a late thanks to Bill for his patience in working with me on a measly PowerBook 100 to do a complex newsletter every day of the convention. If you want to juggle for fun or professionally someday, you can get information on becoming a member of the International Juggler's Association by writing to: Box 218, Montague, MA 01351.

Thanks, of course, to my first QuarkXPress mentor, Lou Ann Hallman, who proved to me time and time again that QuarkXPress was indeed worth learning (and who taught me that if I didn't want to get fired, I would learn it, and learn it well). At that time QuarkXPress was at version 2, and I still don't think it wasn't worth learning then (what with parent/child picture boxes and more printing problems than a suffering Linotronic 200 should have had to deal with at the time).

No set of thank you's would be complete without a round of applesauce for Rob Teeple and Teeple Graphics, for having so much faith in my QuarkXPress knowledge oh-so-long-ago that he called upon me to train new QuarkXPress users.

Thanks to Jim Wiegand at the XChange, who supplied me with most of the great XTensions and XTension demos supplied with the book on the enclosed CD-ROM.

Special thanks to Lori Mercier, head of QuarkXPress tech support, who answered many of my questions and was a lot of help.

Thanks to all the people at Alpha Books, especially my tireless editor, Kelly Oliver, who transformed this book from mere text (most of it grammatically incorrect) to an exciting reading and learning experience. Thanks to Barry Pruett for calling me four times while I was in Ixtapa. And thanks to all the other Alpha Books people involved with this project: Faithe Wempen, Seta Frantz, Heather Stith, Mark Enochs, Audra Gable, and San Dee Phillips.

On Your Mark...

By now you've figured out that my name isn't Alfred M. Pinkleswitch, and you'll soon find yourself in the midst of many other strange goings-on once you have enterd the world of desktop publishing.

You are about to enter the mysterious world of QuarkXPress. Just think, in a short time you too will be able to create full color, professional magazines, books, stationery, business cards, posters, newsletters, advertisements, brochures, and anything else you can possibly print.

Gentlemen (and gentlewomen), start your computers...

Part I
Opening the Box
(and Other Basic Stuff)

These lovely chapters are the best way to avoid the dreaded QuarkXPress Trauma Syndrome that afflicts millions of people every year. I'll take you slowly through the basics, from why QuarkXPress has a capital "P" to the difference between the toolbox and the Measurements palette (one is tall and skinny, the other is flat and wide—I forget which is which just now).

For these first eight chapters, you don't even have to type anything. You can read most of these chapters happily in your backyard hammock, as your devoted spouse rushes another iced tea to you.

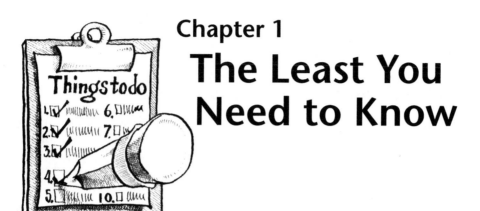

Chapter 1
The Least You Need to Know

The next few pages contain a lot of really important information about QuarkXPress—and quite a few terms that don't mean squat to you at this point. Skim through this chapter now, and then review it occasionally as you read the rest of the book. When you finish the rest of the chapters, come back and read it again; it'll make more sense to you and be very helpful.

10. QuarkXPress is *page layout* software.

I'll repeat that for emphasis: QuarkXPress is a page layout program. Not a word processor, a drawing package, or an image-editing program. The products of those programs come together in the page layout program.

The best way to approach QuarkXPress is to realize that it is the final step in your journey in desktop publishing. You've created breathtaking illustrations using drawing software like Adobe Illustrator or Aldus FreeHand. You've edited photos with Adobe Photoshop. You've typed in hundreds of articles in Microsoft Word or WordPerfect. You then put them all together in QuarkXPress for an award-winning publication.

9. QuarkXPress is easier to use than PageMaker.

No matter what anyone tells you, at this stage in desktop publishing (with QuarkXPress at version 3.3 and PageMaker at 5.0), QuarkXPress is easier to learn, use, and master. It wasn't always this way, but it is now. As an added

bonus, QuarkXPress is actually a slightly *better* product than PageMaker.
I use both; I know. (Remember, you heard it here first.)

8. Know the difference between contents and items.

This is one of the most critical concepts to fully understand when using
QuarkXPress. Everything is either an *item* or the *contents* (inside stuff) of an
item. (See Chapter 8 for more information.)

Table 1.1 lists several elements and shows the category into which they
fall:

Table 1.1   Contents and Items

Content-related	Item-related
Content tool	Item tool
Style menu	Item menu
Text	Text boxes
Pictures	Picture boxes
Left side of Measurements Palette	Right side of Measurements Palette
Line tools	Lines

7. Select before doing.

Before you can change, add, or delete something in QuarkXPress, you need
to tell the program *what* you want to work with. You do this by selecting
something with either the Item tool or Content tool depending on the
function you want to perform. The Item tool can select more than one
item at a time; the Content tool cannot select multiple items. (See Chapter 10.)

6. Change your preferences when you have no documents open.

There are several "default" settings you probably won't care for in
QuarkXPress. You can change most of them using the Preferences

submenu of the Edit menu. The catch is that when you change these preferences, most of the changes affect only the active open document. The next time you create a document, you have to make the changes again. This gets old really fast.

To avoid this potential problem, make permanent preference changes when you don't have any documents open. Whatever changes you make affect all documents you create from that point on, but do not affect any documents you created before the changes were made. (You can add these preferences to previously created documents, but you would have to open each particular document and make the changes.) See Chapter 30 for more details.

5. Always uncheck the "four boxes" in the Page Setup dialog box.

The four boxes in the Page Setup dialog box are Font Substitution, Text Smoothing, Graphics Smoothing, and Faster Bitmap printing. If you uncheck these boxes, your documents print faster, and you can avoid numerous printing problems.

Yes, Virginia, these boxes are always checked, and you need to uncheck them each time you want to print. It is a pain, but it is something you need to deal with. See Chapter 32 for more information.

4. Save Save Save Save Save Save Save Save Save.

The more you save, the less likely it is that you will have to redo work because your computer freezes up on you or because Junior thought it would be fun to take all those wires out of the wall under your desk (or whatever).

The law of saving is as follows:

> *The amount of work you do without saving is directly proportional to the chance of your computer crashing.*

If you save every five minutes, you will lead a happy, fairly uneventful QuarkXPress life. Chapter 5 tells you all you need to know about saving.

3. Use the Content tool to type and edit text.

You must have the Content tool highlighted when typing new text or changing existing text. The Item tool just won't do it. Chapter 8 talks about all the different tools available in QuarkXPress.

2. Most people actually enjoy using QuarkXPress once they get the hang of it.

You will eventually look forward to working with QuarkXPress for page layout even more than you do most other software programs for your computer. It might be hard to believe, but with the helpful tips in this book, you should be able to use the program competently in a matter of days—and begin producing those award-winning publications I keep talking about.

There's even a QuarkXPress users group, which was established several years ago and is publicized as a gathering of QuarkXPress users who enjoy using QuarkXPress. Actually, they are a high tech dependency group of QuarkXPress junkies. They are living proof that using QuarkXPress can be an addiction. Check with QuarkXPress to find out if there is a group in your area, or ask at a local Macintosh User Group to see if they know of a QuarkXPress user group.

1. When writing or typing QuarkXPress, capitalize the Q, the X, and the P—and don't break it into two words.

This seems silly, but nothing makes you look like an amateur more than misspelling the name of the product. Those "in the know" will chuckle, giggle, and probably ridicule those who use the common (and totally unacceptable) spelling "Quark Express."

Chapter 2

And You Thought Quark Was Just a Bartender

In This Chapter

- ☛ Understanding the concept of page layout
- ☛ A briefing on the differences between word processing and page layout
- ☛ QuarkXPress vs. PageMaker: The never ending battle

You've taken the plunge. A shrink-wrapped gray and red container sits on your desk next to the computer, daring you to open it. You're still out of breath from hoisting the QuarkXPress box (which undoubtedly contains lead weights in excess of several hundred pounds) from the floor to your desk, and you give the package the old evil eye.

The box doesn't stir, but you know it's teasing you, trying to intimidate you. "What have I gotten myself into?" you ask yourself.

In a sudden burst of courage, the likes of which you haven't felt since you asked Theresa Jean to the prom thirty years ago, you rip the shrink wrap off the box and pull back the packaging to reveal several thousand manuscript pages and a small stack of floppy disks. Wading through the materials you discover one *User Guide*, one *Reference Manual*, a *Tutorial*, and a *Getting Started* booklet. In addition, there is a shrink-wrapped package discussing a foreign language: EfiColor.

Depression sets in. Your only alternatives at this point are to beg your physician for an anti-depressant or to find some easier way to learn QuarkXPress. So you bought this book, which will inevitably save you thousands of dollars in prescription fees. It will also save you from the rigors of rehab several years from now when you would be up to four or five happy little pills a day.

TECHNO NERD TEACHES...

For the non Trek-watchers, Quark is the name of the Ferengi bartender on "Star Trek: Deep Space Nine." He was named not after this page layout software, but after that tiniest part of matter, the quark. Coincidentally, Quark, Inc., was named after that little piece of matter as well. Even more coincidentally, both the character and the company are made up of countless quarks. See your 6th grade science teacher if you want to know more about quarks.

Getting a Grip on Page Layout

What, exactly, is *page layout*, after all? It is preparing everything that goes onto a printed page—including text, illustrations, and photographs—and making it appear just right. Almost every piece of printed matter that is produced today is created with some type of page layout software or an older method of producing pages. For the most part, newspapers, magazines, books, posters, brochures, business cards, and billboards are all designed with page layout software.

Traditional Printing Methods and Desktop Publishing

The printing process is undergoing a dramatic change in the way that printed media is produced. Until the late sixties, the majority of printed matter was created by manipulating letters, numbers, and symbols in individual lead rectangles to create words, sentences, and paragraphs.

Then, *phototypesetting* gained widespread popularity because more and more systems were created that could electronically produce type automatically in user-specified column widths. At that time, the process consisted of creating columns of type, pasting those columns of type onto an artboard, adding artwork, photographing the artboard, adding photographs to the resulting negative film (stripping), touching up the film (opaquing), creating a blueline for customer inspection, making necessary corrections, and then "burning" a plate. That plate would then be fastened to the printing press, and prints were created.

The film output (negatives) is created by a printer called an **imagesetter**. Using a photographic process, a laser burns images (teeny tiny dots that make up various patterns and shapes) onto the film. The film is then processed by running it through various chemicals (all of which smell terrible) until an image appears as a perfect negative of the computer-designed pages.

With desktop publishing on today's state-of-the-art systems, everything is created on the computer. The customer looks at the prepared manuscript either on the computer screen or on a low-cost laser printout, and the plate is created right from the computer! Not all companies have these advanced systems, but most printshops can at least use an *imagesetter* to create complete perfect negatives with type, graphics, and photos in place. Printing plates are then burned with these negatives.

Comparing Word Processing to Page Layout

QuarkXPress is considered page layout software because it can be used to combine all of the elements on a page: type, illustrations, and photographs. Five years ago, that would have been a satisfactory definition, but nowadays most of the high-end word processors (Microsoft Word, WordPerfect, and Macwrite Pro, for example) have similar capabilities.

But of course, as word processing software has evolved, so has page layout software. Page layout software can place text anywhere, at any angle, in multiple columns, and it can print *four-color separations*, splitting illustrations and photographs into the four process colors automatically.

Four-color process is a term used by printers, publishers, and designers to define a print job that consists of four runs through one printing press (once each for magenta, cyan, yellow, and black) or one run on a four-color press. These four colors combine to create a whole spectrum of colors, creating photorealistic photos in full color.

These features themselves make page layout software substantially more powerful than a word processing program. But these features really just scratch the surface of the program's capabilities.

Page layout software is the final stop for all the objects that have been created elsewhere on your computer. For instance, let's say you're creating a brochure. You have entered and formatted text in Microsoft Word, drawn and designed illustrations in Adobe Illustrator, and scanned and touched up photographs in Adobe Photoshop. You have all the pieces finished, and now you have to put them together. You bring them into QuarkXPress (or some other page layout program), where you can organize them with ease.

What Does QuarkXPress Do?

Sometimes I think it might be easier to say what QuarkXPress *doesn't* do, since it does so many things. As you've learned, QuarkXPress mainly combines existing elements, such as text, illustrations, and photographs. However, the *cool* thing about QuarkXPress is that you can manipulate these elements in almost any way known to mankind, including resizing, rotating, moving, and even skewing (moving the top but not the bottom or vice versa).

QuarkXPress for Macintosh/QuarkXPress for Windows

There are two versions of QuarkXPress: one for the Macintosh and one for IBM-compatibles that run Microsoft Windows. The two versions look the same, work the same, cost the same, and even smell the same (I checked). For the first time ever in the history of QuarkXPress, users of the Windows version (3.3) and the Macintosh version (3.3) can exchange files with ease. Until this point in time, it was difficult and sometimes impossible to take files from one platform to another. Now, exchanging files between platforms is a snap, provided your system has software that enables it to read the other system's disks.

Aldus PageMaker vs. QuarkXPress

Undoubtedly, before you purchased QuarkXPress, you talked it over with friends and/or co-workers; and undoubtedly, some heartily recommended QuarkXPress, and some recommended Aldus PageMaker. In fact, some of them probably told you horror stories of how much more difficult it was to learn one program than to learn the other. You probably heard the "Do yourself a favor, buy…" phrase more times than you care to recall.

Do these people know something you don't? Not really. Prejudice is alive and well in the world of desktop publishing, and there is plenty of discrimination out there. The general attitude I've noticed is that people who have used PageMaker for a few years are *extremely* reluctant to switch, and they start making up reasons why PageMaker is better than QuarkXPress. Also, people who have used QuarkXPress for a few years think that PageMaker is inferior and "beneath" them.

The truth? Well, at this point in time, Quark does have a slightly better product overall. It is faster, its files are smaller, and it is actually easier to learn than PageMaker (I'm not making this up). PageMaker's biggest advantage over QuarkXPress until 1994 was that PageMaker files that were saved in IBM format could be opened on a Mac, and Mac PageMaker files could be opened on an IBM-compatible PC. However, QuarkXPress now does this as well.

The most common fallacy involving QuarkXPress is that it is more difficult to learn than PageMaker. That is not the case anymore. With past versions (version 2.12 of QuarkXPress, version 3 of PageMaker), I would agree that was true. But while each package has become more feature-laden, only PageMaker has become more complex.

There are numerous differences between the two programs. For example, PageMaker has something called a "Story Editor," which is a very basic built-in word processor that enables you to enter and edit text quickly.

I use both products but end up using QuarkXPress far more than PageMaker (although I learned PageMaker and used it exclusively for several years before I used QuarkXPress).

Point the Way to .1, .2, and .3

Why the silly numbers after 3 in the version number? Upgrading software programs using decimal points is all the rage in desktop publishing. QuarkXPress went to 3.0 in 1990. Version 3.3 was published in 1994. Four years, and only a tiny .3 change?

Well, Quark is a little different from the rest of the software industry in that they don't have a new version for every piece of software they put out. So when 2.12 turned into 3.0, Quark decided that there wouldn't be a major version upgrade for quite some time. Instead, they have created several *interim* upgrades, starting with 3.0.1 and going to 3.1, 3.1.1a, 3.1.1b, and 3.1.1c. Then 3.2 arrived, followed shortly by 3.2.1. Finally, we have 3.3, which will undoubtedly get some letter or other number attached to it.

Cross-platform refers to being able to take a file generated on one system, such as a Macintosh, and open it on a different kind of system, like a PC running Windows.

What do these ridiculous numbers mean? Not much. The only thing that is constant is that the higher the version number, the more recent the version. Usually, the version numbers follow this standard: an upgrade to a whole number, like to 4.0, would mean significant changes to the program. A .1 change is a much lesser change, usually dealing with several feature additions. And a change of (this is weird) ..1 is usually a maintenance upgrade, shipped free of charge, to correct problems found in the previous version. Letters? Well, few companies use letters, but they are almost always very minor upgrades, often having to do with compatibility issues for different equipment.

The changes in QuarkXPress from 3.1 to 3.2 in the spring of 1993 were impressive, but limiting. The changes from 3.3 were less impressive, but solved the *cross-platform* problems of old.

The Least You Need to Know

QuarkXPress is better than PageMaker. Now when your PageMaker friends (or, more likely, PageMaker enemies) ask, "Where does it say that QuarkXPress is better than PageMaker?" you can show them this paragraph. Or better yet, when you are finished reading this book you can print out an official-looking press release stating that an independent testing agency has found that QuarkXPress (while harder to capitalize) is easier and more useful than PageMaker.

- ☞ QuarkXPress is page layout software, which means it is a program where words and pictures come together.

- ☞ It doesn't matter if you have a PC or a Mac, QuarkXPress runs the same on both systems. You can even transfer files from one system to another with ease.

Chapter 3
Installing the QuarkXPress Monster

In This Chapter

☛ How to install QuarkXPress the easy way

☛ System requirements for QuarkXPress

☛ Installation options

All those floppy disks. There must be millions of them (actually, there are seven, but it *looks* like a whole heckuvalot more). And as if dealing with all those disks isn't confusing enough, Quark is one of the few companies that uses an installer made in-house to confuse and bewilder all.

As a warning before you start, remember that QuarkXPress' installation can take up to 10MB of your hard disk space. Make sure you have even more than that available.

For best results on a Macintosh, restart it with extensions turned off (press Shift until you see a message that matter-of-factly states **Extensions Off**) before you install QuarkXPress. Failing to do so could cause a number of problems, especially if you have any virus detection software like Disinfectant or SAM running on your system.

What You Need System-Wise

QuarkXPress requires System 6.0.5 or later on a Mac, Windows 3.1 or later on a PC, and at least 3MB of *RAM* available for the program. This minimum configuration makes it possible to run QuarkXPress on the low end of Macintosh systems and most 386 PCs.

The QuarkXPress application takes up 2.5MB of hard disk space, and other necessary files (spelling dictionary, miscellaneous XTensions, and so on) take up an additional 3MB. If you have any additional XTensions or other supplementary files, over 5MB of drive space could be used.

What You *Want* System-Wise

Of course, working in QuarkXPress 3.3 on a Mac Plus or a 386/20 PC is not exactly the ideal solution. In fact, QuarkXPress won't even crawl along at this point (it sort of oozes). The image of the clock/hourglass cursor will become permanently embedded in your skull if you even try to do the simplest activities in QuarkXPress on a machine as limited as this.

RAM (Random Access Memory) is memory that your computer uses for storing the currently running applications (programs) and files (documents). The more RAM you have, the more programs and documents—and the bigger programs and documents—you can open at one time.

My recommendation is that you get at least a Mac II series or 486/20 PC computer, or something even faster. Getting a PowerMac or Pentium-based PC for QuarkXPress is a good idea if you are planning to do complex, long, or four-color documents. The power of these processors will speed along the software, allowing you to get more work done in less time.

In addition, you can never have too much RAM. If you have lots of memory, you are able to create and open bigger and bigger files, keep more documents open at once, scroll faster, draw faster, and so on.

What Happens When You Install the Software

There are many things to do and see while you install QuarkXPress. This section is split up into small, easy-to-digest chunks that explain what goes on during the actual installation process.

To start the installation program on a Macintosh, first put Disk 1 in the drive. Then double-click on the **Installer** icon in the drive's window. To start the installation program in Windows, first insert Disk 1 in the drive. Then pull down Program Manager's **File** menu and select **Run**. In the text box, enter **a:\install** or **b:\install** (depending on which drive the disk is in), and click **OK** or press **Enter**.

So Many Questions: The Pre-Installation Survey

If this is the first time you have installed QuarkXPress on your computer, you will have to fill out an on-line questionnaire (similar in complexity to a 1040 tax form) before the software even begins to load onto your hard drive. The answers to these questions are recorded to the floppy disk called "User Registration," which you send to Quark in a prepaid floppy disk mailer.

The important questions in the questionnaire are on the first screen. The other screens are full of questions that can be ignored; there is no requirement that you answer every question. The tech support people never actually see the information that you enter anyway. (If you don't send in your User Registration disk with the necessary information on it, and you call for technical support, Quark will pretty much question your very existence—let alone your claim of owning a real copy of the software.)

MB Both RAM and hard disk space are measured in megabytes, commonly referred to in print as MB. (Don't ever say "em-bee" though; always say megabytes. Or if you want to sound like you're really on the cutting edge, call MBs "megs.")

XTensions Files that reside in the QuarkXPress folder, which add features, capabilities, and functions that weren't part of the original program. XTensions are discussed in Chapter 35.

Where the Files Are '94

Boatloads of files are loaded onto your hard drive when you install QuarkXPress, and they are loaded into a variety of different places. Most files will be placed in a folder/directory called "QuarkXPress Folder" or "QUARK," which you create by choosing the New Folder/Directory option when the Installer asks you where to place the application files.

What the Options Mean

When installing QuarkXPress, you are presented with a number of options to choose from, as shown below. (In QuarkXPress 3.2 and older, the installation screens look a little different.)

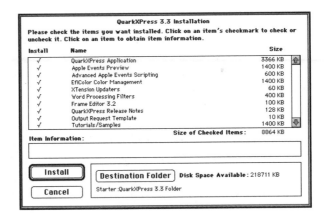

The QuarkXPress 3.3 Installation dialog box.

Here is a brief summary of the options in the Installation dialog box:

Make sure you don't lock (write-protect) either the Program Disk 1 or the User Registration Disk. Doing so will disable the Installer. To unlock the disks, make sure the little plastic tab covers the hole in the corner of each disk.

QuarkXPress Application   This installs the program itself.

Apple Events Preview (Mac only)   Checking this box installs files needed for QuarkXPress to work with other open applications and instantly update information between them.

Advanced Apple Events Scripting (Mac Only)   This method makes it possible for QuarkXPress to use AppleScript—a scripting language from Apple that enables advanced users to automate repetitive, complex tasks like macros.

EfiColor Color Management   This installs a special system for matching colors of the original objects to the final printed page. If you aren't going to be doing color work, you don't need EFIColor.

XTension Updaters   These are files that will update certain third party XTensions that you had in a previous version of QuarkXPress.

Word Processing Filters   Always check this option, as it enables you to open files from most word processors. You may remove any of the several XTensions that are automatically installed after the installation.

Frame Editor 3.2   This handy little utility enables you to create custom frames for picture boxes and text boxes (see Chapter 27 for more information on these features). The only problem with this program is that it can easily create complex frames that can't be printed on a desktop laser printer.

QuarkXPress or ASCII Release Notes   Tells QuarkXPress to install a TeachText file that contains corrections to the manuals and information on which upgrade features QuarkXPress doesn't work with.

Output Request Template   Installs a QuarkXPress file that's set up as an output request template used to instruct your service bureau on which fonts and pictures are included, as well as other important information about the file.

Tutorials and Samples   Installs several tutorial and sample files that are used with the QuarkXPress tutorial manual.

Installing QuarkXPress 3.2 or an Older Version

The Installer on QuarkXPress 3.2 and older asks you if you want the same things, but in a different way. Here are the different options:

Cool Blends   Installing this XTension gives QuarkXPress the capability to print all sorts of really nifty gradients within picture boxes and text boxes in QuarkXPress.

If the Cool Blends XTension is installed on your system and you save a file that uses its features, you will not be able to open that file on a system that does not have the Cool Blends XTension installed.

Balloon Help (Mac Only)   This activates Balloon Help for QuarkXPress so that when Balloon Help is turned on in the upper right of the screen (Macintosh System 7 users only), little messages will pop up all over QuarkXPress, telling you about every menu option, palette, tool, and object in QuarkXPress.

Balloon help is great for about five minutes, and then it becomes the most annoying thing you've ever seen. My advice is, if you want to see what Balloon Help is, install it, run QuarkXPress with it on, and look at everything until you are really bored (remember, this won't take long). Then quit QuarkXPress, open the folder where QuarkXPress is located, and throw out the file called "Balloon Help"—which should save you about 1/4MB of disk space.

Pantone Colors   This XTension is an installation must. It enables you to pick Pantone colors, which are the industry standard for printing colors. Although Pantone colors are numbered with a ridiculous, usually annoying system, they are still the most common and best way to ensure that the colors you would like in your document match the output.

XPress Dictionary   This is one of those files you just gotta have. It contains the spelling dictionary, which enables you to do spel chexs in QuarkXPress. It also contains hy-phen-a-tion in-for-ma-tion, which is invaluable in QuarkXPress.

XPress Help   Like most software programs' on-screen help, this is a misnomer. XPress Help is not of any use when, for instance, you are having trouble printing something, or you are having a hard time selecting something. Instead, it is more of an on-screen reference guide. I have found it useful on occasion, though.

Egad! Where'd All *These* Options Come from?

You would think the Installer would now be able to go on its merry way—installing your program and only bothering you to ask for the occasional floppy disk, right? No, the good folks at Quark have decided to throw you a loop. They wait until after you have inserted the second floppy disk to present you with a screen so ominous-looking that some frightened users-to-be may just click the Cancel button and never use QuarkXPress at all. The box looks like the figure on the following page.

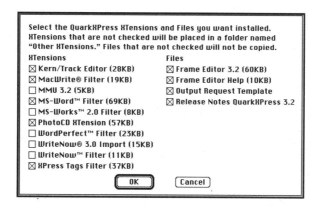

The More Options dialog box (QuarkXPress 3.2 and older).

Yikes! It isn't as scary as it looks, though. Most of the files on the left are self explanatory, and the ones on the right are all fairly basic. In the XTensions column, there are a few XTensions that need some sort of explanation. So, here goes:

Kern/Track Editor   This XTension allows you to really make a mess of things in regards to the spacing of the letters and numbers in your fonts. Don't install this unless you understand the kerning and tracking concepts (discussed in Chapter 15) in depth.

MMU 3.2   This one fooled me the first time I saw it. Being the computer guy I am, I assumed this acronym stood for "Memory Management Unit." Nope. It means "Multiple Master Utility." If you don't have Multiple Master fonts (or you don't know what they are, in which case you probably don't have any), leave this option unchecked.

PhotoCD XTension   This XTension enables you to bring PhotoCD images directly from PhotoCD format into your system. Only check this if you have a CD-ROM drive and use photo CDs.

All the other XTensions should be checked or unchecked depending if you use those particular file types. For instance, if you have Microsoft Word on your system, check the MS Word filter. This XTension enables you to *import* and *export* text files created with Microsoft Word. If a client, co-worker, or friend has WriteNow, you may want to check that option as well, so that you will be able to import and export those text files, and so forth. The import/export functions are based on the filters you have on your system for importing, and on the choices QuarkXPress has for exporting. Not all word processing programs are supported.

SPEAK LIKE A GEEK

Import   QuarkXPress will bring text that was originally created in another program directly into a QuarkXPress document.

Export   You can save a QuarkXPress story in a particular word processor's format and then open it up in that word processor.

One of the nice things about these options is that if you screw up and uncheck something that should have been checked (say you've forgotten that Aunt Betilda uses Macwrite), the XTension will still be installed in your QuarkXPress folder. However, it will be placed in a special folder called "Disabled XTensions," so it can be retrieved at any time and put into the main QuarkXPress folder without having to reinstall the software.

The files on the right side of the dialog box, on the other hand, are either installed or not installed depending on whether the boxes are checked. I covered the options' descriptions earlier in this chapter.

The Least You Need to Know

So now you know what QuarkXPress is and how to install it. Yeah, there's a little more to it, but I don't want to depress you too much at this time. Besides, at this point, the program is installed and ready to go. Life is sweet.

- ☞ On a Macintosh, you must have at least 4MB RAM, System 6.0.5, a Mac Plus or better, and a minimum of 5.5MB of hard drive space available in order to install QuarkXPress.

- ☞ On a PC, you must have a 386, 5MB RAM, and a hard drive with 5MB of available space to install QuarkXPress. And, of course, you also need Windows 3.1 or better.

- ☞ To install QuarkXPress for Macintosh, insert Disk 1 and double-click on the **Installer** icon.

- ☞ To install QuarkXPress for Windows, insert Disk 1, select **File Run**, enter **a:\install**, and then click **OK**.

Chapter 4
Starting QuarkXPress for the First Time

In This Chapter

- ☛ Starting up QuarkXPress
- ☛ Creating a new document
- ☛ Quitting QuarkXPress
- ☛ Using the keyboard versus the mouse

In QuarkXPress, unlike most other software packages, there is much to know before you even see the page you plan to be working on. In fact, a complete understanding of the New Document dialog box (discussed shortly) will save you hours, maybe even weeks of frustration.

Let's go ahead and start up the program so you can see what all this blather about dialog boxes and such means. Then, when you've got QuarkXPress on your screen, we can talk about how you use the program. Shall we?

Firing Up QuarkXPress

Starting QuarkXPress is easy: a few clicks and you're there. Do one of these things:

- ☞ On a Mac, find the QuarkXPress folder and open it. Inside there will be several files. Find the red/gray one that says "QuarkXPress 3.3" and double-click on it.

- ☞ In Windows, find the QuarkXPress group icon and double-click on it. From the QuarkXPress group window, find the QuarkXPress 3.3 program icon and double-click on it.

Depending on the speed of your system and the number of XTensions you have installed, it could take as little as 20 seconds or as long as three minutes for QuarkXPress to start. First the QuarkXPress "splash screen" appears, telling you who this copy of QuarkXPress is licensed to; then you see various XTensions in the lower left corner of that screen.

Eventually, the toolbox appears on the left side of the splash screen. When it does, that means the startup is complete. The splash screen goes away only if you click on it or choose an option from the menu bar.

Staring Blankly at the Splash Screen

If you've used QuarkXPress before and played around in it, there is the possibility that the toolbox won't appear the next time you try to start the program, and you will have that sinking feeling that so often accompanies system crashes. Actually, what has probably happened is that before you last quit the program, you closed the toolbox (usually accidentally).

In this case, look for any of the other palettes that usually appear in QuarkXPress, such as the Measurements palette (along the bottom of the screen or wherever you last placed it), the Document Layout palette, the Colors palette, or the Style Sheet palette. (You learn about these palettes in Chapter 9.) If any of these were open the last time you used QuarkXPress, they should appear the next time you start the software.

If none of them show up, click on the splash screen. If the splash screen goes away, the program is finished loading and is ready for you to create a new document.

For My First Trick ...

To create a new document, select **File→New→Document**. (This means to click on the **File** menu, pull down to the **New** command, and then select **Document**.) Or, better yet just press ⌘-N (**Ctrl+N** in Windows). The New Document dialog box appears, as shown below.

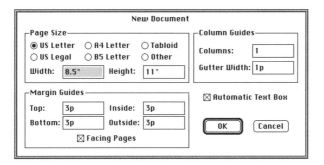

The New Document dialog box.

All sorts of options await you here. If you want to create a document this minute and you don't care about selecting options, go ahead and click **OK**. Just like that, QuarkXPress creates a new document. This probably isn't the best thing to do, though, because you should set up your own specifications for the page with the options in this box.

What's with All These Options?

Glad you asked. Because of the way QuarkXPress is designed, you have to tell it every detail of your page setup *before* you get started. Mind you, all of these options can be changed after you create your document, but it is *much* easier when they are set up correctly before you begin creating your pages. You learn how to use the options to set up your page in the next chapter. For now, you should learn how to get around in dialog boxes by paying close attention to the next section.

Talking Back to Dialog Boxes

The New Document dialog box is a typical example of the kind of dialog box that is found throughout QuarkXPress. These boxes are called "dialog boxes" because they are boxes in which the computer gives you some information or you give the computer some other information; thus, a *dialog* ensues.

There are a few important considerations to be aware of when you work with dialog boxes. The most important one is that the computer demands your attention when a dialog box is showing. In fact, you usually can't click anywhere *but* inside of a dialog box. If you try to click outside of a dialog box, the computer will make a noise. (It might as well say, "I don't think so.")

Most dialog boxes contain a dark-bordered button or a shaded button, like the OK button in the New Document dialog box. This button is your ticket out of the dialog box. You can almost always select any dark bordered button by pressing Enter or Return. Selecting OK tells the computer that you wholeheartedly agree with everything in the dialog box.

But what if you don't like what is in the dialog box, or what if you simply opened it up by accident? Clicking the Cancel button, also found in most dialog boxes, tells the computer to disregard any information entered in that dialog box, and the dialog box disappears from your screen. You can also select the Cancel button by pressing ⌘-. (period) or **Esc** in Windows.

Text Fields Are Everywhere

Probably the most common feature in a dialog box is the *text field*. In a text field you can enter values, measurements, names, or other text. Usually one of the text fields is *highlighted*, which means that whatever you type on the keyboard replaces that highlighted text. If text isn't highlighted, you add text next to where the cursor is positioned.

To highlight a text field in QuarkXPress, double-click on that text field. If you just click once on a text field, the cursor is inserted wherever you click. That's handy if you want to edit the text in the text field.

Option Buttons and Check Boxes

In dialog boxes, you often stumble across areas where you need to choose from several options. In the New Document dialog box, you choose the page size by clicking inside one of six different option buttons (shown below). In any set of option buttons, you can only select one of the buttons at a time. Clicking on an option button that is already "on" (it has a black dot inside of it) does not affect that option button.

Option buttons are sometimes called *radio buttons* because they are sort of like the definable preset buttons on an old car radio. When you push one of the buttons in, the one that used to be pushed in pops out. You can only have one button pushed in at a time. Option buttons work the same way.

In the Page Size section, if the values in the Width and Height text field are different from the five standard sizes displayed there (like maybe 8" × 10"), the Other option button will be selected automatically. Choosing the Other option button while the text reads as one of the five sizes will *not* change those measurements; QuarkXPress assumes you are going to be doing that shortly.

┌─ **Page Size** ─────────────────────────┐
│ ◉ US Letter   ○ A4 Letter   ○ Tabloid │
│ ○ US Legal   ○ B5 Letter   ○ Other   │
│ **Width:** `8.5"`   **Height:** `11"`   │
└───┘

The Page Size section of the New Document dialog box.

Check boxes, on the other hand, often come in sets and can be turned on and off in any combination. The figure below shows the single check box from the New Document dialog box.

☒ **Automatic Text Box**

The Automatic Text check box.

An "X" inside the check box means that the option is on, while an empty box means that the option is currently off. Clicking on a check box toggles it from being on to being off (and vice versa). In addition, you can click on the word next to the option button or check box to turn it on or off. This is almost always easier than clicking in the tiny area of an option button or check box.

Moving Around in a Dialog Box

As you've learned, to select an option in a dialog box using the mouse, you just click on it. Easy enough. You can also use the Tab key to move around in a dialog box. Unfortunately, on a Mac the Tab key only moves you between text fields. In Windows, Tab will take you to the next element, regardless of whether it's a text field.

You can, instead of jumping forward, jump backwards as well. If you press **Shift-Tab**, the previous text field will become highlighted.

On a Mac, if you press the Tab key the next text field is highlighted. This is usually the next logical choice available. For instance, in the New Document dialog box, when the Width text field is highlighted, pressing the Tab key highlights the Height text field. Pressing the Tab key again highlights the Top text field, and you could continue tabbing until the Gutter Width text field is highlighted. Pressing Tab while the Gutter Width text field is selected highlights the Width text field, and around and around it goes, highlighting each successive field.

The Mouse vs. Keyboard Equivalents

Before I write anything else here, let me make one thing perfectly clear: I love using Windows and the Macintosh interface instead of DOS and UNIX. And the mouse is a wonderful tool—a necessity for modern computing. Ah. I feel better. But I have to warn you:

The Mouse can become a crutch.

Gasp! What in heaven's name can I mean by that? Maybe if I was really short or something, but...

There are many things that the mouse does well, but few of those things are found in QuarkXPress. If you quit QuarkXPress by pulling down the **File** menu, the mouse is no longer an asset; it is slowing you down. Mice (mouses? meece? mooses?) are great for drawing, for organizing, for pointing and clicking, but there is a practical limit to their usefulness.

At some point, most users begin to migrate away from the mouse to the different keyboard equivalents available to them in most programs. Well, you might as well start migrating right away. Don't give me excuses like, "But I'm just learning the program, I don't need to be memorizing keyboard equivalents," because I won't have it. No, if you want to use QuarkXPress productively, you will have to use keyboard equivalents. The sooner you get used to it, the easier it will be.

Every time there is a *keyboard equivalent* (or *shortcut key*, as Windows users like to call them) available for some command, I'll note it next to the reference in the text. Look at these keyboard equivalents; don't skip over them. But don't worry about memorizing them, either.

When you are using the software and you want to quit, for instance, ask yourself what the keyboard equivalent is. If you know (or even think you know), press that keyboard equivalent. If you don't know, go to the menu where the command is found, and instead of just blindly choosing Quit, read the keyboard equivalent listed next to it. Next time you need it, you'll probably remember it.

If you press the wrong key, you can always undo the last action by selecting **Edit→Undo** (or pressing **Ctrl+Z**).

Mouse Pain and You

Well, I was tempted to inform you about the medical studies which have discovered that heavy use of the mouse hurries along Carpal Tunnel Syndrome. I also thought that you might be interested to hear that heavy reliance on the keyboard when you have a mouse actually cures arthritis. Instead, let me assure you that heavy use of the mouse can make muscles sore and tender, but only after hours of repetitive movements. It's not going to kill you or anything.

To prevent physical discomfort from any computer-related activity, take *lots* of breaks. That doesn't necessarily mean quit working every twenty minutes and take a five-minute coffee break. It just means move around. Never sit in the same position at the computer for more than an hour. Stop using the computer and do some other kind of work for a bit, or get up and walk around a little. Suddenly you will feel revived, and in the process, you will be preventing all sorts of potential discomfort.

Keyboard Commandos: The Desktop Publishing Nerd

The more keyboard equivalents you memorize, the faster you will be able to use QuarkXPress. You won't have to spend precious time searching every menu for a specific command. Nor will you have to worry about accidentally selecting the wrong command.

To check your nerd factor after you have been using the software for a while, do the following exercise: try to do the Command alphabet. Start with ⌘-A (which is Select All), ⌘-B (Opens the Frame dialog box), ⌘-C (Copy) all the way through the alphabet. Not that I do this regularly or anything, but there is a command for every letter.

If you get them all, try ⌘-Shift-A or ⌘-Option-A. It's lots of fun for the entire family.

In addition, when someone says, "I hate having to pick fonts this way. It is *so* slow." You can blurt out "Try typing ⌘-Option-Shift-M, which highlights the font text field on the Measurements palette." You're sure to get a couple of raised eyebrows for that one.

TECHNO NERD TEACHES...

If you start applying command keys to non-computer events, you've gone too far. Thinking ⌘-Q right before you fall asleep is a common indicator of this level of eccentricity.

I've Had Enough, Already: Quitting QuarkXPress

Fortunately, quitting QuarkXPress is one of the easiest things you can do in the program. It can be accomplished in one of two ways: Either open the **File** menu and select the **Quit** command, or—even easier—press ⌘-**Q** (**Ctrl+Q** in Windows).

If you have any documents open that have not been saved recently (saving is discussed in the very next chapter), a message like the one shown below appears, asking if you would like to save changes before quitting.

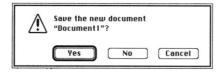

The Save Changes? dialog box.

If you don't care what happens to the document, click **No** or press ⌘-N (**Ctrl+N** in Windows). If you want to save the document but have not done so yet, click **Yes** or press **Enter** (or **Return**). The Save As dialog box appears. Look in the text box with the highlighted text—it tells you the name of the document. If it says "Document1" or "Document2" or something like that, it is unlikely that the document has been saved yet. Refer to Chapter 5 for an in-depth explanation on saving and saving options. If the document has been previously saved, clicking the **Yes** button updates the already saved file with any changes that have been made to the document.

If you change your mind and decide you don't want to quit at this time, click the **Cancel** button. You can activate any Cancel button in QuarkXPress with the keyboard by pressing ⌘-**Period** (the Windows equivalent is the **Esc** key). In fact, pressing ⌘-Period will cancel any operation that is in progress, including printing, opening, and importing. (If you are following along with the book, you'll probably want to keep the program running so you can set up your new document in the next chapter. Click **Cancel** to close the dialog box and keep QuarkXPress running.)

If there were no documents open or the documents have been saved recently, the program quits and disappears in just a few seconds (instantly on the PowerMacs).

TECHNO NERD TEACHES...

A more secret way to quit QuarkXPress on a Mac (besides ripping out the power cord) is to Force Quit the program. This should *only* be done when you are in a situation where nothing else will work. Any unsaved work will be lost and you still may have to restart your system, but at least you can get out of the program. Hold your breath, toss something (small) over your right shoulder, and press ⌘-**Option-Esc**. A message box appears, warning you that unsaved changes will be lost. Nod reverently and click the **OK** button.

If you're using Windows, you can try the old **Ctrl+Alt+Del** routine. That takes you to a screen in which you can press **Enter** to quit the program or press **Ctrl+Alt+Del** again to restart your computer. Try pressing **Enter** first. If that doesn't work, you have to restart your computer. Bummer.

The Least You Need to Know

Well, you still haven't created anything of substance in QuarkXPress, but my, haven't you learned a lot! Besides, all this stuff will be old hat after a session or two of actually using QuarkXPress.

- ☛ Using keyboard equivalents will make you more proficient in QuarkXPress.

- ☛ To start up QuarkXPress, double-click on the program icon or a document created with QuarkXPress.

- ☛ You create a new document by selecting **File→New→Document** or by pressing ⌘-**N** (or **Ctrl+N** in Windows).

- ☛ To quit QuarkXPress, select **File→Quit** or press ⌘-**Q** (**Ctrl+Q** in Windows).

Chapter 5
Setting Up Your Very First Document

In This Chapter

- ☞ Specifying parameters in a new document
- ☞ Understanding the measurement systems in QuarkXPress
- ☞ A word about text boxes

For now, let's return to the New Document dialog box, so we can pick up where we left off in Chapter 4. If you don't have the dialog box on-screen, press the keyboard equivalent to create a new document. (It's ⌘-N on a Mac, Ctrl+N in Windows, in case you forgot.) In this chapter, we move through the dialog box section by section, explaining what every option means.

Give QuarkXPress an Inch, It'll Take a Pica

There are different measurement systems available to you in QuarkXPress. There is the standard inch system that we all know and love, in which there are always twelve inches in a foot, three feet in a yard, and so on. There is also the metric system, in which there are one hundred centimeters in a meter, and one hundred millimeters in a centimeter. QuarkXPress lets you specify if you would rather see measurements as millimeters or centimeters. Another measuring system, which is the preferred method of measurement in QuarkXPress, is common to those in the publishing and printing industry: points and picas. There are only two units to remember, and they can be related to inches very easily.

There are 6 picas in one inch; there are 72 points in one inch. Using a smidgen of my incredible mathematical skills, I can determine that there are 12 points in one pica. That is all you need to know about points and picas to relate them to the measurements you are probably so fond of. QuarkXPress will display almost all of the measurements in whichever measurement system you choose to use.

Measurement Notation

QuarkXPress lets you enter measurements in any measurement system you like, and then it automatically converts that to its *default* system.

Default settings are set at the factory, but you can change them. For instance, QuarkXPress's measurement system defaults to inches. If you would rather work in picas all the time, you can change the default setting to picas instead of inches.

Of course, when you are entering picas, how does QuarkXPress know you mean picas instead of inches? You specify the measurement system by adding a symbol to the measurement. Inches are easy. Just add " to the measurement, and QuarkXPress will know that 6" means six inches.

You indicate centimeters by putting the letters cm after a number. Thus, 4cm becomes four centimeters. Millimeters are indicated by the letters mm, so 92mm is ninety-two millimeters.

Picas are a bit more confusing. The measurement 3p stands for three picas, but p3 or 3pt stands for three points. So the p *after* the number indicates picas, but the p *before* the number indicates points. This makes pica/point measuring easy once you get used to it: 4p6 is four picas, six points.

QuarkXPress will display all of your results in the current measurement system. For instance, if the current system is inches and you enter 1p6, once you press Tab or Return, the value will change to .25".

If you enter a value without a letter or symbol telling QuarkXPress which system you are using, it will assume you want to use the default system. In the inch and centimeters systems, if you enter a 6, QuarkXPress would interpret it as six inches and six centimeters, respectively. But in the pica system, entering a 6 would be interpreted as six points, not six picas. Even when you are in the pica system, you have to enter a "p" after the number to indicate picas.

You may also enter numbers in the pica system that aren't, well, logical. For instance, instead of entering fourteen picas (14p) you may enter one hundred and sixty-eight points (p168). QuarkXPress will know what that means and will show 14p where the amount was entered.

TECHNO NERD TEACHES...

You enter fractions in QuarkXPress by entering the *decimal equivalent*. So you would enter 1/2 as .5, and you would enter 5/8 as .625. This chart should help you with most common fractions:

1/16=.0625	1/8=.125	3/16=.1875	1/4=.25
5/16=.3125	3/8=.375	7/16=.4375	1/2=.5
9/16=.5625	5/8=.625	11/16=.6875	3/4=.75
13/16=.8125	7/8=.875	15/16=.9375	1=1

Big Pages, Little Pages

Page size in QuarkXPress is *really* important. Picking the correct page size before you begin will make your life oh-so-much-easier than if you pick a size at random. There are a few rules to follow when choosing page size. Here they are:

☛ If you don't know the page size, try to estimate a little *smaller* than the size you are thinking of. It is much much much much (four muches) easier to enlarge a page in QuarkXPress than to reduce it. This may be hard to do at first, but trust me, increasing the page size is a snap. Decreasing it has caused many a desktop publisher to hang his head in despair.

☛ Make sure you make the size of the page the same size as the finished (cut and folded) page. If you are designing a brochure that will be 3.67" × 8.5" when folded, make the page size 3.67" × 8.5". Resist the temptation to second guess and make the page size 11" × 8.5" (the unfolded size). You can place three pages next to each other in something called a *spread,* which is better than creating a single 11" wide page.

☛ Note those Width and Height text fields. QuarkXPress doesn't have a way for you to switch between landscape and portrait orientations, so if you want a page that is 11" across, and 8.5" deep, make sure that the width is 11" and the height is 8.5" Selecting Letter will switch those numbers to the portrait (taller) orientation automatically. The Other option button is selected if a landscape measurement is chosen, as shown below.

If you type in a value other than one of the five standard options, the Other option button is automatically chosen.

☛ Even if your measurement system is picas or metric, page size is *always* measured in inches. This is one of those weird things, but all paper in North America is measured in inches (Europe measures paper in millimeters). For example, letter size pages are 8.5" × 11", which is measured as 51 picas by 66 picas. But if you enter 51, QuarkXPress interprets that as 51 inches, not 51 picas— even though you are in the pica system. (However, you can enter 51p, which QuarkXPress will recognize as picas and will convert to inches.)

TECHNO NERD TEACHES...

The A4 and B5 letter sizes are a little different, because they use standard size paper… for Europe. If you are planning to print on European letter-sized paper, choose these options. Otherwise, stay away from them, as they look really strange to an American like me.

The Outer (and Inner) Limits

Page size in QuarkXPress is limited, but those limits are kind of bizarre for the type of work most people do. Unless you are designing thumbnail ads or billboards, you can probably create a document "to size."

The smallest a document can be is 1" × 1", which is a tiny square like this one:

A 1" × 1" square.

The largest document can be up to 48" by 48", which we can't print here. Doing so would make it difficult to fit this book onto bookshelves, as well as in your car to take it home.

Margin On to Glory

If you try to create a document with a dimension larger than 24", you may get a message stating that the dimensions must be no larger than 24". This message will only appear if you have the Facing Pages option checked (at the bottom of the Margin Guides section in the New Document dialog box). Uncheck this box and try again.

The Margin Guides section of the New Document dialog box, shown in the following figure, has always befuddled users of QuarkXPress. The main reason for this is because they put too much emphasis on the word "Margin" and not on the word "Guides."

These settings are *guides* in that they are, for the most part, a visual reminder of an eye-pleasing distance from the edge of the page. Many times, unsuspecting QuarkXPress users have assumed that if they wanted something to butt up to the edge of the page, or actually *bleed* off the page, they would have to set the margins accordingly. What resulted was a lot of unnecessary math, similar to finding derivatives in Calculus.

The Margin Guides section of the New Document dialog box.

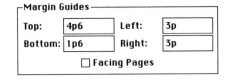

If you don't have Left and Right text fields like the figure does, it is because the Facing Pages option is checked in the dialog box. When Facing Pages is checked, Left becomes Inside, and Right becomes Outside.

These guides do two things: First, they serve as the aforementioned visual reminders as you are laying out your page, and second, they are guides for the automatic text box, which appears when that option is checked in the New Document dialog box.

The measurements in the Margin Guides text fields are distances from that edge of the page. For instance, a measurement of 4p6 in the Top text field indicates that a horizontal margin guide will be placed 4p6 from the top edge of the page.

Facing Up to Your Pages

You may be wondering what this Facing Pages option is that seems to be all the rage. The Facing Pages check box automatically puts left and right pages next to each other in your document so that you can see how these pages will look when the job is finished and those pages are actually next to each other. This option enables you to easily place objects that cross both pages right in the center of the two pages. You can then choose to print the pages together or separately.

Because left and right margins are different on documents that have facing pages, the margins are specified as inside and outside instead of left and right. This makes it possible for left-side pages to have the same inside (right) margin as right-side pages, whose inside margin is on the left side.

The Column Before the Storm

The Column Guides box, shown in the following figure, lets you specify how many columns will be on each page, and what the amount of space between them (called *Gutter Width*) will be.

```
┌─Column Guides──────┐
│                    │
│ Columns:      [1  ]│
│                    │
│ Gutter Width: [1p ]│
│                    │
└────────────────────┘
```

The Column Guides box.

The number of columns you specify are created in the space between the left and right (or inside and outside) margins of your page. The gutter width is subtracted from this amount. In QuarkXPress, you never have to specify the column width; instead, the software does the computations for you, based on the width of the text box and the amount of gutter between columns.

Once again, these are only guides, and they only affect the automatic text box (described below). Just because you typed in 3 columns with 1p6 gutter width doesn't mean that you can't have a page with 2 columns and .75" gutter width. Everything in QuarkXPress is very flexible… if you can find where to make the changes.

OOPS!

Strangely enough, even when you have specified only one column, QuarkXPress does not allow you to enter a value of zero into the Gutter Width field. Instead, you must have a value of at least 3 points (p3 or 3 pt) as the gutter. As to why there must be three points or more, that is anybody's guess.

The Electromatic Automatic Text Box

Sounds pretty neat, doesn't it? If you say yes, you'll like this box, your text magically flows into it and formats itself—and suddenly you have a newsletter. Well, not exactly. In fact, not even close. About the only thing "automatic" about the automatic text box is that it is automatically placed on each page of your document, one edge on each margin and divided into the columns you specified above.

This is, indeed, a great feature. It allows you to set up a document with ten, twenty, even thousands of pages, all with a text box on them automatically. The importance of this will surely elude you at this point, but in the future, you will nod wisely and might even start calling me Obi-Wan (not that I'd want you to).

One nice feature of the automatic text box is that text can flow from one page to another, then another, onto the next, and so on with little assistance from you.

The number one bad thing about the automatic text box is that all too often, people forget about its existence and then find it later accidentally. The number two bad thing about the automatic text box is that no one notices it isn't checked until they try to use a text box that was never put there. All sorts of nasty words are spoken, even shouted, as a result. This is one thing that can't be changed after you create a document, at least not by checking a little box.

The Least You Need to Know

Now you're all set up and ready to start creating your first masterpiece in QuarkXPress. In this chapter, you learned about all the options in the New Document dialog box (and more), including:

- ☞ The New Document dialog box controls the basis of your document setup and should be as close to the final measurements as possible.

- ☞ Margins are guides only; objects can appear outside of them.

- ☞ Use the following notation for measurement systems: 1p = 1 pica, p1 = 1 point, 1" = 1 inch, 1 mm = 1 millimeter.

- ☞ Checking the automatic text box check box creates a text box in your document that has its edges aligned with the margin.

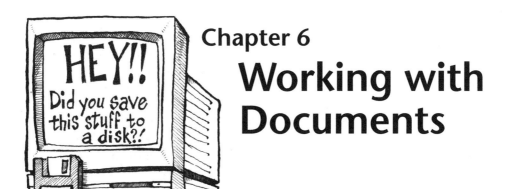

Chapter 6
Working with Documents

In This Chapter

- ☛ Saving your document
- ☛ Undoing mistakes (not that you'll make any)
- ☛ Closing documents
- ☛ Opening previously saved documents

There are all sorts of things that have to be done with documents that are pretty darn *computery* in nature. Before you skip this chapter, let me explain that those things are really easy and are also important to learn (unlike yodeling, which is very difficult and quite inconsequential to learn).

Saving Your Document

Quite possibly the most important thing you can do with a QuarkXPress document is save it. No one listens to me when I tell them about this, but there are tiny little mites inside the QuarkXPress software whose job it is to monitor your work, and when you haven't saved what you are doing for a long period of time, they initiate a system crash.

These mites like nothing better than to wreck your day by relieving you of hours and hours of productive work with a simple crash. The only way you can keep the mites at bay is to save often. Unless you're so busy saving that you aren't getting any work done, you aren't saving enough. There is no good time to save, but here's a guideline. Whenever you do something different, such as import a picture, change a font, open another QuarkXPress document, or switch to another software package, *save your work.*

I may seem obsessive about saving, but I have lost more work in QuarkXPress and other software programs than most QuarkXPress users will ever create.

At the end of the day, make backup copies of your work. Even duplicates on the same drive are better than no duplicates at all. The best thing to do is to save a backup to a part of your system different from where the original document is (such as on a floppy, cartridge, or server volume).

How to Save Your Work (and Your Sanity)

When you create a new document, the first thing you should do is save it on your hard drive. To save, you must have a document on-screen. You can open several documents at one time (which you do by repeatedly using the **File→Open** command covered later in this chapter), but saving affects only the frontmost document. So if you have multiple documents open, you must bring them to the front and save each of them.

To save, select **File→Save** or press ⌘-**S** (**Ctrl+S** in Windows). The Save As dialog box appears, as shown below.

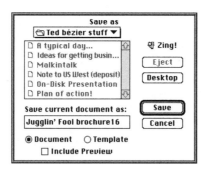

The Save As dialog box.

The first time you save a document, the Save As dialog box appears. You have to do two different things: name the document and determine where it will be saved.

Naming Conventions and That Silly .QXP

The process for naming documents is different for Macintosh and Windows systems. On Windows systems, you can use up to eight letters or numbers, optionally followed by the extension .QXP or .QXT. On a Macintosh, you can throw naming conventions to the wind and name the file anything your heart desires, without regard to anything (except, of course, that it can't be more than thirty-two characters long). Take full advantage of the thirty-two available characters in order to be as descriptive as possible.

Regardless of the system you have, try to make the name of the file resemble the document as closely as possible. Avoid names like "Stupid," "Stuff," "Document1," and other nondescript names. Instead, try to name the file as if the person who will be looking for it next has no idea what you called it, but only knows what the document looks like. Avoid putting dates and times in the document name, since this information is automatically recorded with the document anyway.

Finding a Good Home for Your Document

When saving, pay close attention to the Save As dialog box and make sure that you save your document in the correct location. A good saving strategy is to save documents *outside* of the application folder/directory. Keep only the files necessary for the application with the application, and put files you have created in a different location. Of course, you'll need to remember where the file is being saved, so make the folder/directory name somewhat logical (once again, so that a complete stranger could find this file if he needed to).

Why Would Anyone Else Need My File?

Well actually, no one probably will need your files unless you work in a company where there are several systems with QuarkXPress and work is scattered out among different people. The reason to be so obvious with your file naming and location, is that it may be several weeks, months—even *years*—before you need that file again. Think back just a few days. Can you remember what files you saved by name and location? Probably not. I work with an average of thirty to forty files a day, so in a year that would be almost fifteen thousand different files. I won't remember what is in the files Stuff1, Stufficate18, and HRPuffnStuff3 a year from now.

Undoing a Mistake (Not That You'll Make Any...)

If you happen to make a mistake while working in QuarkXPress, there is an easy way to correct it. Immediately select **Edit→Undo** or press ⌘-Z (**Ctrl+Z** in Windows), and the last thing you did will be miraculously undone—providing you haven't clicked the mouse, saved, or done one of the other million activities that changes the Undo command into the Cannot Undo command.

Remember, this only undoes the *last* thing you did, not something you did two minutes ago, or something you did last time you were in the document.

The power of Undo is massive, but it has strict limitations: there are several things you can't undo. In these cases, you usually are not warned in advance; instead you are greeted with a grayed-out Cannot Undo where Undo used to reside in a nice, healthy black. In addition, you can't undo after you save, and you can't undo something you did the last time the document was open.

Undoing Major Gaffs

Let's say you've "accidentally" replaced all the text in your report on nuclear waste reduction with a spicy love letter to a former girlfriend, Florence. Your current girlfriend (who happens to be madly jealous to the point of occasional convulsions) is walking toward you, having popped into the office just to say "hi." Meanwhile, the phone rings; it's your boss, asking you to refresh him on what the copy reads on page 4. Right now the text on page 4 contains material that wouldn't really enlighten your boss (at least not on the topic of nuclear waste). The clock reads 2:59, and your client, the Nuclear Regulatory Commission, is expecting a fax of the entire report at 3:00.

In a burst of panic you hit ⌘-Z to undo this mess. But instead, you remember the last thing you did was to color your former girlfriend's name ruby red everywhere it appeared in the document. One of those names turns back to black. Sweat beads form and begin cascading down your face. In your state of panic, your eyes start to bulge, and your hands twist into trembling claws. Life as you know it is about to end. Your current girl-friend is now just three steps away.

Fortunately, *The Complete Idiot's Guide to QuarkXPress* is open to this exact page and is lying on your floor, the likely sight of a future chalk line in the shape of your body. You spot the answer in this line of text:

Revert to Saved.

You quickly select File→Revert to Saved, and a dialog box like the one below appears.

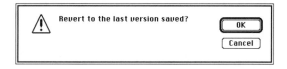

The Revert to Saved dialog box.

You whack the Enter key on your keyboard. The letters to your ex-girlfriend are gone, replaced with your insights on the toxicity of nuclear waste in schoolyards and other matters. You read a line to your boss, smile at your girlfriend, and print a copy to be faxed to the Nuclear Regulatory Commission.

The life-saving Revert to Saved command reopens the last saved version of your document, deleting any changes that were made to the document since it was last saved. Pretty neat, huh? (By the way, you're welcome.)

Closing Documents

Sometimes, beginners have trouble remembering that closing a document is different from quitting the program. Make sure you keep the two com-mands separate in your mind. You can close a document and still keep QuarkXPress running so you can work in another file.

To close a document that you are finished working with, select **File→Close** or press ⌘-**W** (**Ctrl+W** in Windows). In addition, you can click on the upper left corner of the document window in the little box that appears there. That box is called the *Close Box* on a Mac, and it's called the *Control-menu box* in Windows.

If your document has just been saved (which I recommend you do before closing), the document simply vanishes. If you have made any changes since the last time it was saved, a dialog box appears, asking if you'd like to save changes. Click **Yes** to save changes, or click **No** to not save changes. Clicking the **Cancel** button returns you to the document.

Opening Existing Documents

After you've created, saved, and closed a document, you will probably want to open it and work in it again eventually. There are several ways to open existing QuarkXPress documents. Here are a couple of easy ways:

☛ The easiest way to open a QuarkXPress document on a Mac is to find the document on your hard drive and double-click on it. You can double-click a document icon on the desktop or a document listed in the Finder. Even if QuarkXPress is not currently running, double-clicking a QuarkXPress 3.3 document icon runs the program and opens the document that you double-clicked.

You cannot open a document in QuarkXPress that has a higher version number than the version you are currently running. For instance, if you have version 3.2 of QuarkXPress, you will not be able to open files in version 3.3 format.

☛ An easy way to open a QuarkXPress document from Windows' File Manager is to find the document's name in the file list and double-click on it. As long as there is a file association set up between QuarkXPress and documents with the .QXP extension, the program starts and opens the document you double-clicked. (For information on file associations, see your Windows manual.)

☛ Another way to open a QuarkXPress document is to drag the document icon on top of the QuarkXPress application icon and release it. (You can do this on the Mac desktop or in File Manager.) This opens up the document in QuarkXPress and starts QuarkXPress if necessary.

But wait, there's more. Yet another way to open a QuarkXPress document is to pull down the **File** menu within QuarkXPress and select **Open**, or press ⌘-**O** (**Ctrl+O** in Windows). A dialog box appears, as shown in the following figure, enabling you to select the file you want to open.

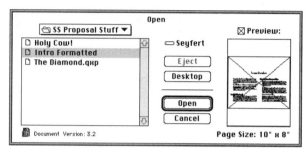

The Open dialog box.

Navigate through this dialog box until the document you are interested in appears. Then select it and click the **Open** button.

Depending on the version of QuarkXPress that was used to save the file you want to open, there may be a preview available for that document. If so, that preview will appear on the right of the dialog box. A note appears under the preview stating the dimensions of the pages in that document.

The Least You Need to Know

You learned plenty of lovely new commands in this chapter. Here's a list of important information to take with you as you delve into the next chapter.

- ☛ You save a document by selecting **File→Save** or by pressing ⌘-**S** (**Ctrl+S** in Windows).

- ☛ You can undo the last activity by selecting **Edit→Undo** or by pressing ⌘-**Z** (**Ctrl+Z** in Windows).

- ☛ You can revert to the last saved version of the current document by selecting **File→Revert to Saved**.

continues

continued

☛ Close a document by selecting **File→Close**, by pressing ⌘-**W** (**Ctrl+W** in Windows), or by clicking in the box in the upper left corner of the document window.

☛ To open a previously saved document, use the **File→Open** command.

Chapter 7
What's All This Stuff on the Screen?

In This Chapter

- ☞ Getting oriented with QuarkXPress
- ☞ Viewing your document at different sizes
- ☞ Showing and hiding various elements

When you first look at the elements on a QuarkXPress screen, you're liable to become very confused very quickly. There seem to be too many menus for one program to have, and all sorts of palettes are floating around the screen.

Although it may not look like it at first, each of the tools, menu items, and text fields on the palettes have specific functions—most of which are quite basic. Initially, the hardest thing to figure out is the difference between the individual tools, markings, and terms used throughout the program. That's what the next couple of chapters are for. They're a reference for most of the things you see on-screen when you first start working in QuarkXPress.

The following illustration shows the elements of a typical QuarkXPress document window and corresponding palettes and menus. If some elements in the following figure don't appear on your screen, don't panic. Later in the chapter, I'll show you how to bring those missing things to the screen.

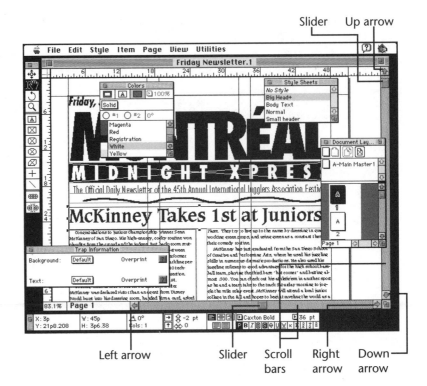

Slider   Up arrow

A typical (though messy) QuarkXPress document window.

Left arrow   Slider   Scroll bars   Right arrow   Down arrow

Scrolling Around Town

Right away you'll recognize the program's familiar *scroll bars*, which appear on the right and bottom edges of the document window. By clicking on the arrows at each end of the scroll bars, you move the document in that direction so you can see more of it. For instance, to see a section of the document below the part that's shown in the current window, click on the down arrow.

Strangely enough, the document moves in the direction *opposite* the direction of the arrow you click. (When you click the down arrow, the document moves up so you can see what's on a lower part of the page.) Remember when you are using the scroll bars that you are *looking*, not moving. The cursor doesn't move when you scroll.

To move quickly through your document, click on and drag the little square slider that appears between the two arrows. The document moves proportionately to the distance you drag. Once again, drag toward whatever you want to see. If you want to see something to the left of the viewing area, drag the bottom slider to the left.

A third way to move through documents with the scroll bars is to click on the gray areas between the slider and the arrows. Doing so moves the document about 80% of the window size towards whichever side of the slider you click. This works with both the vertical and horizontal scroll bars.

Scrolling Without Scroll Bars

The best possible way to quickly scroll around your document, though, isn't by using the standard scroll bars. Instead, hold down the **Option** key (**Alt** for Windows), and the cursor changes into a little hand. (Make sure Caps Lock is not turned on.)

To use this little hand tool, keep the **Option** key pressed (**Alt** for Windows) and then drag, actually pushing the document around inside the window. This becomes second nature the more you do it, and it's much more convenient than using the scroll bars.

If the cursor doesn't change into a little hand, the Grabber Hand option has been turned off. To turn it on, select **Edit→Preferences→ Application Preferences**, and click the **Grabber Hand** check box. (This only affects versions 3.1 and older of QuarkXPress.) Versions 3.2 and newer don't have this option. The Caps Lock key is used to turn the feature off (Caps Lock engaged) or on (Caps Lock not engaged).

Mucho Documento in QuarkXPresso

You can have several documents open at once in QuarkXPress, but only one of them is the active document. The *active document* is the one in front of all the other documents. Its window title bar (along the top of the window) is gray with black letters on a Mac; in Windows, the active document's title bar is blue (if you're using Windows' default colors). Inactive document windows have white title bars with grayed-out letters.

You can only work in one document at a time (unless you are moving objects from one document to another, as discussed in Chapter 11), and that document is the active document. Any menu command, tool, or palette you use will affect only the active window.

To make a document window active, select it by clicking anywhere on the document's window that is visible. You can also choose a window from the **View** menu.

Changing the Size of Your Document... NOT!

In the View menu, there are several options with which you can specify different viewing percentages for your document. Changing the viewing percentage through the View menu only changes how you see the document, not anything about the document itself. So 12-point type viewed at 400% is still 12-point type, it just looks four times as large (48-pt.) when viewed at this percentage.

Only two of the viewing options have keyboard equivalents. You can access Actual Size (100%) by pressing ⌘-1 (Ctrl+1 for Windows). The Fit in Window size is a magnification based on the size of your document window: the document is as large as it can be while still fitting within the window. The key command for the Fit In Window option is ⌘-0 (Ctrl+0 for Windows).

To quickly highlight the viewing percentage in the lower left corner, press **Control-V** on a Mac or **Ctrl+Alt+V** for Windows (V for View).

On the View menu, the other option without a percentage is Thumbnails view, a special small view that's useful for organizing pages within your document. Thumbnails view enables you to see several tiny document pages at once, as well as to move them around within your document. Thumbnails view is also used when dragging pages between two open documents to quickly duplicate a page and everything on it into another document. You cannot edit page content in Thumbnails view.

Using Custom Viewing Percentages

If you like viewing your documents at 130%, you can do it easily by highlighting the viewing percentage in the lower left-hand corner of the document window and typing a new percentage. You don't have to type the % symbol, but it won't hurt if you do. When you press Enter or Return, the document will change to the viewing percentage you have typed.

Of course, looking in this box is also a quick way for you to note what the current viewing percentage is, no matter how it was changed.

The Double-Secret View Change

Pressing ⌘-Option and clicking will change the view from any viewing percentage to 200%. If the viewing percentage is already 200%, pressing

⌘-Option (Ctrl for Windows) and clicking will change the view to 100%. Sneaky, huh?

If you have QuarkXPress 3.1 or older, just press **Option (Alt for Windows)** and click to do the same thing.

Show and Hide

No, this section isn't about a bashful version of the popular children's school activity. Several things on the QuarkXPress screen besides palettes can be hidden or shown. These things are the guides (used for aligning objects), the baseline grid (used for aligning text across columns), the rulers, and "Invisibles" (characters you don't normally see, like spaces or tabs).

When these objects are visible on-screen, the menu item will read "Hide" and when they are hidden, it will read "Show" for each of them.

Showing and Hiding Guides

Guides include margin guides (which you set up in the New Document dialog box), ruler guides that are dragged from the rulers, the X that appears in an empty picture box, and the outlines of unselected text and picture boxes.

Hiding guides is a good way to show how your document will really look, as opposed to the way it normally looks on-screen, with lines and stuff all over it. The following figure shows the difference between showing guides (above) and hiding guides (below).

Rulers in QuarkXPress are the bars along the top and left of the document windows that are split into standard units of the current measurement system, giving them more in common with rulers than just the name. **Ruler guides** are colored lines (dotted on black and white monitors) you can pull from the rulers by clicking on a ruler, holding the mouse button down, and dragging away from the ruler. This creates a guide (a line that is perpendicular to the ruler it was pulled from) that you can place anywhere in the document window. Ruler guides are useful for aligning objects to a common location.

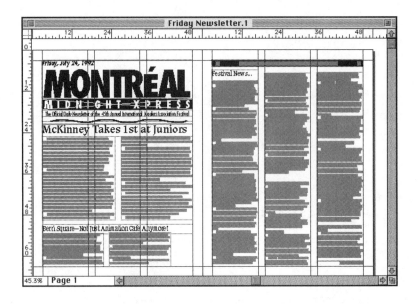

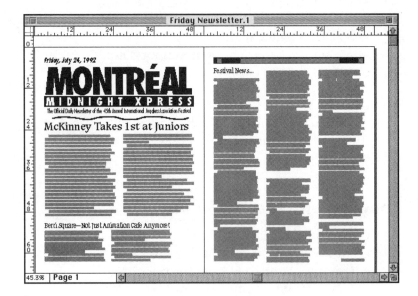

Showing and hiding guides in a typical document.

Showing and Hiding the Baseline Grid

The baseline grid is an advanced feature used for making sure the bottom lines of text in neighboring columns line up correctly. When this option is active, all text will line up to an increment of a preset vertical mark (for example, every 12 pts, starting 3 picas from the top edge of the page). The baseline grid works whether it is visible or not, and seeing it actually can detract from its usefulness.

Showing and Hiding Rulers

This option enables you to hide or show the rulers that normally appear along the left and top edges of each document window. Rulers are shown divided into increments of the current measurement system (which you can change by selecting **Edit→Preferences→ General**).

Even if you have the guides hidden, objects still snap to them as if they were visible. To prevent objects from snapping to guides, you must select **View→Snap to Guides**. When the Snap to Guides check box is empty (the option is turned off), objects will no longer snap to them.

By hiding the rulers, you gain approximately three square inches of viewing area for your document on a standard 13" monitor, and almost twice that on a 21" monitor. As a rule (no pun intended), you should keep the rulers in place, because you can pull down guides from them and you can use them as a handy reference when measuring.

Snap to Guides

When the Snap to Guides feature is activated, a check mark appears next to the option in the View menu. Objects moved to within a few pixels of any guide will "snap" to that guide (the object automatically moves a little so that it aligns perfectly), which makes lining up several objects, well, a snap.

This feature can be annoying when you are trying to move something just a tiny bit, and one edge keeps snapping to a guide. If you want to turn off the feature, uncheck the Snap to Guides option in the **View** menu.

The Least You Need to Know

QuarkXPress gives you several ways to enhance what you see on-screen. By moving around the document, changing viewing magnifications, and showing and hiding different items, you can achieve near complete control over what QuarkXPress is showing you.

- ☞ The easiest way to scroll is to hold down the **Option** key (**Alt** for Windows) and "push" the document around the screen with the grabber hand.

- ☞ When you hide the guides using the command in the **View** menu, the document appears on-screen very close to the way it will look when it's printed.

- ☞ You can view documents in QuarkXPress as small as 10% or as large as 400% of their actual size.

- ☞ To temporarily hide items from view, select **Hide** from the **View** menu.

- ☞ Toggle back and forth between 100% and 200% magnification by pressing ⌘-**Option** (**Ctrl** for Windows) and clicking.

Chapter 8
Tooling Around in QuarkXPress

In This Chapter

- ☞ An in-depth look at the three sections of the toolbox
- ☞ The difference between the Item tool and the Content tool
- ☞ How and when to use the creation tools

The QuarkXPress toolbox (shown in the following figure) is very basic in concept and scope. To use any of the tools, you simply select it by clicking on it, and the chosen tool becomes the active tool.

The toolbox is divided into three major sections: the top tools, a group of four different tools; the creation tools, seven tools used to create items in a QuarkXPress document; and the two linking tools, used to link and unlink text boxes.

If the toolbox isn't visible, select **View→Show**, and it will appear magically. Why wasn't it there in the first place? One of two things could have happened. Either you accidentally closed it by clicking in the little white box (the Close box) at the top left corner, or you closed it by selecting **View→Hide**.

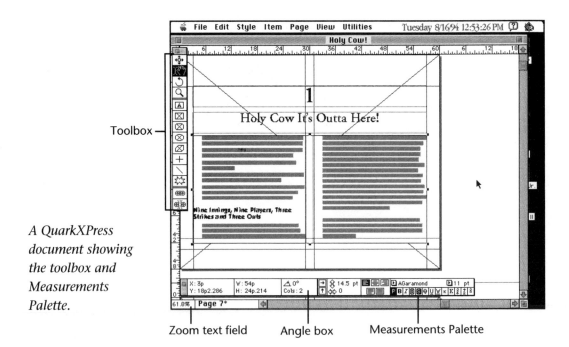

Toolbox

A QuarkXPress document showing the toolbox and Measurements Palette.

Zoom text field　　　Angle box　　　Measurements Palette

Using the Toolbox

As opposed to clicking on the tool you want to use, you can use the keyboard to select tools. To select the next lowest tool on the toolbox, press ⌘-**Tab** (**Ctrl+Tab** for Windows). To select the previous tool, press **Shift-⌘-Tab** (**Shift+Ctrl+Tab** for Windows). To move through several tools, hold down the ⌘ key or the **Ctrl** key (and **Shift**, if necessary), and press **Tab** until you reach the tool you want to use.

A common QuarkXPress technique is to toggle between the Item tool and the Content tool (which are described in the next section) by pressing ⌘-**Tab** and ⌘-**Shift-Tab** (**Ctrl+Tab** and **Ctrl+Shift+Tab** for Windows). You'll find that you flip between these two tools more than any others. When the Item tool is active, press ⌘-**Tab** (**Ctrl+Tab** for Windows) to select the Content tool. When the Content tool is active, press ⌘-**Shift-Tab** (**Ctrl+Shift+Tab** for Windows) to select the Item tool.

I'll talk about each tool in more detail toward the end of the chapter. For now, I'll just give you a brief run-down of the types of tools in the toolbox.

The Non-Conformist Tools

The tools at the very top of the toolbox have various uses, and it is with these tools that you will be spending most of your time in QuarkXPress. The tools are labeled below.

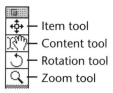

The top tools.

The first two tools are used for moving items, resizing items, and entering and editing text and pictures. Because you use these tools so often, QuarkXPress remembers which of the top tools you are using when you pick any of the lower tools. For example, if you are using the Item tool and you click on a lower tool, QuarkXPress returns you to the Item tool when you finish using the lower tool.

To prevent QuarkXPress from snapping back to the Item or Content tool, press the **Option** key (**Alt** for Windows) when you are selecting any other tool. This prevents QuarkXPress from automatically switching you back, and you can use the selected tool as often as you like. To get back to the Item or Content tool (or any other tool), just select it as usual.

Although QuarkXPress thinks it's being helpful by remembering the tool and returning you to it, sometimes that can be a hassle. For instance, say you're using a tool other than one of the top two tools. You finished whatever action required the lower tool, but you want to use that tool again. However, QuarkXPress has decided that you need whichever of the top two tools you were using *before* you picked the tool you want. It automatically selects the wrong tool.

The third tool is the Rotate tool, which is used to rotate items. The fourth tool is the Zoom tool, which is used to magnify certain areas of your document. The third and fourth tools could actually be ignored; their functions, for the most part, can be performed more productively in other ways (for example, by entering a precise value in the box in the lower left of the document window to magnify at a certain percentage, or by entering the angle of rotation in the Measurements palette).

On the Third Day, Text Boxes Were Created

Those Quark programmers, they're a religious bunch. They've snuck in seven creation tools, one for each day of creation in the Bible. Was this done on purpose? Is it a conspiracy? We won't know until Oliver Stone does a film on Quark...

The seven creation tools shown below (eight if you have the XTension "Stars & Stripes" installed) are used only for creating new items in the document. To use a creation tool, select it by clicking on it, click to tell the computer where the shape starts, and then drag away from that point. The shape gets larger as you pull further away from the starting point. (The Polygon and Line tools work a little differently, as we'll discuss later in the chapter.)

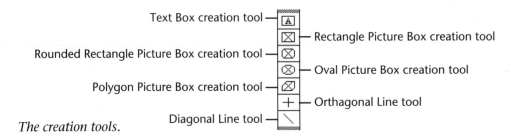

Text Box creation tool —
Rectangle Picture Box creation tool
Rounded Rectangle Picture Box creation tool —
Oval Picture Box creation tool
Polygon Picture Box creation tool —
Orthagonal Line tool
Diagonal Line tool —

The creation tools.

Once you have created an item with a creation tool, QuarkXPress will snap you back to the Item or Content tool you were using before you chose the creation tool. (Unless, of course, you pressed the Option key when you selected the creation tool. In that case, the creation tool remains selected, and you can draw as many more items as you want.)

The (Chain) Linking Tools

The last two tools in the toolbox are used for linking and unlinking text boxes. If you would like text to flow from one text box to another, you use the Linking tool by clicking first in the box the text is coming from and then in the text box the text is going to. When you want to cut that link, you simply click with the Unlinking tool on the end of one link in a text box, and the link is destroyed.

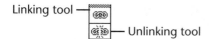

Linking tool ——
—— Unlinking tool

The linking tools.

The Item Tool

The Item tool is used to manipulate items in QuarkXPress. *Items* are text boxes, picture boxes, and lines. The Item tool can be used to move items in any direction or resize these items by clicking on and dragging any of the eight *handles* on text and picture boxes, or on one of the two handles on a line. The primary reason for using the Item tool is to select more than one item at a time.

Handles are the little squares on each corner and on the middle of each side of picture and text boxes. They are also on both ends of a line. Handles are only visible on selected objects.

Item Tool Limitations

The Item tool prevents you from doing several things. When the Item tool is active, you cannot create, edit, or modify the text inside of text boxes. You also cannot import or manipulate pictures inside of picture boxes.

When the Item tool is selected, the Style menu becomes grayed out, and the right half of the Measurements palette disappears, preventing you from using the features in both menu and palette. These limitations make it very frustrating to use the Item tool. Fortunately, there is a better way...

The Secret Pseudo-Item Tool

You can access the Pseudo-Item tool when any other tool is in use by holding down the ⌘ key on the keyboard (**Ctrl** for Windows). The cursor temporarily switches to the Item tool cursor and remains that way until you release the ⌘ or Ctrl key.

The Pseudo-Item tool can do everything the Item tool can do except select more than one item. The real reason to use the Pseudo-Item tool is that when you access it from the Content tool, you can do almost anything that you can do with the Item tool.

The Content Tool: What's Inside?

The Content tool enables you to modify the *contents* of an item, such as the text in a text box or the picture in a picture box. The Content tool is the more powerful of the top two tools, because it can do almost everything the Item tool can do (as the Pseudo-Item tool), and much more. About the only thing it can't do is select more than one item at a time.

With the Content tool, you can resize, move, and rotate items by entering values in the Measurements palette at the bottom of the screen or by changing values in the Modify dialog box (press ⌘-M, **Ctrl+M** for Windows). In addition, you can import, create, and modify text within text boxes, and you can import and edit pictures within picture boxes.

When you have chosen a text box and you pass the Content tool over it, the cursor changes into an I bar. When you have selected a picture box with a picture in it and you pass the Content tool over it, the cursor becomes a hand (similar to the grabber hand that appears to push the page around when you press the Option key). When the picture box is empty, you get the pointer.

The I bar is used to select and move text around within a text box. The grabber hand is used to move a picture around inside a picture box.

The Rotation Tool: What's Your Angle?

In QuarkXPress, you can rotate items to the precise 1/1000 of a degree, which is particularly useful when that client of yours wants to rotate some text exactly 42.387°.

To rotate an item with the Rotation tool, first select the item with either the Content tool or Item tool by clicking on it. Select the Rotation tool, and then click in the center of the item and drag *to the right*. If you drag in any other direction, the item will rotate automatically so that it aligns with the angle you have drawn from the center.

Once you drag to the right, you can drag up, down, or in a complete circle around the point you originally clicked. As you drag (keeping the mouse button down the entire time), note the third field from the left on the top row of the Measurements palette. The number in that field is the current rotation, and it changes to correspond with the angle of the item even as you are rotating it.

The Zoom Tool: Not Just for Kids

In order to see small areas of your document, you can use the Zoom tool to magnify these areas, making them appear larger on your screen and enabling you to adjust elements of your document more precisely. Don't be concerned about how this affects your document's size. The only thing that changes is the amount of detail you get to see in the document.

There are several ways to use the Zoom tool. The first way is to select it by clicking on it, and then to click anywhere in the document. Your document will enlarge on the screen by 25%. You can continue clicking to zoom in further, with each click magnifying your document an additional 25%, until you are at 400% of the document's original size. When you reach 400% magnification, the little plus in the middle of the zoom tool disappears, indicating that you cannot zoom in any further.

The Rotation tool sometimes produces unwanted results when you are playing with it. Press ⌘-Z (**Ctrl+Z** in Windows) to "unrotate" the item back to where it was before its last rotation. To get it back to normal after several rotations, highlight the angle field in the Measurements palette (double-click on it) and enter **0** or the desired rotation. The item returns to its original angle.

Zoomin' Out

To change the magnification in the other way, that is to zoom out and see less detail, press the **Option** key (**Alt** for Windows) when you have selected the Zoom tool. The magnifying glass changes to show a minus sign, which indicates that you can make the document view smaller in increments of 25%.

The current magnification is shown in the little box in the lower left corner of the screen; it's usually followed by a percentage (%) sign.

You can then zoom out all the way to 10% of the document's original size. At this zoom level the page becomes a tiny rectangle, and all type and pictures are pretty much indistinguishable.

If you don't like zooming in increments of 25%, you can change the Zoom tool preferences. To change the magnification level, increase or decrease to a different percentage in the document you are working on, and double-click on the **Zoom** tool in the toolbox. The Zoom tool Preferences box appears, as shown in the following figure. Change the Increment text field to the amount you want the viewing percentage to change each time you click with the Zoom tool. The minimum is 1%, and the maximum is 400%. To change the Zoom tool increments for *all* subsequent documents, make this preference change when no documents are open.

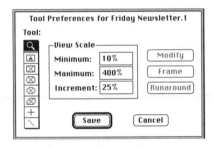

The Zoom tool preferences.

How Cool People Zoom

All this talk of zooming in and out by specific increments is nice, but the best way to zoom isn't by clicking at all. Instead, you drag a *marquee* around the objects you want to magnify. The area within the marquee expands to as large as possible so that you can see everything within that area at a larger size.

Marquee Ever been to the movies downtown? Did you see those lights around the names of the movies that were playing? That's a *marquee*. On a computer, a marquee is a similar beast, but instead of lights it consists of dotted lines.

To draw a marquee with the Zoom tool, select the **Zoom** tool and click and drag the cursor away from the starting point. As you drag, the marquee appears around the area you are dragging. When you release the mouse button, the area within the marquee becomes as large as the document window, as shown in the following figures.

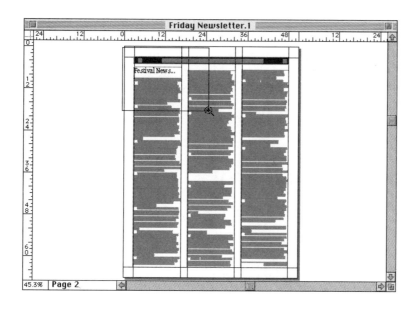

The document as it normally appears (above), and after the zoom marquee is drawn (below).

Don't Select the Zoom Tool

If you prefer to use the keyboard to zoom, you can press the ⌘ key on the keyboard instead of selecting the Zoom tool from the toolbox. (To zoom out, press both ⌘ and Option.) The cursor becomes the Zoom tool. You then proceed to use the Zoom tool just as you would if you had selected it from the toolbox.

The Text Box Creation Tool

Text in QuarkXPress can only exist inside a text box, and the Text Box creation tool is the way to place text boxes on the page.

TECHNO NERD TEACHES...

Actually, the Automatic Text box option in the New Document dialog box (see Chapter 5) is another way to place text boxes on a page.

To place a text box on a page, select the **Text Box creation** tool and click the spot where you want a corner of the text box to be. Drag the cursor across the document to the place where you want the opposite corner of the text box. When you release the mouse button, a text box appears. Note that in QuarkXPress versions 3.2 and older, text boxes can only be rectangular.

The Picture Box Creation Tools

The bulk of the creation tools are the Picture Box creation tools. These tools are used to create "containers" for pictures that are imported into QuarkXPress. Picture boxes can also be used as graphic elements in their own right. You can color any picture box, and put a frame (border) on it as well. (Chapter 22 fills you in on the techniques for making your picture boxes pea soup green and their borders martian-landscape orange.)

The Rectangle Picture Box Creation Tool

Long name, huh? This tool creates rectangular picture boxes. If you press the **Shift** key as you draw the box, you can constrain the picture box to a perfect square.

The Rounded Rectangle Picture Box Creation Tool

Ridiculously long name, eh? As its name indicates, this tool creates rectangular picture boxes with rounded corners. The rounded corners are usually rounded to a radius of .25" (1p6). If you press the **Shift** key as you draw, you can constrain the shape of the picture box to a perfect square (albeit with rounded corners).

The size of the rounded corners is measured by the distance from where the corner normally would be to where the curve starts on the straight edge. This length is the corner radius, shown in the third text field on the bottom row of the Measurements palette. To change the size of the rounded corner, increase or decrease the value in that text field in the Measurements Palette to make the corner larger or smaller.

To change the default rounded corner radius from 1p6 to another size, double-click on the **Rounded Corner Rectangle Picture Box creation** tool in the toolbox, and click the **Modify** button. In the messy dialog box that appears, enter a new value in the Corner Radius text field. All rounded corner rectangles you create from this point on will have the corner radius you specify. If you currently have a document open, this change is only effective in the open document. If no documents are open, this change is effective in all future documents.

The Oval Picture Box Creation Tool

To create ovals and circles, use the Oval Picture Box creation tool. If you press the **Shift** key as you drag, the oval will be constrained to equal height and width creating… a circle!

The Polygon Picture Box Creation Tool

This tool is a little different from the others in that, instead of clicking and dragging diagonally to create a picture box, you have to click to set each individual point of the polygon you want to draw.

The first click sets the first point, the second sets the second point, and so on until the shape is created, as shown below. The only thing to remember is to make the last point in the same place as the first point.

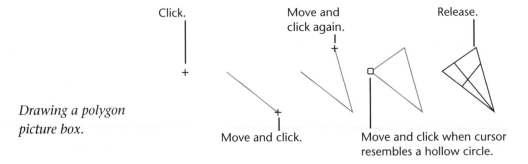

Click.

Move and
click again.

Release.

*Drawing a polygon
picture box.*

Move and click.

Move and click when cursor
resembles a hollow circle.

Once you have drawn the polygon picture box, the points on each corner disappear, and the standard eight handles appear on the outside of a bounding rectangle which is just large enough to include the entire Polygon picture box.

The lines that make up the polygon picture boxes are straight lines. You are limited to two hundred and fifty-five lines per polygon, a number that most QuarkXPress users won't even approach.

The Line Creation Tools

There are two tools that are used to create lines in QuarkXPress. The first has a bizarre name: the Orthagonal Line tool. The Orthagonal Line tool draws horizontal and vertical lines *only*. The other line tool, the Diagonal Line tool, can draw lines at any angle.

The most important difference between the two tools is that you cannot change the angle of a line drawn with the Orthagonal Line tool (except in 90° increments) with the Item or Content tools. You can only change the length and width of the line.

When you draw lines with the Diagonal Line tool, you can constrain them to horizontal or vertical orientation by pressing the **Shift** key as you draw. However, you can change the angle of these lines with both the Item and Content tools. You can also change the angle of an Orthagonal line by editing the angle field in the Measurements palette when the line is selected.

Lines drawn with the Orthagonal line tool are useful for forms and other documents that contain only perfectly horizontal and vertical lines. If you use this tool, you know those lines won't accidentally be nudged into a different angle.

Missing No More: The Link Tools

The two text linking tools have one fairly straightforward purpose: to link and unlink text boxes. Text boxes can be set up so that the text from one text box flows into another, and another, until the end of the story. It doesn't matter where the text boxes are located, as long as the text is linking them together.

You link text boxes by selecting the **Link** tool and clicking on the text box that is the first in the chain of text boxes. Click on the second text box, and the text from the first box flows to the second box.

To unlink text boxes, select the **Unlink** tool and click on the arrowhead or tail feathers in the text box that you want to unlink from the text box chain.

TECHNO NERD TEACHES...

If you want to unlink a text box in the middle of several text boxes without destroying the link between the other text boxes in the chain, press the **Shift** key when using the Unlink tool.

Another nice feature of the linking tools is that when either one is selected after a text box that is part of a chain has been selected, gray arrows appear between the text boxes, showing the path that the text takes as it moves from one text box to another. This linking is shown in the following figure.

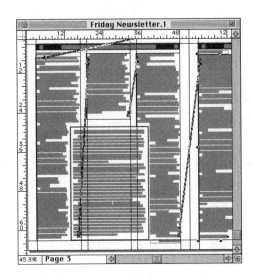

Links between text boxes are visible when a text box in the chain is selected and a linking tool is chosen.

The Least You Need to Know

Maybe it's not your dad's toolbox, but the tools in QuarkXPress have as many (if not more) uses. Getting to know the tools well takes a bit of time, but learning them will help prevent much frustration in the future.

- ☞ The toolbox is divided into three sections: the top tools section contains a mishmash of useful tools, the creation tools section contains tools used to create items, and the bottom section contains the text linking tools.

- ☞ The Item tool only affects items, not the contents of items. The best thing about the Item tool is that it can select more than one object at a time.

- ☞ The Content tool is used to edit the insides of items, such as the text inside of a text box.

- ☞ The Zoom tool increases the viewing magnification of the document, but the document itself is not changed in any way by its use.

- ☞ Holding down the ⌘ key is the same as selecting the Zoom tool.

- ☞ The creation tools create objects.

Chapter 9
A Set of Discriminating Palettes

In This Chapter

- ☛ Understanding the Measurements palette
- ☛ The Color palette
- ☛ The Document Layout palette
- ☛ The other, lesser palettes

QuarkXPress has five main palettes in addition to the toolbox, which is also a palette of sorts. Using commands in the View menu, you can show or hide all of these palettes. In addition, you can display the Measurements palette by pressing a key command that would normally highlight one of the text fields on the palette. The palettes are all *floating* palettes, which means they exist above your document window, and can only be covered up by other palettes.

To move a palette, click and drag on the gray bar that is usually along one edge of the palette. (It looks and acts like a little title bar.)

The Measurements Palette

The palette you will undoubtedly use more than any other is the Measurements palette, shown in the following figure. In this palette, you will make the most precise changes to items, text, and pictures in QuarkXPress.

The Measurements palette.

The information in the Measurements palette changes to reflect the selected items and contents of those items. If a text box is selected, the Measurements palette will show information about that text box, including its location, size, size of type, font, kerning, and other text-box-related information.

To automatically select the first field in the Measurements palette, press ⌘-**Option-M**. If the Measurements palette has been hidden, use this key combination to display it.

TECHNO NERD TEACHES...

When a text box is selected and the Content tool is being used, ⌘-**Option-Shift-M** highlights the font field of the Measurements palette.

Style sheet   A set of styles for text, such as 12-pt. Helvetica Italic with –20 tracking, flush left, auto-leading, with a two-line drop cap. You can apply this set of styles to text instantly instead of having to apply each style individually.

To move around the Measurements palette, use the same Tab and Shift-Tab combinations that you use to navigate through dialog boxes. Tab highlights the next text field; Shift-Tab highlights the previous text field.

When the Item tool is selected, the right half of the Measurements palette will *always* be empty. When more than one object is selected, only X, Y, and the angle of the selected objects will be shown. If nothing appears in the Measurements palette, no items are selected in the active document.

The Colors Palette

The Colors palette, shown in the following figure, is used to apply colors to items, frames of items, and contents of items. (You can only apply gradients to item backgrounds.) In addition, you can specify tints for each color in this palette.

The Colors palette.

Command-clicking on a color (Ctrl+clicking in Windows) opens the Edit colors dialog box, where you may add, delete, or modify existing colors. Chapter 22 discusses this box in more detail.

Fashionable Bed Covers: The Style Sheets Palette

You use the Style Sheets palette, shown in the following figure, to apply style sheets to paragraphs by placing the cursor in a paragraph and clicking on the style you want to change the paragraph to. To remove any local style changes (changes within a style) when applying a new style sheet, press the Option key while selecting the new style sheet.

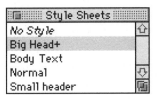

The Style Sheets palette.

Command-clicking on a style sheet opens the Edit Style Sheets dialog box, where you can add, delete, or modify existing style sheets. The style applied to the paragraph that currently contains the cursor is highlighted in the Style Sheets palette. If the style has been modified from the original style specifications, a plus will appear next to the name of the style.

The Document Layout Palette

The Document Layout palette, shown in the next figure, allows you to add, delete, and reorganize the pages within your document. In the Document Layout palette, you can create spreads across several pages (like gatefolds and centerfolds), create several sets of master pages (discussed in Chapter 29), and create new and unusual page numbering schemes.

The Document Layout palette.

Trapping is the process in which QuarkXPress attempts to overcome printer misregistration by *spreading* (expanding) and *choking* (being expanded into) adjacent colors.

The outlined number in the Document Layout palette indicates the current page in your document window. The current page might not be visible, depending on where the contents of the palette have been scrolled. To get to any page quickly, you can double-click on that page. To get to a master page, double-click on the master pages at the top of the palette.

You create new pages by dragging them from the top of the window onto the main layout area, where you can choose a master page, blank page, or blank facing pages. You delete pages by selecting them and clicking the Delete button in the upper right of the palette. If you have version 3.1 or older of QuarkXPress, a trash-can icon takes the place of the Delete button, and you have to drag each page to the trash can to delete it.

The Trap Information Palette

The Trap Information palette, shown in the following figure, is not for the squeamish. It is used to set up custom *trapping* for your document. The most helpful and useful thing about this palette is that it explains to you, in as close to English as trapping allows, what is being trapped and how that is being accomplished.

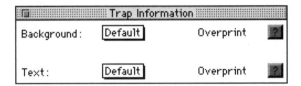

The Trap Information palette.

One way to become familiar with trapping is to go around your document, click on pairs of items, then check the information in the Trap Information palette. Trapping and other complex printing issues are tackled in Chapter 34.

The Library Palette

This is the unsung hero of palettes. The Library palette, shown in the next figure, is an organization haven used to keep track of QuarkXPress-related artwork, headings, articles, and even entire pages. A library is a useful place to organize artwork that has been modified in QuarkXPress as well.

OOPS!

Storing artwork in libraries is not a replacement for saving the artwork files on your hard drive. You will still need to retain a copy of the original artwork in order to print the artwork contained in libraries.

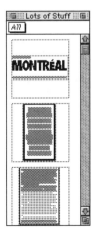

The Library palette. (This library is called "Lots of Stuff.")

The Least You Need to Know

Palettes provide you with several options that are right at hand when you are working in a document. Because you can move, show, or hide palettes at any time while you are working, it is easier and quicker to work with palettes than it is to use their corresponding menu items.

☞ You can show and hide the palettes in QuarkXPress by using the options in the View menu.

☞ You display the Measurements palette by pressing ⌘-**Option-M**.

☞ To close a palette, click on its little white Close box.

☞ The toolbox is a palette.

Part II
Beyond the Typewriter

Like the previous part, you can read these chapters while sacked out in a hammock, though you should have your portable computer out there with you. I've tried typing in a hammock, and all I have to say is "Wow! You'd think the computer case would crack after falling four feet and then being crushed by a two-hundred-pound adult male."

This part is where we get down to brass tacks, which just so happens to be one of the silliest sayings I can think of. Brass tacks? Huh? Anyway, in the following ten chapters, I'll tell you how QuarkXPress handles text, and how you can handle QuarkXPress.

Chapter 10
Why We Must Use Text Boxes

In This Chapter

- Why text can only exist inside text boxes
- How to manipulate text boxes
- Working with columns inside text boxes
- Linking text boxes

In order to work with type, you must create a text box. This chapter deals with creating, using, and modifying text boxes, but read it anyway. It's much more exciting than it sounds.

The Silly Text-in-a-Text-Box Rule

Memorize this line, and your world will be a happier place:

Text can only exist inside of text boxes.

This rule is the number one reason why PageMaker People (an unruly sect who worship overly large document files) say that QuarkXPress is too "boxy." Unfortunately, PageMaker People fail to note that, although its text boxes are invisible, PageMaker poses the same limitation, and one tool is used both to create and to edit the text boxes.

In QuarkXPress, you *must* create a text box in order to enter text into the document. If you try typing without a text box, QuarkXPress beeps maddeningly until you make one.

Text boxes are items that you can move, adjust, and group with other items as long as the Item tool is selected. You create, select, and edit the text inside the text boxes using the Content tool.

Read this section again and again (you can skip the PageMaker People part) until all of it sinks in.

Brand-Spanking-New Text Boxes

You create a text box by selecting the Text Box creation tool (shown in the following figure) and then going to the document and dragging diagonally to draw a rectangle (also shown in the figure). Text boxes can be any size, but they must always be rectangular (at least initially). To constrain the text box to a square, hold down the **Shift** key while you are dragging.

Using the Text Box creation tool to create a text box.

After you draw the text box, the tool will snap back to either the Content or Item tool. If the Content tool is selected, a blinking *insertion point* will appear in the upper left corner of the text box, indicating where new characters that you type will appear. You can place an insertion point anywhere within a block of text by clicking between any two characters that are side by side.

Resizing Text Boxes

To change the size of a text box after you create it, select any of the eight handles (shown in the following figure) and drag them. You can use any tool to change the size of the text box. Dragging the handles on the corners of the text box changes both the height and width of the text box. Dragging the handles that are located in the middle of the sides of the text box changes only the width or the height.

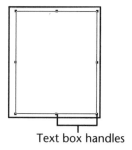

Text box handles

The handles on a text box.

You can convert your text box into a funky shape by selecting it, selecting **Item→Box Shape→Polygon**, and then selecting **Item→Reshape Polygon**. This creates several control points you can use to change the shape of the text box. Read more about reshaping text and picture boxes in Chapter 8.

Shoving Text Boxes Around Your Document

To move a text box, select the Item tool (or press ⌘ with any other tool except the Zoom tool) and click on the text box (anywhere except on a handle). Then drag it in the direction you want to move it. Release the mouse button when the text box is located where you want it.

You can actually perform this action in two different ways. If you click and drag instantly, without pausing between the click and the drag, the image you drag will consist of only an outline of the text box. If you click and then pause until the item blinks (a second or two) before dragging, the contents of the text box will be displayed as you drag it across the screen. This is called a live rotate.

Anytime you drag an object off the edge of the document window, the window will scroll along with you to show you where you are placing the object.

Text Boxes Spinning Out of Control

The only way to modify text so that it appears at an angle other than 0° (as it does in this sentence), is to rotate the text box that contains it. To rotate a text box, follow these steps:

1. Select the text box by clicking on it (make sure the handles are visible on the edges and corners of the text box).

2. Select the Rotate tool and click at the point from which you want your rotation to pivot. Pause for a second (if you want to do a live rotate) while still pressing the mouse button and drag to the left.

3. Keep the mouse button pressed and drag the cursor around the text box. It will rotate as you drag.

4. When you like the angle of the text box, release the mouse button. The text box stays at that angle. (You can see the angle of your rotation in the fifth field of the Measurements palette as you rotate.)

5. When a text box is angled, you may still select and edit text as you did before rotating it.

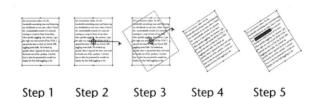

Steps for rotating a text box.

Step 1   Step 2   Step 3   Step 4   Step 5

Using the Measurements Palette with Text Boxes

Instead of using the Item tool, you can also use the Measurements palette to resize, move, and rotate your text boxes. In fact, it is easier to manipulate your text boxes this way than to use the Item and Rotation tools to do the same thing.

In the following example you'll move, resize, and rotate a text box, all with the Measurements palette. To make a text box on your screen look like the one in the following figure, follow these steps:

1. Make sure the text box is selected, then press ⌘-**Option-M** (**Ctrl+Alt+M** for Windows). This key command selects the Measurements palette. The first text field (labeled X) becomes highlighted.

2. The X field (not to be confused with "The X-Files," that very scary TV show) is the distance from the position of the zero point to the left side of the text box. Type **6p** in the text field and press **Tab**. The text box moves six picas to the right.

3. The next field highlighted is the Y field, in which you enter the distance from the zero point to the text box. Type **15p** in this text field and press **Tab**. The text box moves 15 picas down.

4. The W text field is now highlighted; it holds the value for the width of the text box. Enter **25p** and press **Tab**. The text box becomes 25 picas wide.

5. The H field becomes highlighted. This is the height of the text box. Enter **20p** and press **Tab**. The text box is now 20 picas tall.

6. The next field highlighted is the angle field. Normally this is at 0°, meaning that the text box is right side up. Enter **15** in this box (you don't need the ° symbol). This rotates the text box 15° counterclockwise. (Entering a negative number causes the text box to rotate clockwise.) Press **Enter**. All the changes take effect at once: moving, resizing, and rotating.

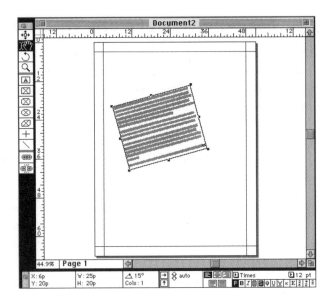

Changing text box attributes with the Measurements palette.

Goodbye, Text Boxes

Pressing the Delete key does not delete a text box... unless you have the Item tool selected. When you have the Content tool selected, pressing the Delete key deletes the last character typed. If there are no characters to delete, QuarkXPress beeps at you.

No matter which tool you are using, you can delete any object, including text boxes, by pressing ⌘-**K** (**Ctrl+K** in Windows). (I like to think of K for Kill, but that's something my therapist is helping me work through.) The menu command for ⌘-K appears in the Item menu, at the menu item Delete. That is because this command, quite logically, deletes selected items.

TECHNO NERD TEACHES...

In version 3.2, the coolest way to delete *any* item, including text boxes, is to press ⌘-Option-K. Instead of your object being deleted instantly, a little alien-like fellow (shown in the following figure) wanders onto the screen and uses his ray gun to blast a hole into your object, causing it to change into several bright colors (on a color monitor) before disappearing. Amazing, the technology today....

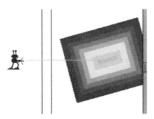

One of the aliens inside your computer, given free reign to blast away unwanted items...

Adding Columns within Text Boxes

You can split any text box into several columns, with text inside of the box flowing from columns on the left to columns on the right, as shown in the figure. Be careful when you're creating columns, though. Having several columns within one text box reduces the number of characters that can be within the text box. Because of this, changing the number of columns after the text has been set can produce unwanted text rewrap, and the text might take up much more or much less space than it did at the previous column width.

Text flows easily through columns within each text box.

Normally, each text box has one column. To change the number of columns in a text box, go to the Measurements palette and select the third field from the left on the bottom (labeled Cols). Enter the number of columns you want to divide the text box into, and the text box is broken up into that many columns. Or go to the Columns field in the Modify dialog box, where you can also specify a gutter value at the same time.

You can also change the amount of space between columns by selecting **Item→Modify** and changing the amount in the Gutter text field. The wider the gutters in your text box, the thinner the columns will be. Gutters must be at least 3 points wide no matter how many columns are in the text box.

This discussion brings us to the interesting dilemma of the one-column text box, which of course doesn't need a gutter. It doesn't matter; the gutter width must still be a minimum of 3 points.

Linking Text Boxes

To make text flow from one text box to another, create the text boxes to house the text. Select the Link tool (second from bottom in the toolbox) and click on the first text box, where the text will start. The edges of the text box will turn into a moving marquee. Then click on the text box to which the text is to flow, and the text flows from the first text box to the next.

Do you want to see how your text flows? If one of the text boxes in the text chain is selected, select the unlinking tool and click on the center of a text box to display arrows that show the direction of the text flow, as the story in the text boxes moves from one to the next.

To link several boxes, press the **Option** key when you select the Link tool. You can continue to link as many text boxes as you want.

To unlink text boxes, select the **Unlink** tool, then click on the tail feathers or tip of the link arrow you would like to break. To remove one text box from a chain of several without destroying the rest of the links, press **Shift** while you click on the link tail feathers or arrow tip you want to remove.

Changing the Text Box Specs

When a text box is selected, choose **Item→Modify** to access the Text Box Specifications dialog box (shown in the following figure). In this dialog box, you can do everything that you can do with the left side of the Measurements palette and more.

Text Box Specifications

		First Baseline
Origin Across:	8p10.327	Offset: 0p
Origin Down:	3p10.177	Minimum: Ascent
Width:	29p1.673	
Height:	25p3.573	Vertical Alignment
Box Angle:	0°	Type: Top
Box Skew:	0°	Inter ¶ Max: 0p
Corner Radius:	0p	Background
Columns:	3	Color: None
Gutter:	1p.024	Shade: ▶ 100%
Text Inset:	0 pt	
☐ Suppress Printout		OK Cancel

The Text Box Specifications dialog box.

In the left column is an item called Box Skew. Increasing this angle *skews* the text box to the right. Decreasing this angle skews the text box to the left.

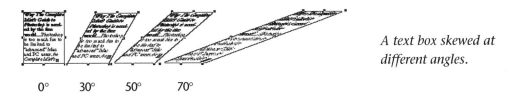

0°   30°   50°   70°

A text box skewed at different angles.

You can add white space around the inside edge of the text box by increasing the value in the Text Inset field. The value you enter will be the amount of white space on each side of the text box. It's useful to put a frame on a text box (see Chapter 27) because it prevents the frame from being too close to the characters.

SPEAK LIKE A GEEK

Skewing results when the top of an item is moved left or right, and the bottom of the item is moved in the opposite direction.

You can also choose a background color for the text box in the Background Color pop-up menu. The text color will not change when you change this setting. (As a result, you might not want to change the background color to black because you wouldn't be able to see the black text.)

The Least You Need to Know

This chapter taught you just about everything you need to know about text boxes. But just so you don't forget anything important, here are the highlights again:

- ☞ Text cannot exist in QuarkXPress unless you first create a text box to hold it.

- ☞ Text boxes are the most common items in QuarkXPress, and the Text Box creation tool is the mother of all text boxes.

- ☞ You resize a text box by dragging the handles on the corners and the edges of the box.

- ☞ You can create any number of columns within a selected text box, so long as the total width of the gutters is not greater than the width of the text box.

- ☞ You can reposition, rotate, and resize text boxes within the left side of the ever-present Measurements palette.

Chapter 11
Entering Letters, Numbers, and Bizarre Symbols

In This Chapter

☛ Entering type

☛ Accessing special characters

☛ Importing and exporting type

The real strength of QuarkXPress has always been its excellent type-handling capabilities. This chapter gives you the lowdown on the basics of typing text in QuarkXPress, and lets you in on where you can find all those nifty symbols everyone *else* seems to be using.

You don't even need to know how to type (though it helps) to learn the concepts in this chapter. All you need is a keyboard with the letters printed on each key. (Did you ever wonder why, in Typing class, there were pieces of masking tape and mom's favorite red Magic Marker?)

Typing Text

You can enter text directly in QuarkXPress by typing it in a text box when the Content tool is selected. If you need a refresher on creating and editing text boxes, flip back to Chapter 10. Otherwise, continue!

Inserting the Insertion Point

The insertion point in a text box is the location at which the next characters you type will appear. You move the insertion point by clicking between any two characters in a text box. An empty text box normally has a blinking insertion point in the upper left-hand corner. You'll only see the insertion point when you have selected the Content tool.

Character   Any single letter, number, or symbol that you type in QuarkXPress. Every time you press a key within a text box, a character is generated. Characters also include spaces, tabs, and returns.

Text entered with the keyboard automatically wraps to the next line, flows from column to column, and flows from text box to linked text box. If you fill up a text box that is not linked to another text box, a small square with an X in it appears in the lower right corner, telling you that there is more text in the text box than can be displayed in the current font and point size.

The Almighty Typesetting Law

If there were typesetting police, they would be handing out tickets left and right to people who break the Space law, which is:

Never put more than one space between sentences.

Just compare one space to two on your printout, and you'll realize that the extra space just isn't necessary. (And if you're using justified alignment, you'll find that it really throws off the spacing that QuarkXPress leaves between words.)

I know your high school English teacher told you in his high-falutin' way that you have to put two spaces between sentences. But this is the same guy who snorted nasal spray (at least you thought it was nasal spray) and gave the class "Blue Mondays" (his term for study hall) when he didn't feel like teaching. So forget what he told you and listen to me. I don't snort nasal spray.

Capitalization

You can capitalize letters using the following methods:

1. Press Shift when typing letters, and all letters will appear UPPER-CASE. Numbers will be replaced by the symbols above them.

2. You can press the Caps Lock key so that you don't have to constantly hold down the Shift key. Engaging the Caps Lock key works like using the Shift key, except that it only affects letters—not numbers or punctuation.

3. You can change text that you originally typed as lowercase to all UPPERCASE by selecting the text and pressing ⌘-**Shift-K** (K for KAPS, this time). If you've changed text to uppercase using this command, you can change it back to lowercase by selecting the text again and pressing ⌘-Shift-K again.

A good habit to develop is to type your text as normal, but instead of typing text in all caps with the Caps Lock key, type it in lowercase or initial caps (where the first letter of each word is capitalized). Then highlight that word and press ⌘-**Shift-K**. This way, if you decide that you really want it in all lowercase or initial caps, all you have to do is select the type and press ⌘-Shift-K, and everything changes back to normal. This is much more useful when you're working with a lot of text than when you've only got a little bit.

The Caps Lock key is like a Shift key that only affects letters. Punctuation, numbers, and other symbols pretend nothing special is happening when Caps Lock is pressed. This is in contrast to the way the Caps Lock on a typewriter behaves, where most if not all keys are "shifted" to the secondary symbols.

Caps Lock is very useful for typing initials, like I.J.A. If I had typed that with the Shift key pressed, it would look like I>J>A>—which is... well, wrong.

Rubbing Out Nasty Characters

To delete the previous character you typed—the one before the insertion point—press the **Delete** key (Plus and DOS keyboards say Backspace) on the upper right corner of the main section of the keyboard. You can also delete the next character, the one after the insertion point, by pressing **Shift-Delete** (Del on an extended keyboard).

When you have selected characters (see Chapter 12 for an in-depth look at selecting), pressing the **Delete** or **Backspace** key will delete all the selected characters. Pressing any other character will replace the selected text with the character(s). Pressing any other character will replace the selected text with that character.

You can delete a return by placing the insertion point on the left edge of the line following the return and pressing **Delete** or by placing the insertion point before the right figure and deleting forward.

Creating Special Characters

In most typefaces, there are several special characters available, including all sorts of symbols like ™, ®, © and ¶. Most of these characters can be accessed on a Macintosh by pressing Option and another key (or in Windows by pressing Ctrl). Others can be accessed by pressing Option-Shift and another key. For a complete listing of the different symbols available, use the Key Caps desk accessory under the Apple menu or the key chart that came with the font. Below is a list of some of the most common "hidden" symbols.

Symbol	Mac key command	Windows key command
™	Option-2	Alt+Shift+2
·	Option-8	Alt+Shift+8
¢	Option-4	Alt+Shift+4
…	Option-;	Alt+Shift+;
– (en dash)	Option-hyphen (-)	Ctrl+=
— (em dash)	Shift-Option-hyphen (-)	Ctrl+Shift+=
®	Option-r	Alt+Shift+R
"	Option-g	Alt+Shift+C
÷	Option-/	Alt+Shift+/

Symbol	Mac key command	Windows key command
π	Option-p	Alt+Shift+P
†	Option-t	

Windows users can see all of the special symbols available in a particular font using the Windows Character Map accessory (located in the Accessories application group). All the characters in that font are displayed. Double-click on the character you want to use, close the character map, and paste that character where you want it to appear in your text.

'Typesetting' "Quotes" vs. "Inch" and 'Foot' Marks

Nothing gives away the fact that a printed piece was created by an amateur more than the use of inch marks (") and foot marks (') for quotation marks (") and single quotes ('). In most word processing software, as well as QuarkXPress, you can turn on an option called "Smart Quotes," which automatically creates curved quotes for you when you type the inch and foot keys on the keyboard.

If you activate this option (by selecting Edit→Preferences→Application and checking the Smart Quotes check box), you won't have to memorize the obscure key commands for each of these curled quotes (listed above). But you will face another problem: what if you need to designate something in inches or feet? What to do then? Panic? Turn the Smart Quotes option on and off each time? Give up all hope?

Actually, you can use the standard inch and foot marks when the Smart Quotes option is on by pressing the Control key and the inch or foot mark. For the inch mark, press ⌘-**Shift**-". For the foot mark, press ⌘-'. So, no need to panic. Typesetters give them authenticity by selecting the character and making it italic. Better yet, use the foot and inch symbols included in the symbol font.

Typesetting quotes are called a number of names, including Curvy Quotes, Curly Quotes, Real Quotes, and strangely enough, Cool-looking Quotes. Inch and foot marks are commonly referred to as Straight Quotes and Typewriter Quotes.

F-Ligatures: Siamese Letters

A *ligature* is a pair or trio of characters that are joined together to create a more eye-pleasing result than if the two separate letters were just smashed together normally as a result of character spacing. Most people are familiar with the a-e ligature, with looks like æ in lowercase and Æ in uppercase. These ligatures are rarely used, and don't represent the true usefulness of ligatures.

Ligatures are only available on Macintosh systems. If you're a Windows user and this bugs you, send a note to Bill G. about it.

There are four standard ligatures that are used in typesetting today, the fl and ffl ligatures (ffl) and the fi and ffi ligatures (ffi). Depending on the typeface used, these may or may not be pleasing to the eye. The ligatures are used because the hook that hangs down on an f often runs into the l or dot of the i awkwardly, making the letters difficult to read.

You can have QuarkXPress create f-ligatures automatically. Simply select **Edit→Preferences→Typographic** and select the **F-ligatures** preference in the dialog box that appears. If you would prefer to type an f-ligature without changing the preferences, press ⌘-**Shift-5** for ffi and ⌘-**Shift-6** for ffl. QuarkXPress considers each of the f-ligatures to be one character.

Symbol Fonts

The standard symbol font, called for some strange reason, "Symbol," contains several special characters including mathematical characters and Greek letters, like the ones shown below.

Key	Symbol
P	Π
\	∴
b	β
p	π
D	Δ
Q	Θ
W	Ω

You can switch from your current font selection and use one character at a time from the Symbol font by pressing ⌘-**Shift-Q** (**Ctrl+Shift+Q** in Windows) followed by the character you want from the Symbol font. The character after the symbol font reverts back to the font you were using before you switched to symbol.

Hanging Around a Bunch of Dingbats

Also known by a select few as "All in the Family" fonts, *Dingbats* come in several varieties. The most common and popular is called Zapf Dingbats, which is a collection of various shapes and little doodads that are rather helpful. The pointing hand symbol that appears in the "In This Chapter" and "The Least You Should Know" sections of this book is a Zapf Dingbat accessed by pressing Shift.

Several of the more popular Zapf Dingbat characters are shown below.

Key	Symbol
3	✓
B	✛
H	★
X	✳
S	▲
o	❑
v	❖
w	❯

Invisible Characters

Now, I admit this all sounds a little far-fetched, and that the only invisible characters we are familiar with are usually of the pixie variety, but there are several characters we type every day that we can't see. For instance, space. "Not fair," you say, "since we know they are there because…" of what? The *space* they create? C'mon, now. Actually, it is quite difficult to tell the difference between one and two spaces next to each other, and even harder to tell the difference between two and three spaces.

For this reason, the View menu has an option called Show Invisibles (⌘-I on a Mac, Ctrl+I in Windows). When Show Invisibles is selected, teeny tiny little dots appear in spaces, one for each space. This way it is easy for you to count how many spaces there are between other more visible characters.

Other characters that are "invisible," but that show up with this option include tabs, returns, line breaks, and End of Page markers (which force text after them to the next page), all of which are discussed in Chapter 7.

Importing Text That You Typed Somewhere Else

People who have QuarkXPress and a word processing program usually don't like typing in QuarkXPress. It's rather slow, and it's full of unnecessary stuff that most people don't want to worry about when typing. If that wasn't bad enough, the width of a letter-sized document doesn't fit on the standard 13/14" screen. When you get toward the end of a line, the whole screen scrolls over. Then it jumps back to the left side of the page when you start a new line. The whole screen is constantly being redrawn, which is very annoying.

Importing is the process of bringing text or a graphic object that has been created in other software into QuarkXPress.

Exporting is the opposite of importing. Instead of bringing text or pictures into QuarkXPress, you save the file to your hard disk in a format that another software program can open and use.

If you're one of those people who doesn't like to type in QuarkXPress, you don't have to. You can *import* just about any text file created with any word processing program. QuarkXPress accomplishes this feat by providing XTensions that convert many different file types into a format QuarkXPress can import. With Microsoft Word you can even import the style sheets (style sheets are discussed in Chapter 19).

Before importing text, make sure that a text box and the Content tool are selected. If the text is being added to the end of an existing story, be sure to place the cursor at the end of that story. (You can do this quickly by pressing ⌘-**End**, or **Ctrl+End** for Windows.) If any text is selected when the file is imported, the selected text will be deleted and replaced with the contents of the newly imported text file. (If you don't want that to happen, make sure you don't have any text selected.)

To import text into QuarkXPress, select **File→Get Text** or press ⌘-**E** (**Ctrl+E** for Windows). The Get Text dialog box appears, asking for the text file. If you click once on the text file's name, information about that file will appear. You'll then have two options: (1) Do you want quotes in text converted into typesetting quotes, and (2) Do you want any style sheets included? Unless there are inch measurements specified within a text file, always check convert quotes. To complete the import, click open or just double-click the file name.

Taking Text Out (Exporting Text)

Sometimes it is necessary for you to *export* text into a text file. Maybe you need the text in another layout program, or maybe you want to work on it in a word processor.

Before you can export text, decide which portion of the story will be exported, and select it. (If you want to export the entire story, don't bother selecting any text.) Then, select **File→Save Text** (⌘-**Option-E**), and the Save Text dialog box appears. In addition to being able to choose between saving only the selected text and saving the entire story, you can use a pop-up menu at the bottom of the dialog box to control the format in which the file will be saved. The list only includes the text XTensions you loaded during installation. Type in the name of the file you're saving and click **OK**. A new file is created on your hard drive that can be opened by a word processor that corresponds to the file type.

The Least You Need to Know

Just when you thought it was safe to hunt and peck, I throw this chapter at you and tell you that you need to know how to type. However, by teaching you to import, I've given you an alternative: You could avoid typing entirely if you could find someone to type for you—and then just import what he types.

- ☞ You can only type when you are using the Content tool and have a text box selected.

- ☞ The Delete key (Backspace on some keyboards) deletes the character to the left of the blinking insertion point.

- ☞ You can create many special characters by pressing **Option** or **Option-Shift** (**Alt** or **Alt+Shift** in Windows) when you press a key.

- ☞ To see all the available characters in a font, Mac users press ⌘-→; Windows users display the Character Map accessory.

Chapter 12
Selecting Text So You Can Do Stuff to It

In This Chapter

- ☛ Selecting with the mouse and the keyboard
- ☛ Deleting and replacing selected text
- ☛ Copying and moving selected text

In order to make changes to anything in QuarkXPress, you must select the object first. If nothing is selected, nothing will be changed. You can't affect it until you select it. The same is true for text. This chapter explains some of the umpteen (18, actually) different ways you can perform the vital task of selecting. It also covers some of the things you can do with selected text, such as move it, copy it, or kill it.

Random Notes on Selecting Text

After reading the introduction to this chapter, you may be wondering why there are 18 different ways to select text. The number one reason is to confuse and frustrate the QuarkXPress novice. The second reason is that there are at least 18 different circumstances in which one way is better than the other seventeen for selecting the text. All these ways have one thing in common, however; you must first select the Content tool before you can use any of them.

Most people latch onto a couple of different ways to make selections, which is enough to get them through most circumstances. However, the more ways you can select text, the faster and easier you'll be able to work in QuarkXPress.

One important thing to note when selecting text is that selecting text and selecting text boxes are two different things. When you select a text box, the container of the text is selected. The content of that text box is only affected in that it may flow differently if the size of that text box is drastically changed.

In order to select text inside of a text box, you must first select the text box then select the text inside it. Selecting the text box is as easy as clicking on it with either the Item or the Content tool. You can then use the Content tool to select the text inside the text box. Here's a handy rule to help you keep it all straight:

Text cannot be selected unless you have already selected the text box it is in.

Selecting Text with the Mouse

There are two basic ways to select text with the mouse: by dragging over characters or by clicking repeatedly on words, lines, and paragraphs. You can combine clicking and dragging for even more effective selecting. This section explains all the ins and outs of using the little rodent.

The I Bar and the Hot Point

When the Content tool is being used in a text box, the cursor changes to more or less resemble the letter "I." You use this cursor, commonly referred to as the I Bar (go figure), to select characters, words, and other stuff.

The I Bar has a "hot point," a certain spot that is the actual point that is being clicked when you press the mouse button. It is imperative that the hot point be at the location you want to click. The hot point is circled on the I Bar which follows.

The I Bar's hot point.

Drag Racing

A common method for selecting text is by dragging. Dragging means to press the mouse button, move the mouse over a particular area, and then release the mouse button. The following paragraphs outline several ways to select text by dragging the mouse.

- ☛ **Dragging horizontally**   You can select characters by dragging horizontally across the characters you would like to select. The more characters you drag across, the more you select.

- ☛ **Dragging vertically**   If you drag vertically, you can select several lines at one time. You can drag both up and down; the selected characters begin where you first held down the mouse button.

- ☛ **Dragging at an angle**   If you drag at an angle, you can select several lines as well as additional characters. The further you get from the location where you first held down the mouse button, the more lines and characters are selected.

- ☛ **Backtracking**   If you start dragging in one direction and then change your mind and backtrack, only the characters and lines between the original clicking location and the current location will be selected. So if you first drag to the right and then, keeping the mouse button down the entire time, drag to the left of the original location, only the characters to the left of the original location are selected when you release the mouse button.

- ☛ **Dragging from page to page**   You can literally drag from page to page if you so desire, selecting everything that your cursor crosses. In addition, you can drag from one linked text box to another, selecting text in several linked text boxes at once.

Double-Clicking

You can select one word at a time by double-clicking anywhere in that word with the hot point of the I bar. (I usually go for the center of the word, which gives me a better chance of hitting it.) To double-click, you need to click two times in the *exact* same location in rapid sequence. This can be just a little difficult at first, but once you get the hang of it, it becomes fourth nature (twice as simple as second nature).

When dragging, you can select only the text in one contiguous story at a time. Even if your cursor travels from one text box to another, the text in the second text box will not be selected unless the text inside is part of the same story (linked).

When you have selected a word by double-clicking on it, the word and the space after it (if there is one) are highlighted. The space after the word is highlighted so that if you delete that word, there are not two spaces between the remaining words.

Clicking More Than Twice

Yes, it's true. You can click three, four, even five times! Why would you want to do such a thing? The following list explains:

☛ **Triple-clicking** (Sheesh)   Triple-clicking allows you to select a line of text at once, as shown below.

Triple clicking selects a line of text.

> the players to learn how to juggle, several of them
> took up the offer and spent not only that evening
> but the rest of the week learning how to juggle.
> Three in particular, Heidi, Anthony, and Michelle,
> have gone beyond the cascade. They are excited
> about learning more, so, Montréal Juggling Club, go
> recruit.
> Not only were the thespians introduced to throwing

Of course, it takes some practice (and coordination) to get the triple-click down. Once you have perfected it, you can do the triple-click drag. No, the triple-click drag is not a wild dance from the '40s; it's a technique that lets you select successive lines of text. To triple-click drag, click three times quickly in the same location, and then drag. (Don't move that mouse between clicks!)

☞ **Quadruple-clicking** (Yikes!) An Olympic event to take place in Atlanta in '96, the quadruple-click (four clicks in the same place) is used to select a paragraph at a time. As with the triple-click, you can combine the quadruple-click with a drag to select multiple adjoining paragraphs.

Really cool QuarkXPress users don't just double-click; they double-click drag. This technique allows them to select several words at once. Here is how you do it: double-click on a word, but on the second click, don't release the mouse button. You can then drag the mouse over successive words, highlighting a word at a time instead of a character at a time. Very hip.

☞ **Quintuple-clicking** (I don't believe it!) Unfortunately, it's true. You can click five times in one location as a means of selecting all the text in the entire story. (Since you are selecting all the text in the story, you cannot quintuple-click drag. Darn.) Remember that if the text flow is linked to other text boxes on pages you can't see, all that text is selected, too.

☞ **Sextuple-clicking** (You've gotta be kidding!) Well, fortunately for you, I am. Clicking six, seven, or any number of times more than five has the same result as five clicks—it selects all the text in a story.

Instead of causing major finger strain by trying to quintuple-click, you can select all the text in a story by selecting **Edit→Select All** (⌘-A). The next section discusses this command.

Selecting with the Keyboard

You can use the keyboard to select text in a number of ways, including selecting all the text in a story, selecting between two mouse clicks, and selecting carefully one character, word, line, or paragraph at a time.

To select all the text in the story, select **Edit→Select All** or press ⌘-A (**Ctrl+A** for Windows). This is one of those keyboard equivalents you should memorize now: ⌘-A = Select All. Like other text selection methods, this command only works when the Content tool is selected. (Note that Select All only selects the text in the selected text box and any linked text boxes.) If the Item tool is selected, Select All selects all the *items*, such as lines, text boxes, and picture boxes.

The following table lists some methods for selecting smaller amounts of text with the keyboard.

Table 12.1   Keyboard Methods of Selecting Text

Press this	To select this
Shift+← or →	Selects one character to the left or right of the blinking insertion point.
Shift+↑ or ↓	Selects from the insertion point to the previous line (up) or next line (down) at that same horizontal position.
Shift+Command+← or → (Shift+Control+← or → for Windows)	Selects from the insertion point to the previous word (left) or next word (right).
Shift+Command+↑ or ↓ (Shift+Control+↑ or ↓ for Windows)	Selects from the insertion point to the top (up) or bottom (down) of the current paragraph.
Shift+Option+Command+ ← or → (Shift+Alt+Control +← or → for Windows)	Selects from the insertion point to the left end (left) or right end (right) of that line.
Shift+Option+Command +↑ or ↓ (Shift+Alt+Control for Windows)+↑ or ↓	Selects from the insertion point to the top of the story (up) or bottom of the story (down).

TECHNO NERD TEACHES...

To change the Mac default highlight color from basic black to something more visible and highlighty (it's a word, look it up in the glossary), select **Control Panels** from the **Apple** menu and choose the **Color** icon. Change the color to any of the presets available in the pop-up menu, or select **Other** to pick a custom highlight color. (Of course, if you don't have a color monitor, you'll end up with a lovely shade of gray.)

For Windows users, open the Color control panel and choose a new color scheme from the pop-up menu. Or, change the Screen Element (upper right corner) to Highlight and pick a new color from the options below.

Deleting and Replacing Selected Text

When text is selected, pressing the Delete key deletes the selected text. That's to be expected. But what many unwary QuarkXPressers don't know is that pressing *any* key when text is selected will delete that text and replace it with the character for the key you pressed.

When text is selected, be careful not to bump, nudge, or otherwise disturb your keyboard, or the selected text could be replaced with anything, including a space, a return, or another invisible character. If this should happen, don't panic. Instead, press ⌘-**Z** (**Ctrl+Z** for Windows) immediately to undo the mistake, say "Whoopsy-daisy!" or something a bit more forceful, and continue working.

Of course, if you do want to replace the text, just select it and type away to your heart's content.

Copying and Moving Text

When an object in QuarkXPress is selected, you can copy it by selecting **Edit→Copy**. Of course, on-screen nothing happens. What you've just done is make a duplicate of the selected object in the computer's RAM. It stores this object on something called the Clipboard.

The Clipboard—which holds objects that have been copied and cut—has a serious limitation: it can only hold one thing at a time. As soon as an object is cut or copied, the object that was previously on the Clipboard is gone, replaced by the object just copied or cut.

Look on your keyboard. Wait! Finish reading this paragraph first. On the bottom row, there are three keys in a row: X, C, and V. The key command ⌘-X is Cut, ⌘-C is Copy, and ⌘-V is Paste. How to remember these? Well, X looks like scissors; therefore cut. C stands for copy. And V is for Velcro—which kinda works like… paste?

When you select **Edit→Paste**, a copy of the object is placed into your document. The original that you copied is still in its original location, as is the copy on the Clipboard. You can paste again and again, creating several of the objects.

If you select Edit→Cut instead of Edit→Copy, the selected object is removed from the document but is still stored on the Clipboard. Keep in mind that you can undo any of the cut, copy, and paste operations (if you undo immediately after the operation).

To practice using these commands, follow along with these steps:

1. Type the words **Fred likes Bozo's bright tie.**

2. Select the word "Fred" by double-clicking on it.

3. Select **Copy** (⌘-C). The word "Fred" remains in the sentence, but a copy of it is placed on the Clipboard.

4. Click in front of the word "tie" and select **Edit→Paste**. Now the sentence reads "Fred likes Bozo's bright Fred tie." Not prose worthy of Dickens, but those of you who wear Fred ties will understand.

5. Next, select the word "bright" and cut it.

6. Click in front of the word "Bozo's" and select **Edit→Paste**. The sentence, a work of literary art, reads, "Fred likes bright Bozo's Fred tie."

You can continue copying and pasting until the sentence makes even less sense and breaks even more grammatical rules if you want to.

Using Cut, Copy, and Paste with Items

Cut, copy, and paste work the same with items as they do with text. Just select the items with the Item tool, and the item will be cut or copied to the Clipboard. If you have the Content tool selected, only the contents of the item are cut, copied, or pasted.

You must have the Item tool selected to paste items; if you have the Content tool selected and a text box selected, you could paste an item into a text box. This is actually a feature called anchored text boxes, which you'll read about in Chapter 31.

Beyond the Clipboard

You can only move text using Cut, Copy, and Paste for so long before you realize there must be something better. And there is something better... much better in fact. That something is called drag and drop.

Now, this may sound like where a guy puts on his spouse's clothing and surprises her when she comes in the door, but it's a very useful feature in QuarkXPress. It allows you to select text, and then simply *drag* the text to a new location by clicking within the selected area and dragging.

As you drag the selected text, a dotted vertical line follows along with your cursor, showing you where the text will go when you drop it (release the mouse button).

Make sure that the drag and drop option is checked in the application preferences menu, or it won't work. To turn it on, select **Edit→Preferences→ Application**. (It is off by default.)

The Least You Need to Know

If you're one of the select few (pun intended) who has now memorized each and every way to select text in QuarkXPress, congratulations! You'll be a QuarkXPress speed demon in no time. If you've only managed to remember a select few (oops, did it again) of the ways to select text, find others like you, and go beat the living daylights out of the nerd who memorized all of them!

- ☛ Always select objects before attempting to modify them.

- ☛ There are a multitude of ways to select objects: for example, you can drag the cursor across text; click several times; use the Shift key in conjunction with the arrow keys; or use the Select All command (⌘-A or Ctrl+A).

- ☛ When text is selected, any character you type will replace the selected text.

- ☛ Cut and Copy create objects on the Clipboard, while Paste makes a duplicate of those Clipboard objects in your document.

Chapter 13
Different Fonts, Different Sizes

In This Chapter

- Making changes to letters and words
- Changing fonts
- Making type bigger and smaller

Now that you know how to select type, wouldn't it be great if you could do something with that selected type? Selecting was the hard part, but making changes to the selected letters is really quite a bit of fun. In this chapter, you'll learn how simple it is to change the font and size of letters, words, or any other series of selected characters.

There are virtually countless combinations and variations of changes that you can make to selected type in QuarkXPress, and you're going to learn how to perform all of those changes in just a few short chapters. Makes you glad to be alive, doesn't it?

Changing Fonts

"Whoever dies with the most fonts wins," is the battle cry of many a desktop publisher. The procedure of zipping from one font to another is a major concern when you have hundreds (some have thousands) of fonts to choose from. Even if you only have the twenty-some fonts that came with your system, soon you too will become infected with what can only

SPEAK LIKE A GEEK

There is usually some confusion as to exactly what a font is versus a typeface, font, or font family. The terms **font** and **typeface** are both the most basic of terms and apply to the name itself—"Times Roman," "Helvetica Bold," and "Palatino Italic." **Font** is simply a confusing term that can mean any of a hundred different things; consequently, we won't be using that term at all. **Font families** are groups of fonts with the same first name, such as "Helvetica," "Times," and "Palatino."

be described as a font-fetish; you will soon want to have more fonts than you can ever possibly use.

QuarkXPress has two methods of selecting fonts. Select each font individually, or select the "base font" of a family and then apply bold and italic styles to change the font. For example, if Times Roman was selected (a base font), it could be transformed into Times Bold by selecting the Bold style.

Most font families consist of the base font plus bold, italic, and bold italic fonts. The base font is usually named the same name as the font family, though sometimes the word "Roman" is tacked ungracefully on the end of it.

Some font families have more than four fonts. These additional fonts are typically additional weights, like "Light" and "Black." Additional fonts in the same family can also be variations of the base font, such as "Condensed" or "Outline." These additional weights are only accessible if you select them directly.

TECHNO NERD TEACHES...

If you're using a Mac, don't use a font that is named for a city, such as New York, Monaco, Chicago, or Geneva. These four fonts are system fonts, and although they print fine on dot-matrix printers, they bitmap on laser printers and imagesetters. Geneva is a fairly ugly version of Helvetica, and New York is a blocky version of Times designed for use with dot-matrix printers.

To Serif or to Sans Serif?

Type usually falls into one of two categories. *Serif* type has little "thingies," called serifs, on the ends of the main letter strokes, while *sans serif* type does not. Traditionally, serif type was used for body copy, and sans serif type was used for headlines because it is easier to read. (Studies have been done on this whole readability thing, I'm told.)

Examples of serif type include Palatino, Times, Cheltenham (the type-face this book is set in), Garamond, and New Century Schoolbook. Examples of sans serif type are Helvetica, Avant Garde, Futura, and Univers (note the headers on this book).

Palatino
Times
Cheltenham
Garamond

Helvetica
Futura
Univers

Font examples (serif at the top, followed by three examples of sans serif).

Using the Measurements Palette to Change Fonts

Take a look at the bottom of the screen at that wide box with all the funky numbers and symbols (if the wide box is lacking all those numbers and symbols, there is no text selected yet). In the upper right corner of the box, known to most as the Measurements palette (although some of us are petitioning to change its name to "That Wide Box with all those Funky Numbers and Symbols in It") is the Font text field, which probably reads **Helvetica** right now. The Measurements palette is shown below, with all the important parts (those relative to this chapter, anyway) labeled. (If the Measurements Palette is not visible on-screen, select **View→Show Measurements Palette**.)

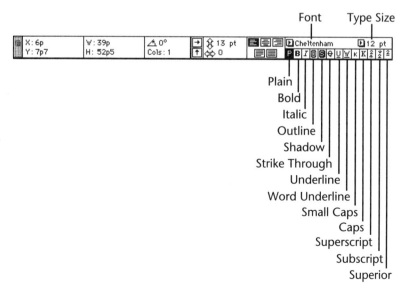

The Measurements palette.

Select the font in the Measurements palette instantly by pressing ⌘-**Option-Shift-M**. You can then type the first few characters of the font and hammer the Return or Enter key—and never even touch the mouse!

To switch to a font other than the one currently in use, click and hold on the little pop-up arrow next to the font name in the Measurements palette, and scroll up or down to the desired font. Selected type changes to that font instantly.

Another way to use the Measurements palette to change fonts is to select the name of the current font and then start typing in the name of the font you want. You don't usually have to type many letters before the entire name of the font appears. This technique (called *clairvoyant*) is helpful when you have several fonts, and you know exactly the name of the font you want to use.

The Double-Secret Font Change

There might be a time when you need to switch to a different font just to create one character (such as a bullet in Zapf Dingbats or Symbol), and then you immediately need to switch back to the original font. You'll find that switching back and forth for these fonts can be very time-consuming and annoying.

Another way to change fonts is to open the **Style** menu and choose **Font**. Choose the font you want from the menu that appears.

QuarkXPress has a feature that enables you to get around this. With a keyboard command, you can switch from the normal font to either Zapf Dingbats or Symbol to create a single character. To do this, place the cursor where you want the Dingbat to go, press ⌘-**Shift-Z** (**Ctrl+Shift+Z** for Windows) and the key for the Dingbat, and then continue typing. Only that one character appears in the Zapf Dingbats typeface. To quickly switch to Symbol, press ⌘-**Shift-Q** (**Ctrl+Shift+Q** for Windows). For more information on these special characters, check out Chapter 11. (Note that this only works if the Symbol and Zapf Dingbats fonts are installed on your system.)

Big Type, Little Type

Type in QuarkXPress can range from 2 points to 720 points. Two-point type is really teeny, and is often used as the point size for legal documents and insurance contracts. 720-point type is used for, well, not a whole lot (though I would imagine some posters, billboards, or other huge signs would benefit from these foot-tall letters).

You can also type at very exacting sizes. Up to a thousandth of a point. So when your client says to you, "Floyd, this type is a little too small. Make it just a weensy bit bigger," you can increase the size by as little as a thousandth of a point—and then ask your client to stop calling you Floyd.

The Mathematics of Type

If you already read Chapter 5, you know that there are 72 points in one inch. So, if we change the point size of the letter "I" to 72 points, it should be an inch tall, right? Of course not. It's actually somewhere between 50 and 55 points tall. The following figure shows the letter "I" with some other letters to show the discrepancy.

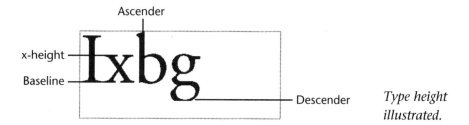

Type height illustrated.

Why this bizarre math? How can 72=50? The answer lies in the word "gjpqy." The bottom parts of the letters in this word (called *descenders*) all extend below the baseline. When type size is measured, these descenders are taken into account. The point size is measured from the bottom of the descender to the top of the ascender (the topmost point of the letters b, d, f, h, k, l, and t) in a given font. If a letter doesn't have a descender or ascender, the point size is still measured from where the descender or ascender would be.

A good rule of thumb is that a capital letter that's about one inch tall will measure approximately 100 points. So if you want letters that are a half inch tall, specify a point size of 50 points. This isn't an exact science, so don't quote me on the results; all I know is that it works most of the time for most typefaces. (In fact, it doesn't work very well at all for script fonts.)

Specifying a Different Type Size

Even though there are millions of different ways to change your type's point size, you really only need to know one of those ways. If you double-click on the Size field in the Measurements palette (upper far right), the type size becomes highlighted. Type in the new point size and press **Return**.

Are you racking your brain trying to figure out how many points in two inches? "Let's see, that's two times seventy-two, carry the eight, subtract the co-tangent of pi..." Just type 2" and let QuarkXPress do the work for you. When you press Return, the value changes to 144 points.

In addition, you can change the point size of the type to one of the "standard" sizes by clicking on the pop-up triangle next to the Size field and selecting the size you want.

A Sneaky Way to Change Type Size

There are a few really cool keyboard equivalents that you can use to change type size. To increase the size of type one point at a time, press ⌘-**Option-Shift->** (**Ctrl+Alt+Shift+>** for Windows). I know, that takes four of your fingers, leaving you with only four free ones (I watch "The Simpsons" too often). To decrease the type size by one point at a time, press ⌘-**Option-Shift-<** (**Ctrl+Alt+Shift+<** for Windows).

The real strength of the up one point or down one point keyboard equivalent is that when you have selected text that contains more than one size of type, the size of each is increased or decreased by one point. However, the characters are not all changed to a single size.

You can increase or decrease the size of type at a much faster rate by pressing ⌘-**Shift->** or ⌘-**Shift-<** (**Ctrl+Shift+>** or **Ctrl+Shift+<** for Windows). The point sizes to which your type jumps don't make much sense, but here they are: 7, 9, 10, 12, 14, 18, 24, 36, 48, 60, 72, 96, 120, 144, 168, and 192. When you get to 7-point or 192-point, this keyboard equivalent causes the computer to beep.

Press the ⌘ key (**Ctrl** in Windows) while resizing a text box, and the text inside it will change in size along with the text box. However, doing so may stretch the type horizontally or vertically, distorting it. To constrain the type so that it does not become distorted, press ⌘-**Option-Shift** (**Ctrl+Alt+Shift** for Windows) as you drag. Don't be surprised if you end up with type in a very fine increment (such as 13.678 pts.).

The Least You Need to Know

Changing the font and the size of type are two things you'll be doing all the time in QuarkXPress, so the good people at Quark have created several ways to do both. You don't need to know all of these ways, of course, but it will dramatically increase your QuarkXPress speed if you know most of them.

- ☞ You must select type before you can make any font or font size changes.

- ☞ A quick way to change fonts is to select type and then press ⌘-**Option-Shift-M** (**Ctrl+Alt+Shift+M** for Windows), which highlights the font field on the Measurements Palette. Type in part of the name of the font and press Enter.

- ☞ In QuarkXPress, type can range from a tiny 2 points to gigantic 720 points (which is almost 10" tall).

- ☞ You can increase or decrease point size by pressing ⌘-**Shift->** or ⌘-**Shift-<**.

Chapter 14
Stylizing Type

In This Chapter

- ☛ Applying style changes to type
- ☛ Making selected characters bold and italic
- ☛ Using the Style toggles on the Measurements palette
- ☛ Removing all the styles with the Plain style

Okay, this isn't the *Complete Idiot's Guide to Fashion*, so why are we talking about styles? In QuarkXPress, styles refer to the look of type—whether it is bold, italic, outlined, or underlined—and a host of other little cosmetic changes. All of the styles can be toggled on and off in the Measurements palette in the area under the font name and type size fields. Reversed options are the ones that are selected. Most of the styles can be used in conjunction with each other, unless there is a blatantly obvious conflict.

Make a Bold (or Italic) Statement

Of all the style changes available in QuarkXPress, bold and italic work a little differently from everything else. When you choose bold or italic, the font changes. If the font is Times Roman and you choose italic, the font becomes Times Italic (the name in the font field won't change).

So what happens when you choose Italic and the font is already Times Italic? On your screen the font will look *more* italic, if that's possible, by slanting even more to the right. There's a catch, of course; it won't print like that. In fact, when it's printed it won't look any different from Times Italic although, depending on the font, the spacing can be changed a bit. If you select both bold and italic styles, Times Roman becomes Times Bold Italic, which is a separate font.

Overall, bold fonts take up more horizontal space than base fonts, and italic fonts take up less horizontal space than their base fonts. Bold italic fonts take up about the same, maybe a little more space than the base fonts.

So you're probably asking, "Should I select the font specifically or should I just apply the bold and italic styles to a base font?" I suggest choosing the base font and applying bold and italic styles to it because flipping between bold and italic versions is as easy as one mouse click. Besides, that way you'll never "accidentally" make Times Italic more italic (causing potential spacing problems).

To apply the bold style to selected characters, click on the **B** in the Measurements palette. To apply the italic style to selected characters, click on the **I** in the Measurements palette. If you prefer keystroking to mousing, press ⌘-**Shift-B** (**Ctrl+Shift+B** in Windows) to make selected characters bold or ⌘-**Shift-I** (**Ctrl+Shift+I** in Windows) to make characters italic. The following figure shows regular type next to its bold and italic counterparts.

Normal (base) type,
and the same type
with bold, italic,
and bold italic
applied.

9 Club Flash

9 Club Flash

9 Club Flash

9 Club Flash

TECHNO NERD TEACHES...

If it were up to me, shadow and outline would be banished. Why? For starters, I think they're just plain ugly. Secondly, these fonts cause letters to be spaced farther apart to allow for the space that the outline stroke or added shadow takes up. Lastly, printing problems can occur when either or both outline and shadow styles are used; letters may drop out or your printer's activity light may start blinking uncontrollably.

If you're still set on using outline or shadow, you can make selected characters outlined by clicking on the **O** in the Measurements palette or pressing ⌘-**Shift-O** (**Ctrl+Shift+O** for Windows); make them shadowed by clicking on the **S** in the Measurements palette or pressing ⌘-**Shift-S** (**Ctrl+Shift+S** in Windows).

Lines Through and Under Letters

Someone somewhere thought it would be great to have the ability to run a great big horizontal line right through the middle of any selected text. That someone is still somewhere, undoubtedly running great big horizontal lines right through the middle of selected text while the rest of us simply nod like that's a normal thing to do. By selecting the strikethrough option in the Measurements palette or pressing ⌘-**Shift-/** (**Ctrl+Shift+/** in Windows), you too can run great big horizontal lines right through the middle of any selected text.

A more useful feature is underline. With QuarkXPress, you can underline every character selected or just the words in the selected area. If you click on **U** (underline) on the Measurements palette, all characters, including spaces, are underlined. Choosing the word underline style (**W**) underlines all characters except for spaces. The following figure shows both underlining styles at work on a sentence. The underline created by these styles is fixed in position at a certain thickness. It runs right through any of the descenders in most fonts.

You can underline all selected characters by pressing ⌘-**Shift-U** (**Ctrl+Shift+U** in Windows) or underline every character except spaces by pressing ⌘-**Shift-W** (**Ctrl+Shift+W** for Windows).

Remember the word "gjpqy" (from Chapter 13)? Well, all the letters in that word have **descenders**, or letter parts that fall below the baseline of the word. These descenders and underlines smash right into each other when the occasion arises.

A sentence with underline (top) and word underline (bottom) applied to it.

From the bottom of the bottle I discern movement.

From the bottom of the bottle I discern movement.

All Caps and Small Caps

When you select the All Caps option from the Measurements palette or press ⌘-**Shift-K**, lowercase letters in the selected text become uppercase letters. Using All Caps differs from using the Shift or Caps Lock key to create uppercase letters in that when you remove the All Caps style, only the letters that were originally lowercase become lowercase again.

Sometimes small caps can look "light" compared to the regular caps in the same line. To fix this, select **Edit→Preferences→ Typographic** or press ⌘-**Option-Y (Ctrl+Alt+Y for Windows)**, and change the small caps HScale to 90%. The letters will be stretched wider than before but will look to be about the same weight as the real caps.

So here's a word of advice: try not to set too much type using all caps. Upper- and lowercase letters blended together are much more readable than uppercase alone. Uppercase is great for titles or other areas of emphasis, but not for lines of copy.

When you select Small Caps from the Measurements palette or press ⌘-**Shift-H (Ctrl+Shift+H for Windows)**, lowercase letters in the selected text are turned into small versions of uppercase letters. The difference between normal type, all caps, small caps, and adjusted small caps (as noted in the Oops! sidebar) is shown in the figure below.

Different capitaliza- tion settings.

Wild Type— Normal

All caps —WILD TYPE

Small caps —WILD TYPE

WILD TYPE— Adjusted small caps

Superscript, Subscript, and Superior

Depending on where your text is located, superscript and subscript may not appear to do anything when you select them (for example, if you apply superscript to text at the top of the text box or subscript to text at the bottom of the text box). All these two styles do is move the selected type up (superscript) or down (subscript) by 33%. To make selected characters superscript, press ⌘-**Shift-+** (**Ctrl+Shift++** in Windows) or select the **Superscript** option from the Measurements palette. To make characters subscript, press ⌘-**Shift--** (**Ctrl+Shift+-** for Windows) or select the **Subscript** option from the Measurements palette.

Making some characters superior to others won't give them a bloated ego. The superior style will instead change selected text to 50% of its original size and align the ascenders in the selected text with other text on the same line. Superior is very useful for creating correctly sized registration marks, trademarks, and exponential numbers. To apply the Superior style to selected text, press ⌘-**Shift-V** (**Ctrl+Shift+V** for Windows) or select the **Superior** option from the Measurements palette. The numbers in the following figure have each of the three styles applied to them to show the differences.

$E = MC^2, \pi r^2 =$ Old Spice^1

$E = MC_2, \pi r_2 =$ Old Spice$_1$

$E = MC^2, \pi r^2 =$ Old Spice^1

The superscript, subscript, and superior styles (respectively), applied to the numbers.

You can modify the superscript, subscript, and superior styles by selecting **Edit→Preferences→Typographic** or pressing ⌘-**Option-Y** (**Ctrl+Alt+Y** for Windows). You can specify the width and height for all three, and change the offset for both superscript and subscript.

De Plain, De... Oh, Never Mind!

The first little box in the row of styles in the Measurements palette contains a little P. Before you rush off to get the paper towels and check to see where the dog is hiding, the P stands for plain. Plain means that no other style attributes are currently selected.

The Plain box comes in handy when you've selected text and made it bold, italic, underlined, and outlined, and then decide to remove all of those styles. Instead of clicking on each and every selected style to deselect it, click once on the **P**, and the type will revert to its original simple form. You can also press ⌘-**Shift-P** (**Ctrl+Shift+P** in Windows) to return selected text to its plain old unstylish self.

The Least You Need to Know

Even if you're not a naturally stylish person, you can make type look absolutely scrumptious with a balanced use of the different styles available in QuarkXPress. Of course, if you get too carried away, your QuarkXPress document will look like a ransom note with hundreds of differently sized and shaped letters pasted on them.

☛ Most styles can be applied by either selecting an option in the Measurements palette or by pressing a ⌘-**Shift** (**Ctrl+Shift** for Windows) key command that uses the first letter of the style with the other two keys.

☛ Selecting Bold or Italic actually changes the font to a bold or italic font. Keeping this in mind, you should never bold a bold font or italicize an italic font.

☛ The Bold style increases the amount of horizontal space taken up by characters; the Italic style reduces that amount of space.

☛ Shy away from using Outline and Shadow; they often cause printers to bomb.

☛ Subscript and Superscript move text with those styles applied up or down but do not change the size of the text.

☛ You can apply most style changes, such as bold, italic, and underline, by clicking on letters on the Measurements palette.

Chapter 15

Doing All Sorts of Other Stuff to Your Type

In This Chapter

- ☛ Moving type up and down without changing the leading
- ☛ Condensing and expanding type
- ☛ Removing and adding space between letters
- ☛ Coloring and tinting type
- ☛ Using the Character dialog box

In addition to making font, size, and style changes, you can do a number of other things to type. In this chapter, you'll learn how to move, condense, expand, and space out your type. For those of you already spaced out, this chapter should be a welcome diversion.

Before you delve into this chapter, remember this: You can't move or manipulate text within a text box with the mouse (except by dragging and dropping it). Instead, there are different techniques for doing these things. You'll learn about these different techniques in this chapter.

Move 'Em Up, Move 'Em Down

To move text up or down, independent of any other characters or paragraphs, you need to adjust the baseline of the text using *baseline shift*.

You can change the vertical position of type by changing the baseline shift. To move type up or down, first select the characters and then choose **Style→Baseline Shift**. Enter the distance you want to move the type vertically. Positive numbers will move text up; negative numbers will move text down. When you're done, click **OK**, and the text moves up or down the specified number of points.

You can also change the baseline shift incrementally by selecting the type and then pressing ⌘-**Option-Shift-+** (**Ctrl+Alt+Shift++** in Windows) to move type up one point or ⌘-**Option-Shift-–** (**Ctrl+Alt+Shift+–** in Windows) to move type down one point.

Baseline shift is extremely useful in situations where it is impossible to center type vertically by normal means. In addition, if a drop cap (a large capital letter at the beginning of a paragraph; see Chapter 18) sticks up too far or doesn't stick up far enough, baseline shift can effectively change the way certain drop caps align with paragraphs. The following figure shows several different baseline shift values applied to one word within a sentence.

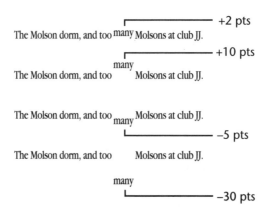

Different baseline shift values applied to one word in a sentence.

Width and Height Changes

Any character in QuarkXPress can be condensed (made thinner), expanded (made wider), squished (made shorter), and stretched (made taller). Some examples of these manipulations are shown in the following figure. You can make these changes with the Horizontal/Vertical Scale dialog box. To access the Horizontal/Vertical Scale dialog box, select **Style→Horizontal/Vertical Scale**.

Distort & Dattort

Distort & Dattort

Distort & Dattort

Distort & Dattort

Horizontally and vertically scaled type.

A pop-up menu in the dialog box enables you to make horizontal and vertical changes between 25% and 400%. When the horizontal option is selected, the value in the text field controls the type width. Percentages less than 100% condense type, and percentages greater than 100% expand type. Entering percentages in the vertical field affects type in the same way, but vertically.

The horizontal scale of selected type can be increased and decreased in 5% increments. Press ⌘-[(**Ctrl+[** in Windows) to decrease or ⌘-] (**Ctrl+]** in Windows) to increase.

Fixing Overlap and Excessive Spacing

Take a look at any magazine ad, and then try to make the same words appear on your screen the same way as they do in the magazine. Even if you have the same fonts, it still looks a little different. Why? The designers in advertising agencies are obsessed with controlling how much space is between the letters in their text.

The space between letters is controlled by both tracking and kerning. *Tracking* works on whole blocks of text at once, while *kerning* changes the amount of space between one specific pair of letters.

Fixing Letter Space Like the Prose

To change the amount of space between all characters in an entire block of text, adjust the tracking. Select one or more characters, and you'll notice that the tracking field on the Measurements palette becomes active. In that field, enter a number less than 0 to bring the characters together, or enter a number greater than 0 to space the characters out.

When letters just barely touch each other, they are **kissing** (awwww). When letters down right run into each other, they are **crashing**.

Kerning is the process of adding or removing space between one pair of letters.

Tracking is the process of adding or removing space between all selected letters.

To change the amount of space between a specific pair of letters, position the insertion point between the letters. The kerning field on the Measurements field becomes active. (The kerning field is in exactly the same place as the tracking field. The difference is that to change tracking, you must have selected a range of characters.) Kerning works independently of tracking.

You can click on the arrows in the tracking/kerning field to change the value in increments of 10. **Option-clicking** (**Alt+clicking** in Windows) on the arrows changes the value by 1. Keep in mind that you cannot make the tracking or kerning more than a value of 500 or less than –500. The following figure shows examples of tracking and kerning with various values.

Oranges

Oranges

O r a n g e s

Squeeze

Squeeze

Examples of tracking and kerning.

Tracking

Kerning

Always change the tracking before you change the kerning. If you do it the other way once, you'll know why I say that.

To quickly change the space between letter pairs (kern) using the keyboard, place the cursor between the letter pair and press ⌘-**Shift-[** (**Ctrl+Shift+[** for Windows) to decrease the kerning by 10 or ⌘-**Shift-]** (**Ctrl+Shift+]** for Windows) to increase the kerning by 10. Press the **Option** key (**Alt** in Windows) at the same time as the other keys to change the increment to 1.

TECHNO NERD TEACHES...

Tracking and kerning amounts are based on a character "em space." The size of an em space has changed over the years from at one time being the width of a capital M, to being the width of the point size of the type, and finally to the width of two zeros. Because tracking/kerning is based on the size of two zeros at the current type size, the changes are consistent if the type size changes. An em space is equal to 200 units in the tracking/kerning field on the Measurements palette.

When to Track/Kern In and Out

The larger the type size, the more tracking or kerning that's necessary because the white space, while proportionately the same, takes up a greater physical distance. Live by that rule, but remember the following rules as well.

You may want to increase the tracking or kerning if:

- ☞ The type is reversed.
- ☞ The type is all caps.
- ☞ The type is smaller than seven points.

You may want to decrease the tracking/kerning when:

- ☞ The type is used as a headline.
- ☞ You are using condensed type.
- ☞ You are using a "light" weight typeface.
- ☞ It will make the type look better (which is a good deal of the time).

For the most part, tracking and kerning correctly is a subjective science. If you like it, it is probably correct. Then again, some art directors I know will tell you, "No, no, it isn't right at all," only to fix it themselves so that it turns out exactly the way you had it in the first place.

Making Tracking/Kerning Changes Permanent

Hidden away deep in the Utilities menu are two options for fixing tracking and kerning problems for good. Before jumping into this, be advised that any changes you make here can drastically screw up your fonts, by making type faces within font families track/kern differently. Also, the whole process is rather time-consuming. It is better than tracking/kerning letters on an individual basis only if you have an enormous amount of tracking/kerning to do.

Be very careful when making these changes. A click here or there in the wrong place can make your type look dreadful. (In fact, I would test this on a machine that belongs to a hated co-worker first.) However, you can replace mangled fonts with the originals.

To change the tracking for a font, select **Utilities→Tracking Edit**. The Tracking Edit dialog box appears (after a good long while if you have many fonts), listing all the fonts installed on the system. Select the font you want to edit, and then click the **Edit** button. A new dialog box appears, showing the tracking values for the selected font. Normally, the tracking values appear as a horizontal line centered on 0. Up to four control points can be manipulated, defining at what point size tracking will be used.

To change the kerning for a font, select **Utilities→Kerning Table Edit** and select the font whose kerning you want to adjust. Another dialog box appears, with a scrolling list on the left containing all the kerning pairs for this font. Select one of them, and their current kerning value appears. By typing in a new value, you can change the distance between this pair of letters. If you type a new letter pair, that pair will be added to the list.

Understanding Auto Kerning

Auto kerning is built into each PostScript font and into most TrueType fonts. There are up to 2,000 custom kerning pairs (letters like Ty that fit together tighter than most) in these typefaces, with specific sets of letters designed to fit up against one another better than they would normally. Auto kerning checks for the existence of these kerning pairs and then places characters the correct amount of space apart, according to the information in the kerning pairs.

For instance, a capital "T" and the letter "y" need to be a little closer together than a "T" and an "h." The "y" can be tucked underneath the "T" a little, reducing the big chunk of white space, which can be distracting or can make the word hard to read. This letter pair is a common one in most fonts' kerning pairs.

PostScript font   A font made by Adobe to take advantage of PostScript printing; the standard in Windows.

TrueType font   A font made by Apple to compete with PostScript fonts; the standard on Macs.

TECHNO NERD TEACHES...

QuarkXPress automatically puts auto kerning into effect for typefaces over 10 points. You can specify a different point size by selecting **Edit→Preferences→Typographic** and changing the Auto Kern Above text field. Don't make the number too high, though. A very high number will essentially turn off auto kerning all together. Set it at 2 if you want all text in your document to be automatically kerned.

Flipping Out

You can *flip* type (reverse it—making it backward and upside-down) in QuarkXPress versions 3.2 and later by selecting the **Flip Horizontal** and **Flip Vertical** commands from the **Style** menu (or the Measurements palette). Note, however, that these options flip the entire text box and all characters in it—not individual selected characters. So don't be too surprised when that letter to General Motors Corporation demanding to know why they stopped making the Pacer in the '70s may turn into total gibberish (assuming it wasn't already gibberish).

One of the really cool things to do with "flipped" type is to send it to others as a secret coded message. The key? Read the text in a mirror or put the page face down on a light. Great fun for the whole office staff.

Type-Dying

You can change the color of individual characters to any of the millions of color combinations that QuarkXPress has to offer. To change the color of type, first select the type. Then select **Style→Color** and select the desired color and the type changes to that color. If you have a black and white monitor, the type will still change color, you just won't be able to see the difference on-screen.

You aren't limited to the colors that are in the menu. You can create your own colors by selecting **Edit→Colors**. For more information on creating colors, refer to Chapter 9.

Not only can you apply color to text, but you can shade (or tint) all colors from 100% down to 0% in .01% increments. For example, you can use a shade of black to make some type of gray. The lower the number, the lighter the color will appear. At 0% black, the color will appear and print as white, not transparent.

Epyt Gnisrever

To reverse type (take a second and read the heading again, very carefully—ti teg?), first select your text and make it white. Then make the text box black by selecting **Item→Modify** and changing the background color to black.

Reversed type.

You may not be able to see your text if it is black and your text box is black. To select the text when you can't see it, click in the text box once with the Content tool and select **Edit→Select All**. The type is selected.

Many times reversed type won't appear to be centered vertically in a text box. This is usually true if there is a lack of descenders in the text, which makes the text appear "too high." Select the text and use the baseline shift function to lower the text until it is centered correctly.

Try to use large type sizes and bold fonts when creating reversed type. If you use fonts with small serifs (fonts with little knobs on the ends of the letters, such as Times), those serifs may be obliterated by the spread of the reverse color. Also, it is much harder to read reversed type than it is to read normal black text on a white or light background.

Character Attributes

The Character Attributes dialog box is a catch-all for character formatting. To access it, select **Style→Character** or press ⌘-**Shift-D** (**Ctrl+Shift+D** in Windows). You can move around in this dialog box by tabbing from one field to the next. To see what you can change in the dialog box, look at the following figure.

```
                        Character Attributes
                          ┌─Style─────────────────────┐
  Font:   ▶ Cheltenham    │ ☒ Plain      ☐ Underline  │
  Size:   ▶ 12 pt         │ ☐ Bold       ☐ Word u.l.  │
                          │ ☐ Italic     ☐ Small Caps │
  Color:  ■ Black         │ ☐ Outline    ☐ All Caps   │
  Shade:  ▶ 100%          │ ☐ Shadow     ☐ Superscript│
                          │ ☐ Strike Thru ☐ Subscript │
                          └───────────────────────────┘
  Scale: │Horizontal│ 100%
  Kern Amount:     0        ┌──────┐  ┌────────┐
  Baseline Shift:  0 pt     │  OK  │  │ Cancel │
                            └──────┘  └────────┘
```

The Character Attributes dialog box.

The Least You Need to Know

Well, if this chapter wasn't just a catch-all for everything under the sun that you can do to type characters, I'll have to dig out my Random House Unabridged dictionary and look up "catch-all."

☞ Baseline shift moves characters up and down, independent of the leading but relative to the position of other characters on the line.

☞ Kerning and tracking change the amount of space between characters; kerning affects one pair of characters at a time, while tracking affects the space between all the letters in any selection.

☞ Selected characters can be colored and shaded using the options under the Style menu.

☞ The Character dialog box (accessed by pressing ⌘+**Shift**+**D**, or **Ctrl**+**Shift**+**D** in Windows) contains almost all the information there is to know about characters and allows you to make changes there as well.

☞ You add space between letters by increasing tracking or kerning.

Chapter 16
Paragraph-Based Changes: A Primer

In This Chapter

- ☛ The difference between paragraph and character selection
- ☛ The magic of paragraph changes
- ☛ Spacing out lines of text using leading
- ☛ Choosing your alignment

Working with paragraphs is different from working with characters in a number of ways. The most important difference is that paragraph changes affect entire paragraphs, not individual characters. Because of this, many people shy away from making paragraph-based changes, and instead try to make all their changes to individual characters—making their lives extremely difficult in the process.

A paragraph is defined by returns. A return signifies that all text after the last return and before the next return is a paragraph. In QuarkXPress, you make most paragraph changes in the Paragraph Formats dialog box, which is accessed by selecting **Style→Formats** or pressing ⌘-**Shift-F** (**Ctrl+Shift+F** for Windows).

Why Paragraphs Aren't Characters

There are certain things that just can't be applied to individual characters, such as alignment (making text flush left, right, or centered) and leading (spacing between lines). If you tried to make such a change to one character, all the other characters in the paragraph would be affected; in fact, they *have* to be affected in order for the change to occur.

This provides an interesting dilemma for QuarkXPress users. How much of a paragraph do you have to select for the change to occur? Here's your answer: You don't have to select anything. "But that's impossible," you say. "It goes against everything I know, everything I believe in..." Well, in a twisted way, you do have to select something but not in the way you're used to.

For you to be able to make a paragraph change, the blinking insertion point must be blinking away inside the paragraph. You can change multiple paragraphs as long as at least one character in each paragraph is selected, as shown below.

Paragraph changes will affect all three of these paragraphs, because at least one character in each paragraph is selected.

> A sparse field of Numbers Championship entrants provided a shorter-than-usual event this year. Team winners were Owen Morse and Jon Wee, who made 140 catches with nine cubs. There were no entrants in the team rings or balls competition. Barry Rosenberg won the Individual championship with 36 catches of seven balls.
> Tighten your seat belt, drain that coffee cup, put those toothpicks in your eyelids and hold fast for one more long day of IJA 1994!
> The jugglers take to the starting line at 9 a.m. on the Molson field track for a whole bevy of races. The Games of the IJA will run from 1-3 p.m. in Berri Square, with small stage performances and juggling lessons running in that outdoor location until 5 p.m.

Leading QuarkXPress Do the Work

When I used my first desktop publishing program (PageStream for the Atari ST back in the mid-eighties), I was able to create some pretty darn nice stuff (for a college kid, anyway). I read about the features, and I started to pronounce the term "leading" as "leeding," which is what it looked like to me. No, I wasn't smart enough to figure out the "led" sound from the spelling even though I grew up outside Reading, Pennsylvania, which is pronounced "redding." (All you Monopoly players out there, note that pronunciation next time you land on the "Reading" Railroad.) Instead I called it "leeding," and for about two years no one corrected me. Come to think of it, there always did seem to be some private joke I wasn't in on.

Being able to change paragraphs without seeing a highlighted area can be a problem if you aren't sure where the blinking insertion point is. Always double-check the location of the insertion point before you make a paragraph change.

TECHNO NERD TEACHES...

The term *leading* was coined from the old typesetting machines that used actual lead strips to separate lines of lead type. Since the advent of phototypesetting and then desktop publishing, very few of these machines are in use anymore.

Now that you know how to pronounce it, I'll tell you what it is. *Leading* is the amount of space between two consecutive lines of type. "Increasing leading" is the process of adding more space between lines, while "decreasing leading" is the process of removing space between lines.

Leading, like everything else in this chapter, affects the entire paragraph in which you make the change. Even if you select one word, the leading of the entire paragraph will change. (If you want to move one word, a few words, or a line up or down, you will need to use baseline shift (superscript, subscript, or superior), which is discussed in Chapter 15.)

Measuring Leading by the Pint

Do you remember me telling you about how type is measured back in Chapter 5? A little confusing, wasn't it? Leading is worse. The leading of a line of type is measured from the baseline of that line of type to the baseline above that line of type, as shown in the following diagram.

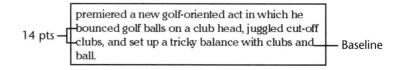

Measuring leading.   14 pts —

premiered a new golf-oriented act in which he
bounced golf balls on a club head, juggled cut-off
clubs, and set up a tricky balance with clubs and — Baseline
ball.

When leading is increased, the current paragraph and the individual lines of type are moved down from the previous line, so the distance between baselines increases. When leading is decreased, the paragraph and baseline of the current line of type is moved *up*. If the leading of the line matches the point size of the text, descenders from the top line may touch ascenders from the bottom line.

Changing Leading in QuarkXPress

The Measurements palette provides you with the easiest way to see what the leading currently is and to change it (see the following figure). The number shown in the leading field is usually the absolute leading, or the actual distance between baselines. If there is a plus or a minus in front of the leading value, the value shown is based on the current point size. If the word **Auto** is displayed, the automatic leading value is in use (see the section on auto leading later in this chapter).

The leading field of the Measurements palette.

Leading field

| X: 10p8 | W: 14p5 | ⏛ 0° | | 🔾 auto | | Caxton Book | 12 pt |
| Y: 7p5 | H: 12p5 | Cols: 1 | | | | P B I ⓞ ⓢ ⓔ ⓤ ⓨ ⓚ K | |

You can't specify leading by percentage. QuarkXPress will not recognize the percentage symbol except when used in preferences for auto leading.

To change the leading to a specific value, double-click on the leading field and type in the leading value you want to use. To reset the leading to auto leading, type **auto** in the space. To set up leading so that it is always a few points more or less than the point size of the type, enter **+1** to increase it by one point, **–2** to decrease it by two points, and so on. This is really useful when you are changing the point size of the type; the leading will always stay a few points more or less than the point size, no matter what the point size is set at.

To change the leading using the keyboard, press ⌘-**Shift**-: (**Ctrl+Shift+**: in Windows) to increase the leading by one point or ⌘-**Shift-**" (**Ctrl+Shift+**" in Windows) to decrease the leading by one point.

So how do you know which numbers to enter? Here's an example: if you want 24 points of space between the baseline of the current line of 18-point Helvetica type and the baseline of the previous line of type, what is the leading you want? Easy enough. It's 24 points. Typesetters and other desktop publishing know-it-alls will tell you that this type is "18 over 24," or they'll write it as 18/24.

Some less experienced people refer to leading by how many points it is compared to the point size of the characters. In the previous example, they would claim that there were 6 points of leading. You should never do this. As we swiftly move into the future, stating leading by the difference in the spacing between lines minus the point size of the type is a no-no. However, it is becoming acceptable to say that there are +6 ("plus-six") points of leading.

If the leading is the same as the point size (18-point leading and 18-point type), it is referred to as "set solid," (once again a reference to the days where chunks of type without leading were set solidly on each other).

The QuarkXPress Measurements palette and leading fields can display leading values either by its absolute (24 points), the amount it is different from the point size (+6), or as the auto amount set in your preferences. The way it is displayed depends on how you enter it.

What Are Those Little Arrows?

You can also use the arrows next to the numerical value to increase or decrease the leading one point at a time. The up arrow increases the leading, which oddly enough pushes the selected line down. The down arrow decreases the leading. Be careful not to decrease the leading too much, or you will find that the lines of text overlap each other. Regardless of the leading value, QuarkXPress will not print or display text lines overlapped.

TECHNO NERD TEACHES...

You can increase or decrease the leading 1/10 of a point at a time by pressing **Option** (**Alt** for Windows) as you click the up and down arrows or by using the ⌘-**Shift-[** and ⌘-**Shift-]** keyboard equivalents (**Ctrl+Shift+[** and **Ctrl+Shift+]** for Windows).

Auto Leading (Or "Making Dad's Chevy Heavy")

Auto leading is a default leading amount set within QuarkXPress' typographical preferences. Normally the default auto leading amount is 20%, which makes the leading 2 points greater than the point size when the type size in the paragraph is 10 points. When auto leading is turned on, one of the leading fields will read **Auto**.

To change to auto leading after other leading is being used, type **auto** into the space in the leading text field. To change the amount of auto leading, select **Edit→Preferences→Typographic** or press ⌘-**Option-Y** (**Ctrl+Alt+Y** for Windows) and enter a different value in the Auto Leading field. You can enter a percentage (be sure to include the % sign) or a value, which is the number of points to be added to the point size of the type. When you have changed the value, click **OK**.

Choose Your Side

Another frequently used paragraph-based feature is alignment, with which you control whether the lines in a paragraph line up on the left or right sides, or are centered or justified (meaning they are pulled to both sides at once). There are five different ways that paragraphs can be aligned, and each of those ways has a corresponding box on the Measurements palette.

The alignment boxes on the Measurements palette.

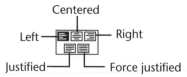

Flushing When You're Done

The term "flush" is used to indicate that all lines of type are aligned on a given side. Flush left means that the lines of type in a paragraph are lined up on their left edge, as are the paragraphs in this book. Flush right is the opposite of flush left in that all lines of text line up on the right side of the column, and the left side appears uneven. Flush right is used most often for captions, not for standard text.

> When text is flush left, the right edge is not controlled; each line stops in a different place, and the right side is usually quite uneven. This unevenness is called *ragged right*.

To immediately change text in a paragraph to flush left, press ⌘-**Shift-L**. To immediately change text in a paragraph to flush right, press ⌘-**Shift-R**.

Not Taking Any Sides

When text is centered, there is an equal amount of white space on either side of it. Centered text is usually used for headlines and titles, as shown below. To center text using the keyboard, press ⌘-**Shift-C**, and text is centered between the right and left edges (or indents if you've applied any) of the text box. If the text box has more than one column, it is centered between the left and right sides of the column it is in.

> John Spurney wants everyone to know that he balanced a Narwhale tusk on his nose in the Bio-Dome. Also, he is going to Costa Rica to pursue Geography and Juggling.
>
> Sandy Brown left for a busy August touring schedule, leaving Monotonovich totally stranded and without a clue.
>
> Scott Morris has a quote: "Juggling, it's not just an art, its a gerund."
>
> Kyla Jacobs saved her parents from certain disaster on the way to the Nationals when she asked, "Are you buckled up?" (niether of them

Text centered in a text box.

Justifying This Whole Alignment Business

Text can be justified two ways in QuarkXPress. The two options are called Justified and Forced Justify (shown in the following figure). The main difference is that with Justified text, the last line in a paragraph is flush left. With Forced Justify, the last line is justified.

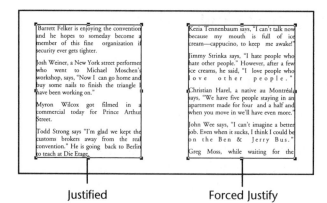

You can justify text using Justified or Forced Justify.

Justified   Forced Justify

To justify text using the Justified method, press ⌘-**Shift-J** (**Ctrl+Shift+J** in Windows). To use the Forced Justify method, press ⌘-**Option-Shift-J** (**Ctrl+Alt+Shift+J** in Windows). The Forced Justify setting is often used when one line of text needs to be stretched out from one edge of a text box to another. The only catch is that you must enter a return after the line of text. In the resulting lines, the spaces between words are huge, and spaces between letters are nonexistent. To fix this, use an Option-Space (press **Option** or **Alt** in conjunction with the Spacebar) instead of using a regular space between words.

The Least You Need to Know

Working with entire paragraphs without selecting everything inside of them is something akin to magic. Keep the following in mind:

- ☞ To justify text on a Mac, press ⌘-**Shift-***letter*, where *letter* stands for the appropriate type of alignment; for Windows, press **Ctrl+Shift+***letter*. (For example, to apply flush right alignment, you would press ⌘-**Shift-R** or **Ctrl+Shift+R**.)

- ☞ Paragraph changes affect the entire paragraph, even if the entire paragraph isn't selected.

- ☞ Leading changes affect the space between each line of a paragraph, measured from baseline to baseline.

- ☞ Changing the alignment forces all the text in a paragraph to hug the left, right, or center, or to be spread evenly from side to side.

Chapter 17
Tab Dancing

In This Chapter

- Understanding how tabs work
- Using the different types of tabs
- Working with tab leaders (dots like you see in a Table of Contents)
- Formatting tab leaders as if they were individual characters

Do you remember the soft drink, Tab, that was around in the 1970s? Tab was a terrible soda… but a great paint remover. Tabs in QuarkXPress are much easier to swallow, especially once you understand the basics.

Tabs are used all the time in QuarkXPress. In fact, one of the easiest ways to see if someone is green behind the ears in QuarkXPress is to see if he uses tabs or a series of spaces. A QuarkXPress veteran never uses more than one space; he always uses a tab instead.

Tabmanian Devils

You create, adjust, and delete all tabs in the Paragraph Tab dialog box, which appears when you select **Style→Tabs** or press **⌘-Shift-T** (**Ctrl+Shift+T** in Windows). The following figure shows the Paragraph Tab dialog box.

*The Paragraph Tabs
dialog box.*

Like other paragraph settings, tabs affect the entire paragraph at once. They are used to create locations at which text aligns in the middle of a line of text. Text can align to these tabs flush left, flush right, centered, or aligned to a special character, comma, or decimal. There can be up to twenty tabs per paragraph in QuarkXPress.

To get acquainted with how tabs work in QuarkXPress, start with an empty text box and the Content tool and follow these steps:

1. Press the **Tab** key on the keyboard, and then type your first name. Press **Tab** again and type your last name. Press **Tab** again and type the number **7**. Your text should look something like the next figure. (Don't worry if your name isn't Ted Alspach. On the other hand, if your name *is* Ted Alspach, drop me a note; that's a pretty unusual name.)

*A text box in which I've
entered my first name,
my last name, and the
number 7, and each is
aligned at a tab stop.*

2. Now, with the insertion point still on that line, select **Style→Tabs** or press ⌘**-Shift-T** (**Ctrl+Shift+T** in Windows) and take a look at the tab ruler above your name and number. It should look something like the following figure.

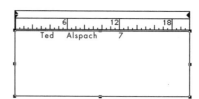

Viewing the tab ruler.

Notice that each word appears to be
flush left at 3 pica intervals. If a word
has several letters (like my last name)
that cause it to extend beyond the
next 3 pica mark, the next word is
placed at the *next* 3 pica mark.

3. Click right above where your last
    name begins and click the **Apply**
    button or press ⌘-A (**Ctrl+A** in
    Windows). You will see all the text
    shuffle off to the right. That's because
    you just created a tab stop (see the
    next figure).

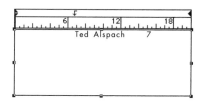

Remember that even when
you don't set any tabs,
there are automatic tabs set
up at every half inch (3
pica) starting on the left
edge of the text box.

Creating a new tab.

When you create a tab stop, all automatic tabs to the left of that
tab (those that appear every one-half inch by default) are elimi-
nated. Therefore, your first name shifts to the position of your
newly created tab, and the last name and number are moved
accordingly to the next available 3 pica marks. (Notice the little
arrow on the very top line in the figure? That indicates the tab.)

4. Click again—this time closer to the left edge of the tab ruler—and
    click **Apply** or press ⌘-A (**Ctrl+A** in Windows). The first name
    jumps back to this new tab stop, the last name goes to the previ-
    ous tab stop you created, and the number appears at the next
    available 3 pica mark, as shown here.

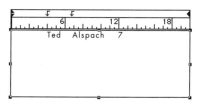

*Text aligned at the
two tab stops you've
created.*

Notice there are two little arrows in the top row of the figure now? Your first name is lined up with the first tab stop, and your last name is lined up with the next tab stop you created. The number is lined up with the next tab stop, which happens to be one of the default tab stops that appear every 3 picas.

5. Click on the tab ruler one more time—this time closer to the right edge of the text box—and click **Apply** or press ⌘-A (**Ctrl+A** in Windows). Your first and last name don't move, but the number is positioned way on the other side of the text box, as shown here.

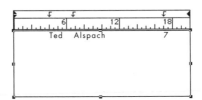

The number scooches over to the right.

Easy enough? I thought you'd think so.

You can also move tab stops around by dragging the little arrows in the top row to the left and right. When you have the arrow where you want it, select **Apply** or press ⌘-A (**Ctrl+A** in Windows), and the words move to the right along with the tab stops.

To delete a tab stop, drag it away from the ruler and release the mouse button. It'll disappear. To delete all the tabs from the tab ruler, Option-click on the tab ruler.

Tab Leaders

"Onward, tabs! Go forth to fight the evils of putting characters together to simulate tabs!" is the cry of the tab leader. *Tab leaders* (pronounced "leeders") are sequences of characters automatically created by tabs for use as underlines, dotted lines, and characters between words.

If you still have the text from the section above, follow along where we stopped (still inside the Tab dialog box).

1. In the tab ruler above the words, click on the third tab (in the top
    row) to select it. Tabs, oddly enough, don't appear selected when
    they are, so you'll have to imagine that it is highlighted or some-
    thing. (The only thing that happens when you click on a tab is
    that its position appears highlighted in the Position field.) The
    Paragraph Tabs dialog box should show the location of the tab, as
    in the figure below. Your location will undoubtedly be different
    than what is displayed there.

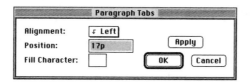

*The Paragraph Tabs
dialog box.*

2. Tab to the Fill Character field and enter a period and a space (.).
    Select **Apply** or press ⌘-A (**Ctrl+A** in Windows). Your text should
    look like the following figure with a row of periods between your
    last name and the number. Amazing, isn't it?

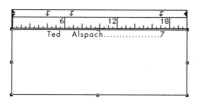

A tab leader.

3. Now select the first tab stop and change the Fill Character to an
    underline (**Shift --**). Click **Apply** or press ⌘-A (**Ctrl+A** in Win-
    dows), and an underline appears from the left edge of the text
    box right up to the first tab stop, where it meets the word (see the
    following figure). Too cool!

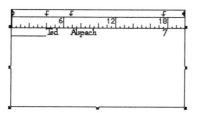

*The underline used as
a fill character.*

You can enter any character for a tab leader, or you can enter
up to two different characters that will alternately repeat
themselves.

Tab Leader Formatting... Huh?

Think your periods are too close together? Are they square (Helvetica
periods are) when you wanted them round (like the periods in Times)?
Want to change the color of an underline tab leader to red?

You can format tabs just as you would any other character. First, select
the tab by double-clicking on it. The tabbed area appears highlighted.
Change the tracking (to increase/decrease space between leader characters),
the font, and the color for the tab. Any change you can make for characters, you can also apply to tabs. For instance, if you wanted to make the
tab green, you would highlight the tab and select Style→Color→Green.
Likewise, if you wanted to increase space between the characters in the tab
leader, you would select the tab and increase the tracking value in the
Tracking text field in the Measurements palette.

Different Tabs, Different Folks

So far all the tabs you've worked with were of the flush left type. However,
tabs come in a wide variety of types. You can also create center tabs, flush
right tabs, decimal tabs, or comma tabs to achieve different results. The
following figure shows the different tabs as they appear on the tab ruler.

*The tab choices available
to you in the Paragraph
Tabs dialog box and on
the tab ruler.*

> ⌐ **Left**
> ↓ **Center**
> ⌐ **Right**
> ↓ **Decimal**
> ↓ **Comma**
> ↓ **Align On:**

The most useful of these different kinds (in my opinion) is the decimal tab. *Decimal tabs* are used to line up decimals for columns of numbers, as shown in the following example. Note that numbers without decimals are lined up as if they did have decimals. This enables you to perfectly align all sorts of numbers, if they have cents or not.

Item	Pink	Turquoise	White
Rings	$12.00	$12.50	$18.00
Silicone balls	$26.00	$26.00	$25.00
Renegade Custom Clubs	$39.00	$40.00	$29.99
Cheapo Clubs	$7.49	$7.49	$7.99
Devil Sticks	$19.99	$19.99	$29.99
Spinning Balls	$15.00	$15.00	$12.00

A flush left tab was used to set up the items, and decimal tabs were used to align the numerical values.

Comma tabs are like decimal tabs except that the numbers align along the commas. This is especially good for my Canadian friends, whose monetary system puts a comma where everyone in the U.S. knows there should be a period.

Centered tabs are most useful as column headers. For instance, they were used for headings in the previous figure. Note that the centered tabs are in use *only* on the first line—not on the other lines, where the left and decimal tabs remain in effect. Select or insert your cursor in the top line only.

Flush right tabs are good for aligning objects along their right sides, although that's not something you'll probably use very often. Everything tabbed to a flush right tab will align with the right edge of the tab.

TECHNO NERD TEACHES...

Decimal tabs act like flush right tabs when there is no decimal.

You can change a tab from one kind to another (for example, change a flush left tab to a centered tab) by clicking on the tab to select it, changing the alignment setting in the Paragraph Tabs dialog box, and then clicking **Apply**.

The Mystical Automatic Flush Right Tab

There is a secret, very useful way to create an automatic flush right tab on any line. Press **Option-Tab** (**Alt+Tab** for Windows), and the next text you type will align with the right edge of the text box or column or the rightmost tab that has been set.

The Option-Tab won't show up in the tab ruler, but if there is another tab stop before the end of the line, Option-Tab will stop there.

Why is this any different (or better) than making the text flush right? Because you can have several things on a line that uses this tab. For instance, one line can start with something flush left, and then to get something flush right on the same line (like in the header of a newsletter) just Option-tab over to it, like in the example below. Another reason to use Option-Tab is to quickly set up two columns in a one-column text box. Type a word, and then press Option-Tab to get the other side of the text box where you can type another word.

After you type the first word, use Option-Tab to jump to the other side (right side) of the text box.

Monday→	July, 1994

Align On *This*

A very specialized tab is the Align On: tab, which is like a decimal or comma tab except that instead of aligning on a decimal or comma, it can align on any character. Select the **Align On:** option from the Alignment drop-down menu in the Paragraph Tabs menu (⌘-Shift-T), and enter the character on which you would like the tabbed words to line up. If the character you specify is not in that word, the tab acts like a flush right tab. (You might use this to align asterisks or percent signs, for example.)

Even More Tab Ramblings

Here are some more helpful tips for using tabs:

☞ You can set the Apply button in the Paragraph Tab dialog box to be turned on all the time by pressing **Option** (**Alt** in Windows)

when you click on it. It will then appear highlighted until you
Option-click on it again. When the Apply button is turned on,
most changes you make in the Paragraph Tabs dialog box are
reflected instantly on-screen. (You don't have to click the tab stop
and then click Apply—you just click the tab.)

☞ Entering a value in the Position text
field in the Paragraph Tabs dialog
box and clicking Apply creates a new
tab at that position, whether or not a
tab has been selected. However, you
can't move a tab using the Position
text field: selecting a tab and entering
a new position creates a new tab at
that position, but leaves the old one
where it was originally. If you're a touch typist, you'll find this to
be the quickest method.

You can press ⌘-**Option-A**
(**Ctrl+Alt+A** in Windows) to
turn the Apply button on
and off.

☞ If it covers something you're working with, you can always move
the Paragraph Tabs dialog box by clicking on the title bar (where
it says "Paragraph Tabs") and dragging it out of the way.

The Least You Need to Know

Learning about tabs seems unnecessarily difficult compared
to the ease of whacking the Spacebar several times, but
making corrections to "spaced-out" characters is an awful
experience—one that I hope you never have to go through.
On the other hand, editing tabbed text is easy, as the following highlights will remind you:

☞ Tabs are used to align text to certain horizontal
positions.

☞ You insert tabs in text by pressing the Tab key.

☞ Tab leaders create a string of characters between
the tabs in text.

☞ Create an automatic flush-right tab by pressing
Option-Tab (**Alt+Tab** for Windows).

Chapter 18
Industrial Strength Paragraph Formatting

In This Chapter

- ☛ Looking at the Paragraph Formats dialog box
- ☛ Indenting paragraphs
- ☛ Creating drop caps
- ☛ Creating space before and after paragraphs
- ☛ Creating paragraph rules between paragraphs
- ☛ Changing the hyphenation and justification settings

Sometimes leading, alignment, and tabs just aren't enough. When it comes time to pull out the big guns for paragraph formatting, you need the Paragraph Formatting dialog box. In this chapter, we go "just too far, darn it," and look into everything that you can possibly do with paragraph formatting.

A Paragraph Formatting Extravaganza

The Paragraph Formats dialog box (shown in the following figure) is where everything happens—at least everything relating to paragraph formatting. You open it up by selecting **Style→Formats**.

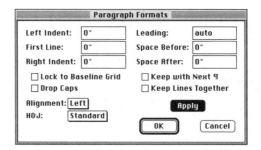

The Paragraph
Formats dialog box.

Okay, so it's a plain-looking little dialog box, with not a lot of flash. But bear with me. Let's see what it can do.

Moving It Over—Indented Text

Indent is a professional-sounding word for scooting text over in one direction or another. It was no doubt invented by some typesetting person who felt it was beneath his dignity to say "scoot." Text can be indented three ways:

- ☛ The left side can be indented from the left edge of the text box.

- ☛ The right side can be indented from the right edge of the text box.

- ☛ The first line can be indented more or less than the other lines in the paragraph.

The first two ways are fairly straightforward. But that third point can really get your head spinning like Linda Blair on a bad day, as you'll see later in this chapter.

Triangle Trouble

The part about the Paragraph Formats dialog box that confuses people the most isn't actually even in the Paragraph Formats dialog box. Instead, it's what happens in the paragraph formats ruler above the text. For each of the three indents, there is a triangle. You might have noticed similar markers in the tab ruler earlier.

On the left, there are two small stacked triangles. The top one represents the first line indent, and the bottom one represents the indent for the rest of the paragraph. On the right, there's one whopper of a triangle that represents the right indent. These triangles just sit there, minding their own business at the edges of the text box until you change an indent. And then everything goes haywire.

Okay, it isn't really that bad. But it *can* take some getting used to. The following figure shows a typical set of triangles, with text underneath showing how the text aligns with them. To the right are the indent values as entered in the Paragraph Formats dialog box. You won't ever see it this way on your screen, of course—I'm just showing it here so you can see the relationship between the parts.

There's no option in the dialog box for tabs, but when the Paragraph Formats dialog box is open, the tab ruler appears, and you can add additional flush left tabs to the ruler. You can also move and delete existing tabs of any alignment. Conversely, you can change margin settings in the Tab dialog box.

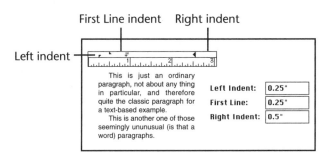

This shows you the relationship between the triangles, the Paragraph Format dialog box settings, and the paragraphs themselves.

Left and Right—The Easy Indents

The left indent is fairly simple to change. Enter a value in the Left Indent text field, or drag the bottom left triangle on the tab ruler, and the text will be indented that distance from the left edge of the text box. The right indent works the same way—enter a number in the Right Indent text field or drag the big right triangle on the tab ruler—except that the right edge is affected, and the distance is measured from the right edge of the text box.

First Line—The Indent from Hell

You probably have figured out the actual mechanics of setting the First Line indent. Either drag the top left triangle on the tab ruler, or change the First Line setting in the Paragraph Format dialog box. Simple enough.

Notice in the following figure that the first line indent's triangle is at position 0 on the tab ruler; that's because the Left Indent number minus the First Line indent number equals 0. This simple math is a quick way of determining where your First Line indent will actually end up.

Unfortunately, few things in life are simple. It's easy enough to change the setting, but to change it to the setting *you actually want* requires some calculation. The First Line indent is confusing because the measurement you enter is in relation to the location of the left indent. For example, if you entered a value of 3p in the First Line text field, the first line indent would move 3p to the right of the left indent—wherever that might be.

To add to the confusion, when the left indent is changed, the *value* of the first line indent remains the same (i.e. the number in the First Line indent text field), but the *location* changes. This happens because the location is based on the position of the left indent. If the left indent is 6p and the first line indent is 3p, the first line indent will appear to be at the 9p mark (3p + 6p = 9p). When the left indent is moved to the 12p mark, the first line indent is located at the 15p mark (3p + 12p = 15p). Whew! It's a lot of nastiness, if you ask me—at least until you get used to it.

Just Hanging-Indent Around...

But wait—the nightmare continues. The most confusing and misunderstood indent of all is the hanging indent, where the first line extends to the left of the left indent. With a hanging indent, the first line indent is a negative number. The following figure shows an example.

This is just an ordinary paragraph, not about any thing in particular, and therefore quite the classic paragraph for a text-based example.
This is another one of those seemingly ununusual (is that a word) paragraphs.

Left Indent: `1p6`
First Line: `-1p6`
Right Indent: `3p`

With a hanging indent, the first line "hangs" off the left edge of the paragraph.

To create a hanging indent, you have to first set the left indent, so the hanging part will have somewhere to hang. For instance, if you want a –6p first line indent, you first have to set at least a 6p left indent.

The most common kind of hanging indent you'll see is the bulleted (or numbered) indent. The bullets (or numbers) become the "hanging" characters, and the rest of the text aligns with the left indent. The figure below shows bulleted indents using the same text and settings from the last figure. When you are using bullets with hanging indents, type the bullet, press **Tab**, and then type the text.

❖ This is just an ordinary paragraph, not about any thing in particular, and therefore quite the classic paragraph for a text-based example.

❖ This is another one of those seemingly ununusual (is that a word) paragraphs.

❖ Unbelievable, yes, but this is the third one of these alarming unalarming paragraphs.

For this bulleted indent, the Left Indent is set to 1p6, and the First Line indent is set to –1p6.

Space Between Paragraphs (The Final Frontier?)

These are voyages of the Starship No Extra Returns. Its mission: to prevent QuarkXPress users from using multiple Returns when they could add space between paragraphs using the Paragraph Formats dialog box.

Uh oh, you know what's coming next... (no, not the Borg). Another italicized line apart from the rest of the text. That means another rule.

Never type more than one return between paragraphs.

Ouch! What if you want to put an extra line between them? The Space Before and Space After text fields can fix these spacing dilemmas much easier and faster than you can by inserting extra returns. What's more, once you set up extra space between paragraphs, you never have to worry about it again.

Choosing Between Space Before and Space After

One of the most perplexing dilemmas for beginners can be determining which of these two settings to use. Or should you use both? Actually, when setting up style sheets (see Chapter 19), you will have occasion to use both. Otherwise one or the other will be fine. There is a great controversy among QuarkXPress users regarding the merits of each, but it really doesn't matter which. I like Space Before—just because it takes fewer tabs to move to that field.

If you do use both Space Before and Space After, remember that the values in each text field are added with your leading, and paragraphs are separated by the combined amount. If you want it to look like there's an additional line between paragraphs, enter the amount of leading you are using (found right above the Space Before text field) in the Space Before or Space After text box.

Drop Caps (Reason #534 to Be Glad You Don't Use PageMaker)

PageMaker bashing, one of my favorite hobbies of late, came into full bloom when I tried PageMaker 4.0's Drop Cap "Addition." While waiting for it to work, I had enough time to get up, go for a short walk around town, shop at two different malls (looking for the ever-elusive Beatles "White Album" on CD) and play a few hands of video poker at the nearby illegal casino. But eventually the Drop Cap Addition worked... although not very well. You see, a drop cap in PageMaker is a separate text box that the rest of the text flows around. It makes for a confusing and frustrating text effect.

QuarkXPress has a drop cap feature that actually makes people go "ooooh" and "aaaahh" at demos of the feature (yes, it really happens). Checking the Drop Caps check box in the Paragraph Formats dialog box makes the entire dialog box larger, as shown below.

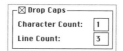

The Drop Cap box in the Paragraph Formats dialog box.

You can specify up to eight characters to be part of a drop cap (the Character Count setting), and that drop cap can be between two and sixteen lines high (the Line Count setting). The following figure shows some examples of drop caps at different settings.

Three versions of that classic fairy tale, The Cheapskate Disco Princess.

Getting a Grip on Baseline Grid

The baseline grid is another one of those underused, underappreciated QuarkXPress features. It is used to automatically line up copy that exists in two or more side-by-side columns or to align lots of items quickly. The baseline grid (you can see it by selecting **View→Show Baseline Grid**) is a series of horizontal lines spaced a certain distance apart.

If you check the Lock to Baseline Grid check box in the Paragraph Formats dialog box, the baselines of the text in the selected paragraph(s) will align to the baseline grid. Of course, this works best when the space between the lines in the baseline grid is set to match the leading you would like to use. You can set that spacing by opening the Typographic Preferences dialog box (press ⌘-**Option-Y**, or **Ctrl+Alt+Y** for Windows)

The Baseline Grid can only have *one* increment per document. If you use text that has two different leadings, you have to fend for yourself manually on one of them.

and changing the Baseline Grid Increment to whatever leading you are using for that copy. Be sure that your leading is not greater than the baseline grid, or text lines will jump down to the next gridline.

The following figures show a multi-column document with the baseline grid on and with it off. Look from line to line across the columns to see the irregularities in the top figure.

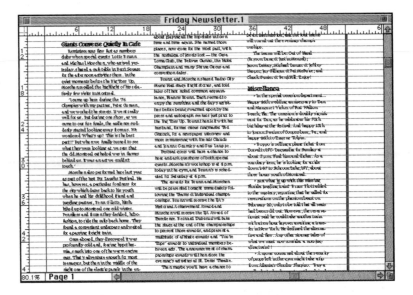

Baseline Grid off (top) and on (bottom) on a multi-column page.

Don't forget that Lock to Baseline Grid is a paragraph setting—that is, if you check the box in the Paragraph Formats dialog box, the change affects only the paragraph(s) for which you specify it. It doesn't affect the whole document automatically. Actually, that's a good thing, though—it's a good strategy to have the Lock to Baseline Grid option checked for body copy only, as headings may develop obscenely large chunks of white space in between lines.

Keeping Things Together

It's every book editor's nightmare. Somewhere in the middle of the book, where proofreaders fear to tread, lies a lonely heading at the bottom of the page. The text that was supposed to have gone under it has been bumped onto the next page by that last-minute text insert several pages before. Don't you just *hate* when that happens?

Fortunately, there are a couple of ways in QuarkXPress to control how paragraphs flow from page to page. The first is useful for heads and sub-heads like the one in the sad tale just described: Keep with Next ¶. The second, Keep Lines Together, is used to prevent the odd stray line from appearing all by its lonesome at the top or bottom of a page. Both of these options are *extremely* useful when setting up style sheets, as you'll see in the next chapter.

First, let's take a look at the Keep with Next option. When you create a heading, nothing is worse than seeing it flow to the bottom of a page, while the accompanying text is floating at the top of the next page. To make the heading jump to the next page to be with the next paragraph, select the **Keep with Next** option in the Paragraph Formats dialog box. The heading will never leave the paragraph again.

Next, there's the whole tawdry issue of killing off the widows and orphans. Before you hide this book from your children because of its violent content, the widows and orphans I'm talking about deserve to be killed—mercilessly.

An **orphan** is the first line in a paragraph that stands all by itself at the bottom of a column or page. A **widow** is a line on the top of a page or column that is separated from the rest of its paragraph on the preceding page or column.

To prevent these freaks of typesetting nature, select the **Keep Lines Together** option. When you do so, the dialog box expands to include extra options, as shown below.

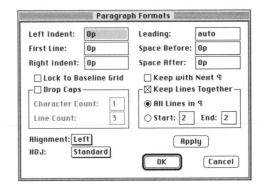

The Keep Lines Together options, in their full glory.

You can choose between All Lines in (which will make the entire paragraph stay together), or you can specify how many lines must start the paragraph at the bottom of the text box and how many lines must end the paragraph at the next text box. Common typesetting practice is that it's nice to have three lines on each, but two will do in a pinch. Enter 2 and don't change it unless someone complains.

When your paragraph doesn't meet the criteria of enough lines at the top or bottom, the entire paragraph is shifted to the next column or page. The same thing happens when you choose the Keep With Next ¶ option, and the heading and paragraph don't fit in the column. Both will appear in the next column/page.

How Do You Want It Aligned?

Clicking the Alignment pop-up menu in the Paragraph Formats dialog box displays the five different alignments available in QuarkXPress. Choose one of these options to have your text aligned Flush Left, Centered, Flush Right, Justified, or Force Justified within a text box. Chapter 16 covers these alignment options in much more detail.

Real Advanced Stuff—H&J Tables

Normally, you only have one hyphenation setting: Standard. However, if you're wanting to get exceptionally fancy, you can create custom hyphenation settings that control how words break apart and how words are stretched across the page when justified. Once you have different hyphenation settings set up, you can apply them via the Paragraph Formats dialog box. Just select that hyphenation and justification setting from the pop-up menu called simply "H&J."

Setting Up Custom H&J Tables

You can set up custom H&Js, as they are called, by selecting **Edit→H&Js** or pressing ⌘**-Option-H** (**Ctrl+Alt+H** for Windows). If this is your first time through H&Js, a dialog box appears, asking if you would like to edit the current H&J standard table, duplicate the existing one, create a new one, delete a setting, or append settings from another document. Click the **New** button to create a brand new H&J setting. The Edit Hyphenation and Justification Tables dialog box appears, as shown below.

The Edit Hyphenation and Justification Tables dialog box. Pretty intimidating, huh?

Before you mess around with the settings, type in a name for the settings. If these settings are going to be used in body copy, type in something to remind you of that, like "body copy." The left side of the dialog box deals with hyphenation requirements, while the right side has to do with justification options. We'll look at hyphenation first.

Hy-phen-a-tion Op-tions

You have a great deal of control over what can and can't be automatically hyphenated in QuarkXPress. If you turn on Auto Hyphenation, QuarkXPress will attempt to hyphenate as well as it can throughout your document following the guidelines you set below.

The Smallest Word text field lets you specify the smallest word, in number of characters, that can be split. Usually a word with less than five characters won't be split, but there are always exceptions (like on-ly), that may be acceptable to some.

In the minimum before and after fields, you control how many charac-ters must be before and how many characters must be after a hyphen for a word to break. Two letters is the absolute minimum you should use.

If the Break Capitalized Words option is checked, proper nouns and the first word in sentences can be split by hyphens. Both are a traditional no-no, but if you aren't traditional, here is the place to show it.

Below that is where you decide what the maximum number of hyphens are that can appear one after the other. Usually the limit is two, because any more can look rather odd (sort of like someone has leaned a small ladder up against your column of text).

The Hyphenation Zone is measured from the right margin. QuarkXPress uses this number to determine whether or not to hyphenate. If you have a hyphenation zone of, say, 1/4", QuarkXPress will only hyphenate if the word previous to the last word on the line ends before the 1/4" mark *and* if the last word has a suitable hyphenation point based on your setting. If you enter 0 as the hyphenation zone setting, QuarkXPress will either hyphenate the last word or move it to the next line, regardless of how close the previous word is to the margin. (This works well for flush left text only.)

Justification Options

The six text fields grouped together in the justification options section on the right side of the Edit Hyphenation and Justification Tables dialog box allow you to specify the minimum, maximum, and optimum amounts of space to be added between both words and characters.

The Flush Zone is how close you have to be to the bathroom in order to hear someone using the toilet. No, not really. Actually, the Flush Zone text field determines how close the last character on the last line of a paragraph has to be to the right side of the paragraph in order to be automatically justified. A good value for this is 1 pica, but it depends on the width of the text box.

If Single Word Justify is checked, when a word is by itself in a column, that word will be justified across the column (providing that the paragraph the word is in is set to justify). This is a matter of taste, or—some would say—bad taste. It doesn't bother me as long as there are four or more letters in the word.

When you get done playing around with the settings, select **OK** to save your changes or select **Cancel** to cancel (of course).

Paragraph Rules—Not Laws but Lines

Okay, that's enough fun with paragraph formatting for one day; it's time to do something else. Close the Paragraph Formats dialog box (if it's still open) by clicking the **OK** button.

Let's take a look at Rules. No, not as in rules-and-regulations, but rules as in a fancy word for "lines." Geez. Typesetters sure like to have fancy names for stuff, don't they? You'd think it would kill them to talk like regular people.

Anyway, you can create paragraph rules (lines) above and below the currently selected paragraph by selecting **Style→Rules** or pressing ⌘-**Shift-N** (**Ctrl+Shift+N** for Windows). The Paragraph Rules dialog box appears, as shown below.

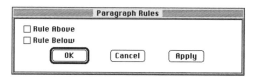

The Paragraph Rules dialog box, plain and simple.

Looks pretty simple, doesn't it? Click on the check boxes and watch the options multiply like rabbits.

```
┌─────────────────────────────────────────────┐
│              Paragraph Rules                  │
│ ☒ Rule Above         Style:  ┌──────────────┐│
│ Length:   ┌────────┐         │• • • • • • • •││
│           │Indents │         └──────────────┘│
│ From Left:│0p      │ Width:  ▶ 6 pt          │
│ From Right:│0p     │ Color:    Magenta        │
│ Offset:   │0%      │ Shade:  ▶ 100%          │
│                                               │
│ ☒ Rule Below         Style:  ┌──────────────┐│
│ Length:   ┌────────┐         │══════════════││
│           │Text    │         └──────────────┘│
│ From Left:│3p      │ Width:  ▶ 1 pt          │
│ From Right:│0p     │ Color:    Blue           │
│ Offset:   │25%     │ Shade:  ▶ 60%           │
│     ┌────────┐  ┌────────┐    ┌────────┐     │
│     │   OK   │  │ Cancel │    │ Apply  │     │
│     └────────┘  └────────┘    └────────┘     │
└─────────────────────────────────────────────┘
```

The Paragraph Rules dialog box grows to monstrous proportions when you select a check box or two.

The Length option controls how long the rule will be from left to right. "Indents" means that the rule will extend from the left to the right indent. "Text" means that the rule will extend only the length of the text on the topmost or bottommost line, depending on which rule is chosen. For example, if you've got a one-word heading on a line by itself, and you want it to look underlined, "Text" is the way to go. If you want it to look like it's sitting on top of a full-width line, "Indents" is your option of choice.

Don't like either option? Okay, choose **Indents** and indent the line itself further. You can shorten the line length by entering values in the From Left and From Right text fields. These values are subtracted from each side, shortening the rule. If you have paragraph indents applied, you can use negative numbers here so that the rules extend outside the text indents.

You can change the Offset value to move the rule up or down from the selected paragraph. A setting of 0% means that the rule is butted right up against the baseline of the paragraph; 50% means that it is between the selected paragraph and the adjoining paragraph (based on paragraph spacing values, not returns); 100% will make the rule butt up against the descenders of the adjoining paragraph.

You can also enter an offset value as a measurement, but you must specify the form of measurement after it or QuarkXPress will assume you want to make that a percentage. If you set a negative number, you can actually print the paragraph text on top of the rule (make sure they are different colors or tints, or you won't be able to read the text).

The Least You Need to Know

The Paragraph Formats dialog box is just full of surprises. By artfully using the Apply button (⌘-**A**, or **Ctrl+A** for Windows), you can change your paragraph settings and watch while your text formats itself. Ah, the life of desktop publishing doesn't get much easier than this.

- ☛ Left and Right indents measure from the edge of the text box or column to the text.

- ☛ First Line indent is a measurement beginning at the Left indent.

- ☛ Create a drop cap by checking the **Drop Caps** option in the Paragraph Formats dialog box and specifying the number of characters and height of the drop cap.

- ☛ Space between paragraphs is in addition to the leading for that paragraph.

- ☛ You can create multiple hyphenation and justification settings for use in any document.

Chapter 19

Keeping in Style with Style Sheets

In This Chapter

- ☞ Understanding and using style sheets
- ☞ Creating style sheets the easy way
- ☞ Creating keyboard equivalents for those style sheets

Read this chapter.

Well, that isn't one of the typical QuarkXPress rules, but it is something you should do. For whatever reason, people avoid "Style Sheets" like they would avoid Michael Bolton on a bad hair day. Yikes!

However, there's no need to avoid style sheets; they make your life easier. I'm basically a lazy person, and the thought of anything making my life easier does perk my interest. (I say this as I sit in my hammock and type, drink at hand—just a Peach Iced Tea Snapple. I avoid alcohol because of those ads that always tell you not to drink and hammock.)

SPEAK LIKE A GEEK

A **style sheet** is a set of preset character and paragraph information, like fonts, style attributes (bold, italic, underline), tracking settings, indents, space between paragraphs, tabs, paragraph rules, and anything else that can be applied to characters or text.

You can have a style sheet for each of the types of text in your document. Look at the text in this book. Style sheets have been created for the following: headings, subheads, body copy, sidebars (such as Speak Like a Geek and Techno Nerd Teaches), captions, and bulleted lists (like The Least You Need to Know).

Each of these style sheets contains information about the character and paragraph attributes of a particular type of text. For instance, body copy is 10-point text with 14-point leading, flush left, with so many points before each paragraph.

Instant Style Sheets

How hard is it to create a style sheet? It takes three (count 'em, three) clicks of the mouse. To create a new style sheet, follow along with these steps:

1. Format some text with the attributes you want to assign to a style. Give the text character and paragraph attributes that make it exactly the way you want it to appear.

2. Put the cursor somewhere in the middle of the paragraph (style sheets are paragraph-based, so you don't have to select anything) and select **Edit→Style Sheets**. The style sheet listing dialog box appears, as shown below. The bottom of this dialog box tells you all about the selected paragraph (yours will look different than mine).

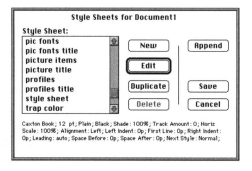

The style sheet listing dialog box.

3. Click the **New** button. The Edit Style Sheet dialog box appears, as shown in the following figure.

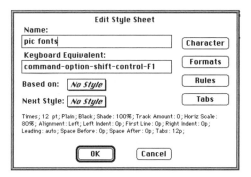

The Edit Style Sheet dialog box.

4. Give the style sheet a name and click **OK**. The style sheet listing dialog box appears once more, but this time your style sheet appears in the list next to the buttons.

5. Click the **Save** button, and the style sheet is added to your document. You can see it and select it by selecting **Style→Style Sheets→Your Style**.

You can create as many style sheets as you want this way, setting up a separate one for each style you use in your document and then following the steps outlined above.

Applying Style Sheets

Applying a style sheet is easy. That's the whole point of using style sheets, after all. To apply a style sheet to a paragraph or paragraphs, put the insertion point inside the paragraph (or select several paragraphs to format a bunch of them at once). Select the style sheet by selecting **Style→Style Sheet** and then clicking on your style. Violà! The selected paragraphs take on the attributes of that style sheet.

Even though you created the style sheet from the paragraph that contained the insertion point, that paragraph has not had the style applied! You will need to select the style and apply it to the paragraph (see "Applying Style Sheets," later in this chapter). And you really do need to do this, so that any changes to that style affect the source paragraph.

When Styles Go Out of Style

You can change the information in a style by selecting **Edit→Style Sheets** and double-clicking on the style in the style sheet listing dialog box. The buttons on the right side of the Edit Styles dialog box (Character, Formats, Rules, Tabs) correspond to the selections in the Style menu. When pressed, each of those buttons displays the corresponding dialog box. For instance, the Character button displays the Character Attributes dialog box.

If another style sheet was applied to your paragraph before you applied the current style, sometimes the style won't change all of the attributes of the paragraph. To prevent this, hold down the Option key as you choose the new style sheet, which will remove any previous settings before applying the new style sheet.

Make your changes in whichever areas are appropriate and click **OK**. Click **Save** in the style sheet listing dialog box. When the changes are made, they affect all paragraphs that have that style applied to them.

Changing a style can be extremely useful. For example, let's say you create a magazine for a client, and then realize that the typeface you used for body copy is Garamond—which is, coincidentally, the last name of the man who ran over your client's cat the other day. You can change all the body copy to another font simply by modifying the style sheet for body copy. This process takes only seconds; it's much more efficient than selecting each block of text and changing the font.

Give Style Sheets Keyboard Equivalents

Most people create a lot of style sheets, but end up using only a few of them. If that's your situation, it makes a lot of sense to assign keyboard equivalents to the style sheets you use most. That way, instead of wading through the menus every time you want to apply the style sheet, you can just press a couple of keys.

To give a style sheet a keyboard equivalent, select **Edit→Style Sheets** and double-click the style sheet to which you are assigning a keyboard equivalent. Click inside the Keyboard Equivalents text field, and type the keyboard shortcut for that style exactly as you will type it when applying it. For instance, if you wanted ⌘-F1 to be the keyboard equivalent, you would press ⌘-**F1**.

When assigning keyboard equivalents, you can use F-keys (F1, F2, and so on) and the numeric keypad on your keyboard only if those keyboard combinations don't conflict with existing shortcuts in QuarkXPress. You can use the ⌘, Shift, Option, and Control keys, or any combination of them (including all four!), with the F-key or numeric keypad key.

To apply the style using your new keyboard equivalent, select the paragraphs to be changed and press the keyboard equivalent. Pretty simple. But then, that's the whole point. In case you forget what keys you've assigned, the key combination for the style appears in both the Style Sheet submenu and the Style Sheets palette. "What is the Style Sheets palette?" you may ask. Well, keep reading.

The Style Sheets Palette

If you have the screen space for it, the Style Sheets palette (shown below) is extremely useful. All the styles are listed in this expandable palette. You can apply styles simply by clicking on the paragraph you want to format, and then clicking on the name of the style sheet.

Give yourself a break and use the Style Sheets palette.

Copying Isn't Cheating—Basing Styles on Other Styles

Give up the old notions hammered into you in grade school that say you always have to do your own work and that copying is cheating. Instead of reinventing the style sheets each time you need a new one, you may find it easier to create style sheets that are based on other style sheets. This has the double benefit that when you change one style sheet, all style sheets based on it will be changed as well.

Command-clicking on any style sheet name listed in the palette takes you to the style sheet listing dialog box. Option-clicking removes any other local formatting from the paragraph and applies the style.

Because you can change the style sheet of something so it's based on a different style sheet than it was originally, be aware that you can't base a style sheet on a style sheet that is based on the one you are trying to change. Doing so would create a paradox in the space-time continuum, which would very likely send you back in time to when there was no indoor plumbing.

To base a new style sheet on an existing one, select the **New** button in the style sheet listing dialog box. Name the style sheet, and select the style sheet to base it on from the pop-up menu in the Edit Styles dialog box.

You can set up chains of these style sheets based on other style sheets based on other style sheets, if you so desire. And if you do, the style sheets stay linked. For example, if you base the Indented Body Text style on the Plain Body Text style, and then you change the font of the Plain Body Text style to Courier, the Indented Body Text style changes to Courier as well.

Next Style, Please

One of the coolest features of style sheets is that you can "program" them to create a string of different style sheets each time you press the Return key. For instance, if you always create a heading, press Return, and then type a few paragraphs of body copy, you can set up the heading style sheet to automatically go to the body copy style as soon as you finish entering the heading. To do this, go to the Edit Styles dialog box and change the Next Style option to the style sheet you want that style sheet to change to when you press Return.

Sucking Styles from Other Documents

Instead of recreating styles each time you create a document, you can use styles that exist in other QuarkXPress documents, by clicking the **Append** button in the style sheet listing dialog box. A standard Open dialog box appears, and when you select a document, the style sheets from the source document appear in the document you are using.

The Least You Need To Know

Now, all this style sheet stuff may seem a little intimidating, but using style sheets instead of applying each individual style to paragraphs can save eons of time.

- Style sheets are combinations of character and paragraph attributes that can be applied to any paragraph.

- An easy way to create a style sheet is to format a paragraph in your text, select it, and create a new style sheet (which will automatically have all the formatting in your paragraph).

- You can use the F-Keys in combination with ⌘ and Control to create keyboard equivalents that you can use to apply style sheets.

Part III
Picture This!

Cheeeeeez. It's picture time, and in this part we look at how you work with pictures in QuarkXPress. I'll tell you about the Picture-in-a-picture-box rule, about picture formats, about how to make your pictures look different in QuarkXPress, and even how to create new colors and apply them to your QuarkXPress items.

Chapter 20
You Oughtta Be in Picture Boxes

In This Chapter

- ☛ Creating picture boxes
- ☛ Creating custom picture boxes
- ☛ Working with the different shaped picture boxes
- ☛ Changing the size of existing picture boxes
- ☛ Changing from one type of picture box to another

QuarkXPress is a tough program; there's no sneakin' around when you're in QuarkXPress. To prove this, just try to disobey the rule below about picture boxes and pictures... QuarkXPress didn't think so. Picture boxes are going to be part of your Quarking as long as you have pictures to place in the program.

Feeling Boxed In?

Text and pictures have one thing in common in QuarkXPress: both need to be in boxes. And when dealing with pictures, you must obey a rule similar to the one in Chapter 10:

Pictures can only exist inside of picture boxes.

Sounds familiar, doesn't it? Well, it happens to be one of those hard and fast rules that you just can't ignore. The only way to bring a picture into QuarkXPress is to create a picture box for it first. No picture box, no picture.

Once you have that concept down, everything involving pictures *should* just fall into place. Unfortunately, it doesn't, which is why I've devoted this entire chapter to creating, editing, and modifying picture boxes, as well as how actually get the picture into the box.

Making Your Own Picture Boxes

You've got four picture box creation tools to work with, and they're located smack dab in the middle of the toolbox.

Rounded-Corner Rectangle Picture Box ⎯ Rectangle Picture Box
Polygon Picture Box ⎯ Oval Picture Box

The four picture box creation tools.

You create any of the first three picture boxes by simply dragging from corner to corner. You use the Polygon Picture Box tool to create individual points that are automatically connected to form a shape. You'll learn more about each tool shortly.

TECHNO NERD TEACHES...

Once you create a picture box, your mouse cursor changes back to the Item or Content tool, whichever you were using last. If you want to draw another picture box, you have to reselect the picture box tool. If you know in advance that you'll be drawing more than one picture box, hold down the **Option** key (**Alt** for Windows) when you select the picture box tool of choice. The picture box tool will stay selected until you select another tool.

Just Your Basic Rectangle...

The rectangular picture box is the most boring one, but it's also the most common. (Go figure.) To use it, select the **Rectangle Picture Box** tool, and drag from one corner to another to create a rectangular picture box.

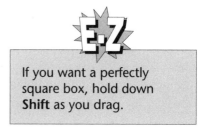

If you want a perfectly square box, hold down **Shift** as you drag.

When you release the mouse button, the picture box appears, as shown here. The X in the middle of the box means that there's no picture in it yet.

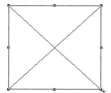

A typical rectangular picture box that was just drawn.

A Not-So-Basic Rounded-Corner Rectangle Picture Box

Why would anyone want to put rounded corners on a picture box in the straight-corner nineties? Well, someone somewhere uses this feature—otherwise QuarkXPress wouldn't include it.

Draw the rounded-corner rectangle picture box just like a regular rectangle box, from corner to corner. It should look something like this figure.

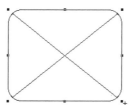

A rounded-corner rectangle picture box.

After you've drawn this box, take a look at the Measurements palette. The third field from the left on the bottom row is the size of the rounded corner. This is considered the rounded-corner radius.

How much radius would a rounded corner have if a rounded corner could be a circle? Or something like that. The rounded-corner radius is the radius of the circle that the corner is a part of. An easy way to work with this is to imagine that this value is the distance from where the corner would be if it was a straight corner, to where the curve begins, if that makes sense (see the figure below).

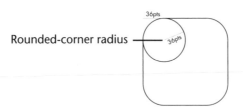

Rounded-corner radius

A corner radius explained.

After you create a rounded-corner rectangle picture box, the corner handles used for resizing the polygon actually exist outside the original shape. This can be a tad disconcerting at first, but you'll get used to it.

Okay, so now you know that the Rounded-Corner Rectangle Picture Box tool enables you to draw rounded rectangles. Now I'm going to tell you that you actually never need to use this tool at all. Instead, just use the regular Rectangle Picture Box tool, then modify the corner radius.

To change the default size of the rounded corners that are created with the Rounded-Corner Rectangle Picture Box tool (normally 1/4" or 1p6), double-click the Rounded-Corner Rectangle Picture Box tool (Sheesh! What a name!) and click the **Modify** button. Change the rounded-corner radius value to whatever you would like it to be. It will remain at that setting while you are using the current document.

Remember, to make changes that last forever (not just while the document is open), you have to make those preference changes while there are no documents open.

A (Basically Round) Oval Picture Box

The third picture box tool is the Oval Picture Box creation tool, which, not surprisingly, draws ovals and circles. (You knew that.) To create an oval, drag from one corner to another. (Okay, it's not exactly a corner; ovals don't have corners. Humor me.) To constrain the shape to a perfect circle, press the **Shift** key while you drag. An empty oval picture box is shown here.

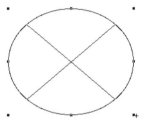

An oval picture box.

The corner handles on an oval picture box are usually nowhere near the oval itself (as you can see above), which makes adjusting the oval seem a little awkward. Therefore, it's a lot easier to adjust ovals than to adjust polygons, as you'll see in the next section.

The Oddly Shaped Polygon Picture Box

If QuarkXPress offered just the normal kinds of picture boxes, it wouldn't be any better than an ordinary, run-o'-the-mill desktop publishing program. (PageMaker immediately springs to mind.) But no, QuarkXPress picture boxes created with the Polygon Picture Box creation tool can have any number of sides and almost any shape.

To use the Polygon Picture Box creation tool, select it from the toolbox, and click in one location. When you release the mouse button, a line follows your cursor, extending from the place you last clicked. Click again and the same thing happens, and again and again. When you want to finish your polygon, go back to the place you first clicked, and your cursor changes into an open circle. When you see the open circle, click again. The shape changes into a standard 8-handled picture box, though it may look a little unusual. (Or you can double-click anywhere to close the path.)

The following figure shows a number of different shapes that you could create using the Polygon Picture Box creation tool. Yes, they're all picture boxes, and they can all hold your graphics—albeit some more weirdly than others.

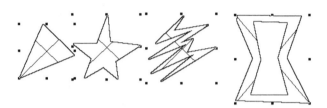

Different polygon picture boxes.

Note that the polygon on the right has a "hole" through it. The picture would go in the outside (the "donut" part), and anything underneath the picture box would show through the "hole" part.

All Polygons Are Rectangles?

It's a statement that would make your 8th grade math teacher shudder. But in QuarkXPress, it's partly true. The handles that surround a polygon always form a rectangle, even if the shape itself looks like a half-eaten burrito. Here are some examples:

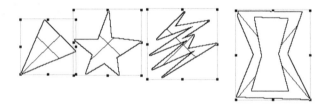

Rectangles surround polygons, no matter how twisted the shape.

Handles appear on this outside rectangle just like they do on other shapes. Dragging these handles to resize the polygon affects the shape inside the rectangle just like it would if you were resizing a more conventional shape.

Bending, Stretching, and Shaping Your Polygon

Sure, you can resize a polygon using the handles just like any other shape. Piece of cake. But did you know you can also change the actual shape of it on the fly? To reshape the polygon, select it and select **Item→Reshape Polygon** (be sure that there is a check mark). The handles outside the shape disappear, and handles appear for each point you clicked when creating the shape. Each of those points can be pushed, pulled, and twiddled with until the polygon doesn't look anything like it did originally. You can also click on the line segments between the handles to drag the entire segment (two handles' worth) at once.

Want more handles? Command-click on a line segment. When you press the ⌘ key (**Ctrl** in Windows) and the cursor is positioned over a line segment, the cursor changes to an open circle (actually a rounded corner square, to be technical). You can click then to create a new handle.

Too many handles? No problem. Hold down the ⌘ key and position the cursor over a handle. The cursor changes to an open circle with an X going through it. Click to remove the handle. When you are finished distorting your polygon, select **Item→Reshape Polygon** again. The polygon once again shows the standard eight handles.

OOPS!

Polygons are limited to 255 sides. (Yeah, like you're going to need more than that.) To give you an idea of how much that is, 255 sides would create enough lines for a fairly detailed floor plan of a 4,500-square-foot house.

Transmogrifying Picture and Text Boxes

Transmogrifying? What kind of a word is that? It's one of those big fancy words that erudite (another fancy word) people use to intimidate others. It means "changing." Now you know.

Any picture or text box can be changed into almost any other shape with just one menu item selection. Sound too good to be true? This is one of those all-too-cool features in QuarkXPress. Select any picture or text box (yes, this works with text boxes in version 3.3 as well as picture boxes), select **Item→Box Shape**, and select one of the options there. Those options are identified on the following page.

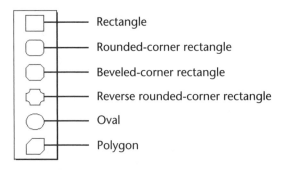

The Box Shape options.

Changing curved shapes to polygons makes the curved edges into several small straight segments. You can't create a curved segment on a polygon. (You can make many small straight segments give the appearance of a curved line, but that's not quite the same.)

When you click one of these options, the selected box changes its shape. Well, usually. If you select the polygon shape, the box will not change in shape, but instead you will be able to access the Reshape Polygon option to change the shape into anything your little heart desires.

The third and fourth shapes in the box shape list (Beveled-Corner Rectangle and Reverse Rounded-Corner Rectangle) cannot be created with any of the picture box tools. (Well, maybe with the polygon tool, but not easily.) Instead, to create one of these shapes, you must create the picture box first and then change it to one of these two shapes.

What Is the Measure of a Picture Box?

The following falls into the "interesting but not critical" category, so feel free to skip it if you're in a hurry to get to the end of this chapter and take a break. When a picture box (with no picture) is selected, the Measurements palette shows the same type of info as you would see when a text box is selected. The main difference is that instead of a columns (cols) option, there is a rounded-corner radius text field for rectangles and rounded rectangles. Here's a typical Measurements palette for a rectangle:

X: 15p3	W: 16p3	⊿ 0°	
Y: 17p9	H: 9p8	⋒ 0p	

The Measurements palette when a rectangle picture box is selected.

The X represents the distance from the left edge of the page; Y is the distance from the top of the page. W is the width, and H is the height. And the third field on the top row is the angle text field. Got it? Good. No, there won't be a quiz.

The Least You Need to Know

In QuarkXPress, you can't avoid picture boxes. But they are pretty darn easy to create and modify, so you might as well use 'em. (Batter's boxes on the other hand, aren't used much at all in QuarkXPress.)

☞ You create picture boxes with any of the four picture box creation tools.

☞ Pressing the **Shift** key while creating rectangles, rounded rectangles, and ovals will make the height and width of the picture boxes equal.

☞ To change from one type of picture box to another, select **Item→Box Shape**, and then select the shape of the box you want the picture box to be.

☞ Even bizarrely shaped picture boxes are bound by a rectangle that defines their size and location.

Chapter 21

Getting Pictures from There to QuarkXPress

In This Chapter

- ☛ Importing pictures

- ☛ A listing of the ridiculous number of graphic formats that QuarkXPress can import

- ☛ How to resize pictures within picture boxes

- ☛ How to make pictures fill the inside of picture boxes

- ☛ Modifying and manipulating pictures within QuarkXPress

All right. Your QuarkXPress document is full of picture boxes. They're obscuring the rest of the page, and the document is now reminiscent of your eighth grade art final. Now it's time to put some real art inside the picture boxes you've created.

For those of you who are skipping around, in the last chapter you learned how to create an empty picture box. And since picture boxes are the only way to use graphics in QuarkXPress, you need to know how to work with them before you go any further. That means if you skipped Chapter 20, go back and read it now.

Back already? Good. To put a picture into your picture box, and mess with it, you use the Content tool. Sounds pretty simple, doesn't it? Well, it is; but there are a few restrictions and caveats you need to know, so you'd better read this chapter, too.

More Than You Ever Wanted to Know About Graphic Formats

QuarkXPress doesn't accept all that many different types of graphic formats, but fortunately, it does take the ones that are really important to Macintosh users. (The Windows version, not surprisingly, takes the formats that Windows users deal with most often.) Here, then, is a list of all the formats that you can import into the Macintosh version of QuarkXPress, what their SAs (Silly Acronyms) mean, and a brief description of each.

- ☞ **TIFF (Tagged Image File Format)**   Pronounced "tiff." This format was created by Aldus right after PageMaker began to take off. It became the pseudo-standard in the late eighties, but when DCS (see below) was announced, it lost some ground. Almost all scanning software can save files as TIFFs, since TIFF can be black and white, color, or grayscale, and almost any size.

- ☞ **EPS (Encapsulated PostScript file)**   This format was created by Adobe, and it usually comes in two basic formats: bitmap (pixels) images and vector (line-based) images. Most software that can import graphics can import EPS. EPS files are larger than TIFF files, but tend to print faster to PostScript printing devices.

- ☞ **PICT & PICT2 (Picture file)**   Pronounced "Pict." Pict files are the most common graphics file types on the Macintosh, but in general you should avoid printing them from QuarkXPress since they are a common cause of PostScript printing errors.

- ☞ **RIFF (Raster Image File Format)**   Pronounced "riff." RIFFs are a very uncommon format whose popularity peaked around 1990. You won't find many graphics files saved in this format, so don't worry about it.

☞ **JPEG (Joint Photographic Experts Group)** Pronounced "Jay-peg." A JPEG file actually removes much of the color and detail information from the file, making it much smaller for storage on your hard drive. You can save in this format in Photoshop, for example, and in so doing specify the level of compression (and thus the amount of lost information) in each image. You can import and print JPEG images out of QuarkXPress only if the JPEG XTension is installed.

☞ **PhotoCD** This format was developed by Kodak as a means of taking standard film and creating files on Compact Discs that can be viewed by a number of systems. PhotoCD is an inexpensive way to get prints as well as (almost) permanent backups of that disastrous ice-fishing trip to Mexico. The PhotoCD XTension must be installed for these files to be imported and printed.

☞ **Paint** Paint files are usually black and white rough images. The first graphics software on a Macintosh was MacPaint. Nobody who's anybody uses Paint format anymore.

☞ **DCS (Desktop Color Separations)** DCS files are actually a set of five EPS files linked together. Designed especially for high-end desktop publishing, a DCS file contains one file for each color to be printed (Cyan, Magenta, Yellow, and Black) and another (preview) file used as a placeholder in QuarkXPress. The number-one reason for using DCS files is that the preview file is pretty small, while the other four files together could take up several megabytes on your hard drive. The four-color files can be kept separate from the preview files, linking up with them only when the file is printed.

Alright, you made it through that file format stuff alive—unless you skipped it. Armed with that knowledge, you should now have a pretty good idea of the file formats you want to import, versus the file formats you want to avoid.

Now that you've read all that, I'll give you the bad news: many times, you don't have any choice. Someone gives you a graphic file to work with, or your favorite piece of clip art comes in only one format. You take what you can get. But at least you now know enough to be happy or unhappy about it.

Ready, Set, Import!

Enough theory—let's get down to business. To import a picture file in QuarkXPress:

1. Select a picture box with the Content tool.

2. Select **File→Get Picture** or press ⌘-E (**Ctrl+E** for Windows). The Get Picture dialog box pops up, as shown here.

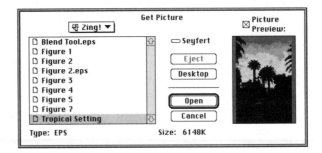

The Get Picture dialog box.

3. Select the picture file from its location on your hard drive. If the Picture Preview box is checked, the picture appears in the right-hand side of the dialog box so you can browse your pictures before you pick one to import.

4. Click the **Open** button to import the picture. That's it—you're done! The dialog box goes away, and the picture appears in the picture box in your document.

If the menu item reads "Get Text" instead of "Get Picture," that means you have a text box selected instead of a picture box. If neither is available, you probably selected the Item tool. Read step 1 again.

You can't have multiple pictures in a picture box! Many gallant users have tried and failed. Give it up. If Get Picture is selected when there is a picture in the picture box, the current picture will be replaced with the new picture. If you really have to have two pictures in the same picture box, you will have to combine those two pictures in the software they were saved in before you bring them into QuarkXPress.

Odd Things You Can Do to Pictures

Once you have imported a picture into QuarkXPress, you can do all sorts of things to it (the poor, innocent picture) as it sits benignly inside its picture box. In this section, we'll discuss how to move it around as well as how to resize, slant, and color it. (Chapter 8 discusses ways of manipulating certain types of graphics too. Skip back there if you need more info.)

If you don't see the picture in the picture box, maybe it's just off-center. Press **⌘-Shift-M (Ctrl+Shift+M** for Windows) to center the picture.

Pushing Pictures Around in Their Boxes

Okay, so you've got a picture in a picture box. You can move the box itself, as you saw in Chapter 20, but you can also move the picture within the picture box. Think of your picture box as a window that your picture peeks through. Moving the picture behind the window changes what's displayed in the window.

There are two ways you can move pictures around: manually (by using the Content tool to push the picture around) and numerically (by entering values in the Measurements palette).

To move a picture around with the Content tool (you know, the one that looks like a hand with an I-bar), first make sure the Content tool is selected. Then click anywhere within the picture box and drag in the direction you want to move the picture. Your cursor changes to a hand.

Using this method, you can actually move a picture right out of a picture box, so it isn't visible at all. How is this possible? The picture must be inside the picture box, and when part of it extends outside the picture box, that part is not visible on-screen or when it's printed. It's like moving the picture so it doesn't peek through the window anymore. If you don't want the picture to print, delete it—don't just move it.

Now let's look at the Measurements palette method of moving pictures. The Measurements palette looks a little different when a picture box with a picture is selected, as shown below.

The Measurements palette when a picture box with a picture in it is selected.

| X: 15p3 | W: 16p3 | ◿ 0° | → X%: 100% | ✥ X+: 0p | ◿ 0° |
| Y: 17p9 | H: 9p8 | ◸ 0p | ↕ Y%: 100% | ✥ Y+: 0p | ◿ 0° |

The next two fields are where you can move the picture around. X+ is how far to the left or right the picture is from its original position in the upper left corner of the box. A positive number means that the picture is to the right of its original location, while a negative number means it is to the left. The amounts are displayed in the current measurement system.

You can change the location of an object by selecting the X+ or Y+ field and typing in new values. Keep in mind that 0 in both X and Y fields will put the picture in the upper left corner of the page.

Rotating, Skewing, and Other Twisted Actions

The rightmost fields on the Measurements palette for pictures are for rotating and skewing pictures within picture boxes. If both values are at 0, the picture has not been rotated or skewed at all.

To rotate the picture, enter the degrees of rotation in the picture rotation text field (third from the left on the top row) and press **Enter** or **Return**. Remember that rotating in QuarkXPress works on a counterclockwise principle: rotating a picture 90° will rotate it 90° to the left.

To skew a picture, enter the amount of skew (between −75° and 75°) in the skew text field (right below the picture rotation field). A positive number skews the picture to the right, and a negative number will skew the picture to the left, as shown below.

The same picture skewed four ways.

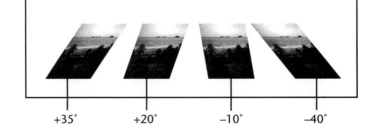

+35°   +20°   −10°   −40°

Blowing It Up, Shrinking It Down

There are two ways (aren't there always?) to resize pictures: by using the Content tool and by entering information in the Measurements palette. But before you start resizing willy-nilly, here's a warning: watch out when resizing bitmap images, such as those that were scanned. If those images are enlarged too much, pixelization occurs. (Sounds like some horrible plague, doesn't it?)

Pixelization is another fine two-dollar word that graphics professionals use to scare the rest of us into thinking desktop publishing is harder than it actually is. Scanned images are made up of thousands of little pixels, which blend together to form photographs and pictures. When you enlarge a picture, each of the tiny pixels is also enlarged. Well, technically the pixels aren't enlarged; they are duplicated. Where you once had one black pixel, you now have a 2×2 square block of them, for instance. If enlarged too much, the pixels (usually square in shape) become quite noticeable, as in the example below.

The original image is on the left, and the enlarged, pixelized image is on the right.

First, let's look at the manual way (the difficult way) of resizing. To manually resize a picture in QuarkXPress, Command-drag one of the handles on the picture's picture box. As you drag, the picture inside the picture box changes in size along with the picture box. To constrain the picture to its correct proportions, press ⌘-**Option-Shift** (**Ctrl+Alt+Shift** in Windows) and drag on the handles. To constrain a picture and picture box to a square shape, press ⌘-**Shift** (**Ctrl+Shift** in Windows) to change the size.

Notice that these commands are the same as for resizing text and picture boxes, but the ⌘ key has been added.

The easier way to resize a picture is with the Measurements palette. The X% and Y% text fields enable you to see the current size of the picture, and to change it to your specifications. The X% is the width of the picture compared to its original width. At 100 percent, the picture is the same size as it was originally. Y% is the height of the picture compared to its original height. Enter new values (you don't have to type the percent sign) to change the percentages of pictures.

You can't make a picture less than 10 percent (1/10) of its original size or more than 1000 percent (10 times) the original size. If that's a problem, open the picture in the program it was originally created in, and resize it there. But remember: drastically resized pictures can look N-A-S-T-Y.

Bonus: Resizing When It's Gotta Be Precise

So far, what you've seen probably doesn't lead you to believe that you can resize a picture to exact dimensions, as least not without a calculator. Well, you can. It just takes a different procedure. To do precision resizing, follow these steps:

1. Select the picture and picture box with the Content tool.

2. Change the picture box to the exact size that you want the picture to be. (I use the Measurements palette for this.)

3. Press ⌘-**Shift-F** (**Ctrl+Shift+F** in Windows), and boom! The picture becomes the exact size of the picture box. (Think of F for Fit.)

This method usually works, but occasionally there will be problems (for instance, if the picture is saved in its graphic program with additional white space around it). In this case, the picture and the white space will become the size you've specified. This is another prime example of the computer not being all that much smarter than your standard doorknob.

To fix this, you must get rid of the white space in your graphic file in the program it was created or edited in.

Making Your Picture a Centerpiece

There is also a key combination that you can use to center a picture inside of a picture box. It doesn't matter if the size of the picture and the picture box are totally different—this keyboard equivalent will put the center of the picture in the center of the picture box.

Sometimes this keyboard equivalent will distort the picture by increasing the width more than the height or vice versa. In that case, use the combination **⌘-Option-Shift-F** (**Ctrl+Alt+Shift+F** in Windows) to resize the picture without changing its proportions.

So what is this key combo? (You thought I'd tell you all about it, and then leave it out, huh? I thought about it.) Press **⌘-Shift-M** (**Ctrl+Shift+M** in Windows) to center the picture. You must have a picture box selected and be using the Content tool for this to work.

Item Modify for Pictures

The Picture Box Specifications dialog box is not very different from the Text Box Specifications dialog box, in that most of the text fields are exactly the same. That being the case, I won't belabor the similar features—just turn back to Chapter 10 if you need a refresher on it. The Picture Box Specifications dialog box is shown below. To access it, select the picture box, and then select **Item→Modify** or press **⌘-M** (**Ctrl+M** for Windows).

Picture Box Specifications			
Origin Across:	15p3	**Scale Across:**	100%
Origin Down:	17p9	**Scale Down:**	100%
Width:	16p3	**Offset Across:**	0p
Height:	9p8	**Offset Down:**	0p
Box Angle:	0°	**Picture Angle:**	0°
Box Skew:	0°	**Picture Skew:**	0°
Corner Radius:	0p		

☐ Suppress Picture Printout

☐ Suppress Printout

─Background─
Color: *None*
Shade: ▶ 100%

(OK)   (Cancel)

The Picture Box Specifications dialog box.

the picture box, and then select **Item→Modify** or press ⌘-**M** (**Ctrl+M** for Windows).

The only things that are different, actually, are the fields on the right side, which are (get this!) the same as the six fields on the right side of the Measurements palette. Déjà vu. So, yes, you guessed correctly. You can use this dialog box instead of the Measurements palette whenever you like.

The most useful thing (in my opinion) that you can do in the Picture Box Specifications dialog box is change the background color. And if you use the Color palette (see Chapter 22), even *this* isn't very useful. That's why I saved this box for late in the chapter; for most people, it's a less convenient way of doing the same stuff that comes easier elsewhere.

The Least You Need to Know

So now you've got pictures inside those picture boxes. If you only had pictures of boxes inside your picture boxes, you would have an electronic version of that old box-inside-a-box gag, huh?

- ☛ To import pictures, use the Content tool.

- ☛ When importing pictures, make sure that the Content tool is active.

- ☛ You can move pictures within picture boxes by clicking and holding the mouse button when the Content tool is active, and then dragging.

- ☛ QuarkXPress can import picture files in almost any graphical format (save TULIP—Ted's Unpatented Large Image Process).

- ☛ Learn how to make those pictures look better than ever by buying *The Complete Idiot's Guide to Photoshop* (coming soon from Alpha Books) by Ted Alspach, who paid for this brief advertisement.

Chapter 22
Color Your World

In This Chapter

- ☞ Creating new colors
- ☞ Working with the Colors palette
- ☞ Creating gradients

One of the most powerful features in QuarkXPress is that it enables you to create any color you would like and apply it to certain types of pictures, as well as to the backgrounds of those pictures. You can even create and apply gradients as backgrounds! Kind of makes you feel like Picasso, doesn't it?

Creating New Colors

You've probably looked at the color list available in QuarkXPress and thought to yourself, "This is it? What?" and "Where are my favorite colors? No Periwinkle? No Mauve? What a chintzy piece of software."

Well, no, colors like Burnt Umber and Sky Blue aren't in the color list, mainly because this isn't *CrayolaXPress*. QuarkXPress really isn't that incredibly stingy (well, at least not in regard to colors). You can pick from literally thousands of colors (not preset), but most of them are hidden so you aren't overcome by the sheer number of them.

In order to add colors to your color list, you must select **Edit→Colors**, at which time the following dialog box appears.

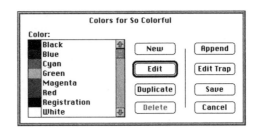

The Colors for Document *dialog box. ("So Colorful" is the name of the document that was open when the dialog box was opened.)*

You can go directly to the "Colors for *Document*" dialog box by pressing ⌘ (**Ctrl** for Windows) while clicking on any color.

The Color scrolling list on the left side of the dialog box shows the colors that are available to you currently. Select a color from this list and click the **Edit** button (or simply double-click a color), and you can change that color. The **Duplicate** button will make a copy of that color for you to change. As it does in other Edit dialog boxes (Style Sheets, H&Js, and so on), Append enables you to suck colors from other QuarkXPress documents. Delete removes colors from your list. The Save button saves any changes you've made, and Cancel cancels any changes.

At this time we're going to press the New button to create a new color. Clicking this button brings up the Edit Color dialog box, shown below.

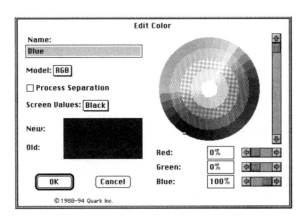

The Edit Color dialog box.

Before you do anything else, you need to determine the *color model* you want to use to create this new color. The next section will explain how to choose a color model. Read on.

Choosing a Color Model

To use one of the color models, select it from the Model pop-up menu. The dialog box will change and conform instantly to reflect the options available for each color model.

Several color models are available, but since I elected to write this book, and not *The So Completely Thorough That It's Ridiculous QuarkXPress Encyclopedia*, I'll only tell you about the four important ones.

RGB   While this is important, it really isn't one of the better choices for most color selections. The main reason it isn't a good choice is that a good number of the available colors *can't* be produced by four-color printing. Use the RGB model (shown below) for picking spot colors that will be printed on their own color plates. Red, Green, and Blue colors already in the standard color list are based on the RGB model.

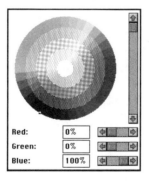

The RGB color model.

CMYK   This is the best overall color model when you will be printing four-color separated documents. Using this model, you know exactly what percentages of each of the process colors (cyan, magenta, yellow, and black) to use when creating each color.

Edit Color

Name:

Model: CMYK

☐ Process Separation

Screen Values: Black

New:

Old:

OK   Cancel

© 1988-94 Quark Inc.

Cyan: 30%
Magenta: 50%
Yellow: 60%
Black: 30%

The CMYK color model.

Pantone   This is a popular favorite, especially when you are going to use spot colors, four colors, or a combination of both in your document. You can print Pantone colors on individual plates or as a four-color separation (although that may not produce an accurate color representation). Another unique thing about Pantone colors is that you can match them to color swatch books supplied from Pantone (for $50, last time I checked). This way you know exactly what color will appear on your "Sly Stallone for Governor" posters. The Pantone color model is shown below.

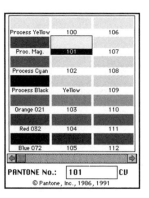

Process Yellow	100	106
Proc. Mag.	101	107
Process Cyan	102	108
Process Black	Yellow	109
Orange 021	103	110
Red 032	104	111
Blue 072	105	112

PANTONE No.: 101   CU

© Pantone, Inc., 1986, 1991

The Pantone color model.

Trumatch   This color system was developed *Xpressly* for desktop publishing. It is based on another color sample book that displays, in somewhat better order than the Pantone book, colors that correspond to CMYK percentages. More and more people are using the Trumatch system. The Trumatch color model is shown on the following page.

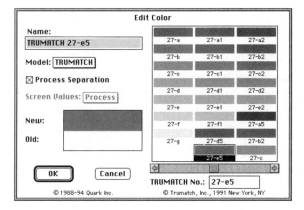

The Trumatch color model.

Naming Your Colors

Once you have determined the color model and the color itself, it is time to name the color. Make sure you give your color a good descriptive name in the text field in the upper left of the dialog box. Sure, it's lots of fun to make a color called "Really Dark Black" if it's actually white, but make sure you don't use this when printing or you might be rather unhappily surprised.

There is one very special color called Registration. This color is special because anything given this color will appear on every color plate that is printed.

EfiColor

When installing QuarkXPress, you have the option of installing EfiColor, a color-calibration system developed to help ensure that what you see on-screen is what you get when you print the document, at least in terms of color.

EfiColor tackles this problem by slightly altering colors on your screen to reflect the way colors normally appear on your monitor and output device. A few problems make it almost worthless:

Problem #1: Not enough monitors are supported. You just got a great deal on the latest Ikegami monitor. In the EfiColor preferences dialog box, you need to select Ikegami, but it isn't there. Hmmm.

Problem #2: Not enough printers/print systems are supported. You have a QMS 230 color printer, but only QMS 100 is listed. So you pick QMS 100 (sounds logical, doesn't it?), and then you spend hours with tech support wondering why everything has a deep magenta tint. It happened.

Problem #3: No two monitors/printers are the same. This says it all. EfiColor may work great on your system, but on your co-worker's (who's got the same monitor), the colors look different. It happens.

In some production environments you can get this to work well, but you have to make sure that all the programs in which you create objects (graphics, photos, and so on) use EfiColor. If one program doesn't use EfiColor, who knows what will appear. Maybe Alec Baldwin knows about the evil that lurks in the hearts of men, but nobody knows what will come out of a non-EfiColor program, when everything else is EfiColor-compatible.

All this negative stuff sounds bad, doesn't it? Well, actually EfiColor is quite useful. As a paperweight? No, because one other thing that EfiColor does is show you the printable colors for each color model. Very useful, and very hip. The next figure shows the RGB color model with a kind of funny jaggedy line running through it. That line separates printable colors from unprintable colors.

The jagged line is EfiColor's way of telling you which colors won't print the same as you see them on your monitor.

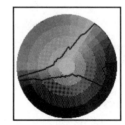

Using the Colors Palette

With the Colors palette (shown below) you can easily apply colors to text and picture boxes, frames, lines, text, and pictures. To display the Colors palette, select **View→Show Colors**. There are two ways to apply colors to objects with the Colors palette: by selecting objects and then selecting the color from the palette, or by dragging the color swatches from the palette to the object.

The Colors palette.

When the Item tool is selected, you cannot color the contents of items. However, when the Content tool is selected, you can color anything. My advice? Use the Content tool when coloring.

Creating Way-Cool Gradients

You can create *gradients* for the backgrounds of text and picture boxes by selecting the word **Solid** in the Colors palette and pulling down to **Linear blend**. You have other blend choices with the Cool Blends XTension.

Once you have selected the first color in the gradient, click on the #2 option button and pick a different color (a different shade of the first color or white) for the gradient to blend to. By default, gradients blend from left to right (at 0°). To change the angle of the gradient, enter a new amount in the angle field (right next to #2). The following figure shows some example gradients and their settings.

Gradients are *GRAD*ual var*IANTS* of different colors or tints across an area. Okay, so the spelling is a little bit off....

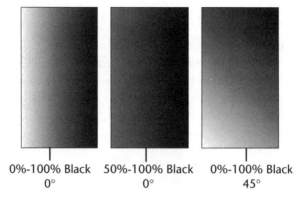

*Different gradients
created with the
Colors palette.*

0%-100% Black   50%-100% Black   0%-100% Black
        0°   0°   45°

The Least You Need to Know

If you don't need to create colors, you can use the Colors palette to take care of all your coloring needs. If, however, you want a permanent green tint on everything you see in QuarkXPress, you can do that quite easily with a big fat Forrest Gump green magic marker.

☞ Create new colors by selecting **Edit→Colors** and clicking the **New** button.

☞ You can use the Colors palette to apply colors to anything in QuarkXPress that can be colored.

☞ Try to name your colors with representative names, avoiding such non-descriptive titles as "Nasty," "Ugly," "Gruesome," "Gunk-like," and "Bleahh."

☞ Iffy-color (EfiColor) is so nicknamed due to the questionable results achieved with this technology.

Chapter 23
Playing with Pretty Pictures

In This Chapter

☞ Changing the color of pictures

☞ Changing picture contrasts and screens

☞ Applying colors to picture boxes and pictures

Within QuarkXPress are the capabilities of a miniature editing program, hidden away in the Style menu. You can do all sorts of things to pictures to make them look cooler in QuarkXPress, including change their color, contrast, and line screen.

Why the Style Menu May Be Gray

Most of the picture changes you'll see in the first part of this chapter require the use of the Style menu. If the Style menu isn't available (grayed out), you can't do these things. Sometimes, for no apparent reason, you cannot access anything in the Style menu. The reasons you may not be able to access the Style menu include:

☞ You have the Item tool, not the Content tool, selected.

☞ You don't have a picture box selected.

☞ There isn't a picture in the selected picture box.

☞ The graphic is formatted as an EPS and can't have changes made to it in the Style menu—unlike graphics formatted as RIFF, TIFF, or B & W bitmap.

So if the Style menu is gray, correct the problems above to make it available—or you'll be left out of the fun we're going to have in this chapter. Get to it!

Coloring and Tinting Pictures

Okay, here's a tough question for you: What types of graphics can't have their colors changed? Stumped? The answer is really annoying: color graphics. The only types of graphics that can be colored or have their colors changed are black and white and grayscale pictures. Hey, I didn't write the software.

If that isn't bad enough, you can change the color of the following formats *only*: TIFF, PICT, and Paint.

Giving Pictures Different Colors

Now you know the limitations of coloring a picture. If you're still in the game, here's how you can change colors in pictures.

1. Select the picture with the Content tool.

2. Select **Style→Color** and choose the color from the pop-up menu that appears.

3. Drag to the color you want the graphic to change to.

Almost too easy, isn't it? When the picture prints in color separations, it will print on that color plate. Color printing is discussed in detail in Chapter 34.

Keep in mind that when you color a grayscale picture, it has several different shades of that color within that picture to represent the different gray shades of the picture.

Tinting Your Pictures

If you think the limitations on coloring pictures are tough, tinting takes it a step further. Not only do all the requirements for coloring a picture apply, but the picture must be black and white. No tinting of grayscale pictures is allowed.

On the other hand, you can tint any black and white picture that you've changed the color of. To change the shade of a color (normally 100%), select the picture with the Content tool, and select **Style→Shade** and the shade (in .01% percentages) you'd like the picture to be. A 100% tint (shade) of a color makes that color solid. A 50% tint is about half the normal color, and 10% is 1/10th of the normal color.

TECHNO NERD TEACHES...

Selecting **Other** enables you to type in the exact percentage tint you want to use. As with most values in QuarkXPress, you can type in any number in increments as small as 1/1000 of a percent. Why would you need to be so exact? It is unlikely that you ever would, but PageMaker can't do it—and therein lies the basis for most of QuarkXPress' feature set.

No matter what tint you choose, anywhere the picture is not void of color (in original) will always be opaque. So if you place a 50% tinted cyan picture over a copy of the same picture that is tinted 50% Yellow, you won't end up with a light green (cyan + yellow = green). Instead, you'll end up with a picture that is 50% cyan, since that is on top of the yellow. See Chapter 34 for more of this nonsense.

TECHNO NERD TEACHES...

Selecting 0% tint of a color makes that color become white. Furthermore, the "white" is opaque and will cover up anything under it.

Changing Box or Background Colors

Any picture box or text box can have a background color applied to it. For the rest of this section, I'm only going to call them picture boxes, but you'll know that I mean text boxes as well.

To change the color of the background of a picture box (remember, that includes text boxes too), select it and select **Item→Modify**. Select the background color pop-up menu, and select a color from the list. After you have selected a color, you can apply a shade to that color by picking one from the pop-up menu or by typing in a custom value.

When using white as a background color, you don't have to specify a shade for it. After all, what the heck is 30% of white? A lighter white?

Selecting the color "None" from the color pop-up menu makes the background of the picture box *transparent*. This is useful when you don't want to cover up things under a picture box.

TECHNO NERD TEACHES...

White is the default color for picture (and text) boxes. I personally hate white backgrounds in my picture and text boxes. It gets in the way and covers up everything under it. Annoying! To prevent this, close all your documents and double-click on the text and picture box creation tools. For each one, click the **Modify** button, and change the background color to **None**. All new documents will have transparent text and picture boxes.

The Negative Look

Now here's a cool look for your pictures. You can print some pictures as their negative by selecting the picture and selecting **Style→Negative**. Press **⌘-Shift-hyphen** (**Ctrl+Shift+hyphen** for Windows) to set the contrast to negative. Press it again to change back to positive.

Contrast Adjustments

You can adjust the contrast of many different types of pictures in two ways: by selecting one of the three presets, or by selecting the **Other Contrast** option and fooling around with all the nifty controls there.

The default preset contrast is **Style→Normal**, which pretty much leaves the contrast alone, leaving the picture as it was originally scanned or illustrated. Selecting **Style→High Contrast** makes the light areas white and all other areas black. Selecting **Style→Posterized Contrast** changes the image into six distinct levels of brightness.

Although I personally like picture boxes to have a background of None, QuarkXPress has set the background to white for a reason. Even though that reason doesn't stand up to much scrutiny, the tech support people say that having the background transparent makes it more difficult to print in QuarkXPress, and that more printing errors occur when the background is not opaque. However, in the thousand-plus years I've worked with QuarkXPress, changing text and picture boxes from None to White has never made it possible for me to print a document that I couldn't print otherwise.

As a rule, the preset contrast settings in QuarkXPress work fine, but they don't offer near the screen resolution for you to tell if that is the effect you are looking for. It's usually better to use the custom settings or do your contrast adjustments in Photoshop.

Custom Contrasts

Selecting **Other Contrast** or (⌘-Shift-C) (**Ctrl+Shift+C** for Windows) displays the Picture Contrasts Specifications dialog box, which you can use to adjust the contrast of the selected picture in almost any way imaginable.

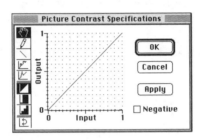

The Picture Contrast Specifications dialog box.

Press ⌘-**Shift-N** (**Ctrl+Shift+N** for Windows) to set the con-trast to normal. Press ⌘-**Shift-H** (**Ctrl+Shift+H** for Windows) to set the contrast to High. Press ⌘-**Shift-P** (**Ctrl+Shift+P** for Windows) to set the contrast to Posterize.

The first five icons on the left control how you interact with the dialog box. The first is the Hand, which enables you to push the levels to the right. The next is the pencil, which lets you draw exactly what you want on the graph. The third is the diagonal line, which you can use to draw straight lines on the graph. The fourth icon is the Levels icon, which enables you to adjust several levels across the graph. The last icon is the spike icon, which lets you set up the graph as a series of spikes.

The next three icons are the presets you can choose from the Style menu. In order, they are Normal, High, and Posterize. The last icon reverses the graph's X coordinates. That's a fancy way of saying that it flips over.

If you check the negative option in the menu, the Negative box appears checked. If you check the box here, the negative option will be on when you exit the dialog box.

Playing Around with the Contrast Graph

Be careful when messing around with the graph in the Picture Contrast Specifications dialog box. It can have some unfortunate effects if you use the wrong settings. I personally think that this is how the *Minnow* ran aground.

Your changes may have very unfortunate, unexpected results on the pictures you are changing. This is mainly due to the inability of QuarkXPress to display an accurate representation of the picture. It doesn't do too badly, but you are definitely better off making these changes in other software designed for this type of thing (such as Photoshop, for example). If QuarkXPress displays poorly, it may also be your monitor, in which case changing programs won't improve the display.

The best way to "play" with the contrast graph is to turn on the **Apply** button (⌘-**Option-A**, **Ctrl+Alt+A** for Windows). Then move the dialog box out of the way so you can instantly see the effects you are having on your picture.

As with the paragraph dialog boxes, you have an Apply button here. Press ⌘-**A** (**Ctrl+A** for Windows) to see your changes before you click **OK**. Press ⌘-**Option-A** (**Ctrl+Alt+A** for Windows) to toggle the Apply button on and off. This Apply button doesn't connect to the paragraph Apply buttons; if you turn this on or off, it doesn't affect the Apply buttons in the paragraph dialog boxes.

Using the Contrast Graph for Real

The contrast graph works on the principle that there are several gray levels in your picture, and that you can take any one gray level and make it any other gray level. For instance, you can make 25% gray become 100% gray by adjusting the proper slider. Here is another look at the contrast graph.

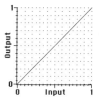

The contrast graph in the Picture Contrasts Specifications dialog box.

The horizontal grid goes from 0 to 1, with 0 being white, and 1 being 100% black. The vertical grid counts from 0 to 1, with 0 being white, and 1 being 100% black.

A "Normal" contrast is where 0=0, .5=.5, 1=1, and so on. Once these values change, you are altering the contrast. Posterized contrast changes the input values so that input values from 0 to 16 are output at 0 (white), 17–33 are output at 17, and so on. This reduces the gray levels to 6. High contrast makes everything above a certain level black, and below a certain level white.

Screening Briefing

This is one of those sections that should have that deeelightful Techno-Nerd stamp all over it. It's an ugly subject, but it is important and quite helpful if you understand it. That's why I'm here—to help you understand it.

Screens in QuarkXPress deal with the way dots are laid out on a printed page that contains different tints of gray. Screens are measured in *lines per inch.*

TECHNO NERD TEACHES...

When a printer asks you what percent screens you are using, he is probably "out of the loop" and is referring to the tint or shading values you've used in blocks. In the old days (a few years ago by now), sheets of film with tints on them were used to create blocks of different grays. These sheets were called *screens* (and still are, in the smaller printing houses). When a printer asks you what type or kind of *line screens* or *halftone screens* you are using, he is in the loop and talking about the screens we're discussing here. Tell him the answer in lines per inch.

The greater the number of lines per inch, the more detail and clarity in a photograph. The lower the lines per inch, the more gray values the photograph may display, but the dots may be visible.

Your concern when deciding what line screen to use is usually based on the printer you're getting the final copy from. If it's a high-end imagesetter, you can specify a high line screen of up to about 175. If you print the final copy to a 300 dpi laser printer, you are stuck with a line screen with a maximum value of 60. In Chapter 33, there is more information on selecting and using the proper line screen value.

Different Pictures, Different Screens

One of the reasons that QuarkXPress lets you play around with different screens here (the Style menu) rather than when you are setting out to print the job (you do it there, too, but not with the same involvement) is that you may want to use different screens for different pictures.

Huh? Well, let's say you were going to use a picture of your nephew. You want the highest amount of grays possible in the photo, in order to see him in all his living glory, but you're also using several text blocks with 50% tints behind them (a little dark, but well suited for your nephew). You want those tints to be as fine as possible when you print to your 600 dpi laser printer. The ideal situation here is to have the photo of Jon printed at a screen of 90 lpi (lines per inch) and the backgrounds of the text printed at 120 lpi.

Well, you can't change the line screen of the text boxes, but you *can* set the entire document to print out at a 120 line screen. Then you can select the photo of Jon by clicking on it with the Content tool, and selecting **Style→Other Screen** (**⌘-Shift-S**, **Ctrl+Alt+S** for Windows) and set the line screen to 90. You can then print out the brochure 8 ½" × 11" paper, fold it, and send it out.

The Standard Screen Options

Besides Normal Screen (the default screen setting that uses the value in the Page Setup dialog box), QuarkXPress has three other standard screens and gives you the ability to create custom screens.

To select a standard screen, select the picture you want to change with the Content tool, and select **Style→** and one of the following: 60 Line Line Screen/0°, 30 Line Line Screen/45°, or 20 Line Dot Screen/45°. The first number, 60 Line, refers to the lines per inch. The second and third words, Line Screen or Dot Screen, refer to the type (shape) of screen. The angle is the angle that the screen appears at. For grayscale images, the standard is 45°.

Not many users of QuarkXPress find the three "standard" settings to be that useful. Instead, they often create custom screens, as described next.

Using a Custom Screen

You can make a screen exactly the way you want it for any picture by selecting the **Other Screen** (⌘-**Shift-S, Ctrl+Shift+S** for Windows) option in the Style menu. Here is the Picture Screening Specifications dialog box.

Picture Screening Specifications

┌─Halftone────────────────────────────┐
│ Screen: 20 (lpi)   Angle: 45°   │
│ ┌─Pattern────────────────────────┐ │
│ │ ⦿ Dot   ○ Line   ○ Ellipse   ○ Square │
│ │ ○ Ordered Dither   │ │
│ └────────────────────────────────┘ │
└──────────────────────────────────────┘

☐ Display Halftoning   [OK]   [Cancel]

The Picture Screening Specifications dialog box.

If you want to mess around with these settings, go right ahead (just make sure you save first). The topics are beyond the scope of this book, but you can look them up in your QuarkXPress manual if you are so inclined.

QuarkXPress has some powerful image-editing capabilities that are appropriate for a number of quick fixes, but to make your images really stand up and bark, leave the image editing to a Photoshop user who can do amazing things to your images. If you would like to become a Photoshop user, pick up a copy of *The Complete Idiot's Guide to Photoshop*, available wherever you got this book (provided that you didn't get this book from young men selling it for 50 cents out of the back of a truck in some depressed section of town, that is).

The Least You Need to Know

In this chapter, you learned about some of the alterations you can perform on your images in QuarkXPress. These include the following:

☞ Black and white and grayscale pictures can be colorized in QuarkXPress.

☞ The line screen determines the size, shape, and angle of the dots that make up shades of gray when you print the document.

Part IV
Laying Out the Pages

Pages here, pages there, move this page, delete that page, line these pages up, and then put the stuff on this page onto that page. No, not that page, that page.

Conversations like these take place in your head as you go through this part, rearranging items on pages and rearranging the pages themselves. I'll even show you how to customize QuarkXPress to your liking in this part.

Chapter 24
Don't Forget Your Lines

In This Chapter

☞ More stuff than you can shake a six-point line at

☞ How to draw and modify lines

☞ Stylizing your brand new lines

You probably think you know everything about everything that can go on a QuarkXPress page, right? Ha ha ha. This chapter tells you about lines, which we have conveniently ignored in the last hundred or so pages.

We've created text boxes. We've created picture boxes. Now, with only two creation tools left, and the title to this chapter screaming out to you, you may have guessed that it is time to create lines. Excited?

Keeping QuarkXPress in Lines

You learned in Chapter 8 that QuarkXPress creates lines with the two line creation tools, known formally as the Orthogonal Line tool and the Diagonal Line tool. The difference between the two? Old Orthy draws lines that are perfectly horizontal or vertical, all the time.

This slight difference causes even the most educated people to call the Orthogonal Line tool the "Straight Line" tool. While I can't argue with the undisputed fact that it draws straight lines, the title "Straight line tool" isn't very specific because the Diagonal Line creation tool also draws straight lines.

If the line is not part of a picture box, you can't draw a curved line in QuarkXPress—unless you are using QuarkXPress 4.0, and the year is 1996. If that's the case and you just now got this book, write to the publisher and tell her to get me to update the book. Thanks.

Call the Orthogonal Line tool anything you want, just as long as you remember that it draws horizontal and vertical lines, and that you cannot change the angle of those lines by dragging one end with a tool, as you can with a line created by the Diagonal Line tool. The only way to change the angle of a line created with the Orthogonal Line tool is to enter a new measurement in the angle text field of the Measurements palette (third from the left on the top row).

Creating Your First Line

To create a line, follow the steps below.

1. Select one of the line drawing tools.

2. Click where you want one end of the line to be located and drag the cursor, keeping the mouse button down.

3. Release the mouse button where you want the other end of the line to be located.

You've just drawn a line. Did you notice that after you first click the first point, a grayish line appears from there to the cursor? That line follows the cursor around until you release the mouse button to set the second point.

To draw several lines, don't waste your time clicking on the line tool of choice before you draw each line. Instead, just press **Option** when you select the line tool the first time. The line tool you've selected will remain until you choose another.

And the Category Is...

By the way, did I mention that lines are items? Well, you're right. I didn't mention it. That's because even though lines are decidedly items, they act a heckuva lot like contents.

Remember that QuarkXPress divides text boxes and picture boxes into two nice, separate categories of items and contents, with a fairly logical division between the two? Well, lines have a dividing line too, but that line is really blurry (which, as a matter of fact, is a type of line you *can't* create in QuarkXPress). The location and size of lines are the item qualities of a line, and the *style* of the line is the contents of that line.

What style? A black line? It has no style! Well, style (for a line) refers to the color, thickness (weight), and *pattern* (dashes, and so on) of the line. That's its style. Choosing the style of a line is discussed later in this chapter.

Which Palette View Is Right for You?

Bad poetry aside, most of the changes that you can make to lines are available in the Measurements palette. The trouble is, there are four different ways of displaying the location of a line via the Measurements palette. Here are the four different displays, with labels, of one line.

| X1 : 5p6 | X2 : 19p4.569 | Endpoints |
| Y1 : 17p | Y2 : 26p6 | |

| X1 : 5p6 | ∠ -34.388° | Left Point |
| Y1 : 17p | L : 16p9.844 | |

| XC : 12p5.284 | ∠ -34.388° | Midpoint |
| YC : 21p9 | L : 16p9.844 | |

| X2 : 19p4.569 | ∠ -34.388° | Right Point |
| Y2 : 26p6 | L : 16p9.844 | |

The four different views of the Measurements palette when you select a line.

By selecting the pop-up menu in the Measurements palette, you can choose any of the four views. The first way of viewing lines using the Measurements palette is the Endpoint view. Viewing by endpoints shows the location of both endpoints (X1,Y1; X2,Y2) where X is how far from the left edge of the page that end is, and Y is how far from the top of the page that end is. The numbers refer to the first and second points. The advantage to this display is that it lets you look at the locations of both points at the same time.

All this X and Y stuff is annoying, isn't it? Well, remember that X means horizontal; Y (because we *like* you) means vertical. And you thought you'd never use all that silly stuff you learned in Mrs. Dull's geometry class.

However, I never use the Endpoints view. I have found it is the least useful of the four views, since it doesn't display the angle or the length of the selected line.

The next view is the Left Point view. This view (my favorite) shows the location of the leftmost point (X1,Y1), the angle, and the length of the line.

Center Point shows the center of the line at XC,YC, as well as the angle and the length of the line. Of course, there is no real center point visible on the line, so this can be helpful (for what, I do not know, but that is what the friendly Quark person told me the last time I talked to him).

The last view is Right Point, which shows the location of the rightmost point (X2,Y2), as well as (you guessed it!) the angle and the length of the line.

Keeping Your Lines in Style

You can make most style changes to lines on the right side of the Measurements palette, shown in the following figure. The first option you can change is the *weight*, or thickness of the line. By double-clicking in the field to the left of that pop-up menu, the current line weight will become highlighted, after which time you can type in a new value. Using the pop-up menu, you can choose any of the preset line weights.

The style options in the Measurements palette for lines.

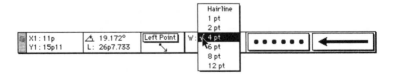

Lines can be as little as 0 (zero) points, or as big (thick) as 864 points, which is equal to 12 inches. The weight of the line never changes the *length* of that line, so you could actually have a line that is 2 points long, but 200 points wide. If nothing else, it can be a fun way to confuse other QuarkXPress users....

The next option that you can change is the line style, which you can change to any one of 11 preset patterns. The width of the line specified in the previous field is the *total width* of the line, as shown in the examples below.

5 points thick

The width of a line contains the style of the line.

The third option on the style side of the Measurements palette when you select a line is the Endcaps pop-up menu. By selecting an option from this pop-up menu, you can apply arrow heads or tailfeathers to either or both ends of a line.

Color and Shade Options

You can color and shade every line just like other objects in QuarkXPress by first selecting the line and pulling down the **Style** menu to **Color** or **Shade**. Then pull over to the color or shade you would like to use. You can also use the Color palette to change the color and shade of selected lines by clicking the color in the palette and typing a tint value in the % text field.

The Least You Need to Know

Hopefully by now you have a handle on lines. Actually, you should have two handles on each line, which would result in you having several handles on all your lines.

- ☞ You can create lines with the two Line tools in the toolbox.

- ☞ You can alter lines created with the Diagonal Line tool in any way.

- ☞ You can't change the angle of lines created with the Orthogonal Line tool (the one that draws horizontal and vertical lines only) by dragging a handle; instead, you have to change the angle in the angle field of the Measurements palette.

- ☞ You can move lines by clicking on their centers with the Item tool and dragging.

Chapter 25

Measurements Palette Secrets

In This Chapter

- ☛ An in-depth look at the Measurements palette
- ☛ Learning QuarkXPress shortcuts
- ☛ How to get QuarkXPress to do your math homework

There are all sorts of things you can do with the Measurements palette that few people know. Yes, the 5th Century Chinese documented most of these features, but in a dialect familiar to few. Since you aren't as fluent in that dialect as I am, I'll spend this chapter acting as an interpreter, giving out all the secrets and shortcuts those amazing people with their funky hats wrote down 1500 years ago.

Hopalong and Hop Back

Whenever you highlight a field in the Measurements palette, you can highlight the *next* field by pressing the Tab key. Continue pressing the **Tab** key until you reach the last field (on the far right), and then press **Tab** once more to skip to the first (leftmost) field. Where you can Tab ahead in QuarkXPress, you can also **Shift-Tab** backward. Shift-Tab highlights the *previous* field.

When you finish jumping around the Measurements palette with the Tab and Shift-Tab commands, press **Return** or **Enter** to put all of your changes into effect.

The Tab and Shift-Tab commands aren't only for the Measurements palette. In fact, you can use Tab and Shift-Tab in all QuarkXPress dialog boxes that have text fields.

Getting There with the Keyboard

Many times you are busy typing and need to make a change on the Measurements palette, but you grumble in disgust at the thought of having to remove your hands from the keyboard to get the mouse. There are two nifty key commands just for these occasions.

Pressing ⌘-**Option-M** (**Ctrl+Alt+M** for Windows) selects the first field on the Measurements palette. From there, you can press **Tab** or **Shift-Tab** to continue moving around within the Measurements palette, and whack the **Return** or **Enter** keys when you finish.

You can select the Font field by pressing ⌘-**Option-Shift-M** (**Ctrl+Alt+Shift+M** for Windows) when you have a text box selected with the Content tool. When you have any other object (picture box, line) selected, and you press ⌘-**Option-Shift-M**, you select the first field in the Measurements palette.

If You Don't Have the Time to Figure Out How Many Points Are in a Centimeter

QuarkXPress is lightning fast when doing conversions. If you are working in one measurement system (let's say inches), you can enter values in any measurement system, and QuarkXPress will figure out what that is in inches.

For instance, say you have a photograph that you want to crop to a size of 13 picas by 10 picas, but you are working in the inches system. Select the picture box for that picture and change the width (W) to **13p** and the height (H) to **10p**. When you press **Return** or **Enter**, the values will change to 2.167" and 1.667". If you don't care what those measurements are in inches (I doubt you will, since you don't need those values for anything else), just don't read what they changed to.

Math the Easy Way

There is a secret, built-in calculator in the Measurements palette. Just as quickly as QuarkXPress converts inches to centimeters to picas, it can also tell you what 2.3" ÷ 2 is equal to (1.65"). How can it do this amazing math?

All you have to do is enter the equation you want to find the solution for into one of the first four text fields on the Measurements palette, and QuarkXPress provides the answer. Seem confusing? It's not, really.

Let's say that your text box was currently 8.75" wide, but you decide you want a text box that is half that width. Simply click after the 8.75" in the W field of the Measurements palette and type /2. When you press **Return** or **Enter**, the value will change to 4.375".

You can use addition (+), subtraction (–), multiplication (*) and division (/) when creating equations, and you can also use parentheses to change the order of the functions. That way, 2*(3+1)=8, whereas 2*3+1=7. The calculator always completes the instructions inside the parentheses first, from left to right.

Wacky Equations

If that isn't just plain fun enough, you can also mix and match measurements. Want to know what 3cm+2.5"–2p is? Type that equation, just like I printed it here, and QuarkXPress converts it to the measurement system you are using.

OOPS!

When you are multiplying or dividing by something, make sure that at least one of the numbers involved is a measurement. For instance, 2"/3 is fine, but 2"/3" is not. The reason for this is that QuarkXPress needs to convert everything into a measurement, and 2"/3" would result in a value of .66, which isn't a measurement at all. If you screw up really badly, you can always press ⌘-Z (**Ctrl+Z** in Windows) to revert the values to their previous settings.

Partial Views of the Palette

Sometimes, it can be frustrating to determine why certain parts of a palette aren't available or are just entirely blank. The following figure shows examples of this.

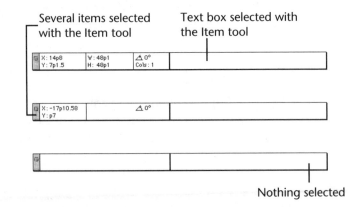

Partial views of the Measurements palette.

A good rule of thumb is that when you select the Item tool, the right side of the Measurements palette will be empty. The exception to this rule is when you select a line with the Item tool; the right side is both visible and editable.

Another rule is that whenever you select more than one item (a group), the only things visible in the Measurements palette will be the location of the selected items and the *least common angle* of those items. The least common angle is the smallest angle that all of the selected items rotate. If you don't rotate one of the items, the value reads 0. If you rotate the first item 10°, the second 25°, and the third item 15°, the angle displayed would be 10°, which is the lowest of all the angles. All the items, in this case, rotate at least 10°.

When the Measurements Palette Disappears...

If the Measurements palette disappears, one of several things has happened. Some of the most common reasons include:

☞ You accidentally clicked just off of the document or palette, and while you can see your document, the palettes have disappeared.

You have accidentally switched to the Finder or another application. Palettes are visible only when you are in QuarkXPress. To remedy this, simply click on the document, and the palette reappears.

☛ You accidentally clicked on the Close box (upper left box) in the Measurements palette. The palette reappears when you select **View→Show Measurements Palette** or press either ⌘-**Option-M** or ⌘-**Option-Shift-M** (**Ctrl+Alt+M** or **Ctrl+Alt+Shift+M** for Windows).

☛ The Measurements palette hides behind another palette, usually the Document Layout palette or the Library palette. Move the other palettes out of the way or press ⌘-**Option-M** to bring the palette to the front.

☛ Leprechauns have invaded your home (or business) and they are just having some fun with you. Call an Irish exorcist.

The Least You Need to Know

While the Measurements palette *can* do some amazing things with math, it won't replace your calculator any time soon. The following are some of the important points in this chapter:

☛ Use the **Tab** key to move to the next text field and **Shift-Tab** to move to the previous text field.

☛ Enter the equations in the fields of the Measurements palette or any other dialog box (for example, Paragraph Formats), and let QuarkXPress do your math.

☛ Press ⌘-**Option-M** (**Ctrl+Alt+M** for Windows) to highlight the first field in the Measurements palette, even if it isn't showing on-screen.

☛ Press ⌘-**Option-Shift-M** (**Ctrl+Alt+Shift+M** for Windows) to highlight the font field in the Measurements palette.

Chapter 26

Moving Items in 3-D

In This Chapter

- ☞ Depth perception and your QuarkXPress documents

- ☞ Moving your stuff around on a page

- ☞ All sorts of rather useless, yet entertaining, features

First, get the 3-D glasses that came with this book, and flip the pages quickly, looking at the lower left corner. You'll see a hula dancer at her computer and... what? Budgetary constraints? No glasses? Oh. Ahem.

Items in QuarkXPress (you know, picture boxes, text boxes, and the like) can be moved left, right, up, down, and—get this—backwards and forwards. By the way, looking at your computer screen with 3-D glasses on can give you a splitting headache.

Selecting and Deselecting Items

You can select items in three ways: by clicking on them with the Item or Content tools, by drawing a marquee around the items you want to select, or by pressing ⌘-A (**Ctrl+A** for Windows) to select all of the items (this last one only works when you select the Item tool).

To deselect all selected items, press the **Tab** key or click in an empty area on the page or pasteboard. To deselect specific items, hold down the **Shift** key and click on the items to be deselected, or hold down **Shift** and drag a marquee around the items to be deselected.

Understanding Front and Back in Layers

Before we get into the 3-D stuff, you need to understand how QuarkXPress arranges things on the page. QuarkXPress locates every item on its own level above the page surface. No two items are on the same level. The first thing you create is on the bottom, the next thing created is right on top of that, and so on, until the last thing created is on the very top. The next figure shows this *layering* of items.

Objects as they normally appear in QuarkXPress (left) and how the layers of that document stack up (right).

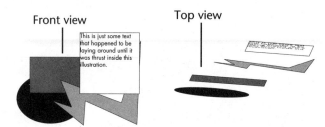

Of course, this whole layering system would be rather limiting if you couldn't move the items around from layer to layer. QuarkXPress lets you move items in two ways: moving an object to the very next layer (up or down) or moving an object directly to the top or bottom.

Moving Items from Top to Bottom and Bottom to Top and Middle to Top and Middle to Bottom

Well, that's what the standard commands do, even though it sounds a wee bit absurd. Let me rephrase it. This section tells you how to move an item to the top or bottom of the layers, regardless of where it is now.

To do this almost-magical act, select the item you want to move by clicking on it, and then select **Item→Send To Back (Shift-F5)** or **Item→Bring to Front (F5)**. The selected item will move to the back or front, depending on which option you choose.

TECHNO NERD TEACHES...

You need not limit yourself to moving one item around at a time. Selecting more than one item (remember, you must use the Item tool to select more than one object) will move all selected objects to the front or back, with their positions relative to each other as they were before you moved them.

Moving Items Just a Smidge

Sometimes, you want to move an item just a bit, instead of moving it to the way top or way bottom of the page. To move objects above or below the next object only, press **Option** (**Alt** for Windows) when selecting **Item→Send to Back** or **Item→Bring to Front**. The menu items change to **Send Backwards** and **Bring Forward**. When selected, these options move the selected item behind or in front of the next item.

Selecting Objects That Are Under Other Objects

What happens when you want to select an object that you covered up partially or entirely with one or more other objects? Well, you can select the other objects and move them or send them to the back, but that would require a lot of shuffling or other nasty work that you just don't have time for.

Instead, select the item that is directly above the item you want to select. Press ⌘-**Option-Shift** (**Ctrl+Alt+Shift** for Windows) and click, and you have selected the item on the bottom. You can continue to select items buried under other items by ⌘-Option-Shift clicking until you have selected the correct item.

OOPS!

Be sure to press **Option** before you click on the Item menu, and hold it until you display the Item menu. Releasing the Option key after you select the Item menu will still enable you to select Send Backward and Bring Forward.

The selected item that is buried under other items won't appear in front of the other items if you have the regular Item tool. You can usually tell which item you selected in a stack by looking at the handles that appear.

Why Everything Seems to Disappear on Occasion

All QuarkXPress users (except you, since you are two steps ahead of the competition by reading this book) inhale sharply when using QuarkXPress at some point early on when they see everything on their page disappear. The only thing left is a little blinking insertion point going on, off, on, off in the upper left corner of the page.

What happened in these instances is that when the users had the Content tool, they accidentally clicked on the automatic text box that covers most of the page. You see, even though there is an automatic text box on the page (if they checked that option in the New Document dialog box), many people still draw their own text box that may or may not cover the automatic text box entirely. When they select the automatic text box (usually accidentally) with the Content tool, it appears above all other items on the page, hiding everything under it.

This happens because QuarkXPress assumes that when you're typing or working with text, you don't want other items sticking up and getting in your way. So it shows you any selected text box in front of everything else while you have it selected with the Content tool. It doesn't move it up or down through the layers; technically an automatic text box is initially on the bottommost layer until you move it or other items below it.

How can you fix this? Simply select the Item tool or click on an empty area in the document. The document's object returns to normal. Even better, if you aren't going to be using that text box, get rid of it by selecting **Item→Delete** (**⌘-K, Ctrl+K** for Windows).

Moral of the section? If you aren't going to use that Automatic Text box, don't check the check box for it in the New Document dialog box. (To get to the New Document dialog box, press Command-N. In Windows, press Ctrl+N.)

Moving Stuff Up, Down, and Sideways

You can move all items around, both on your QuarkXPress page and off, by dragging them with the Item tool. Move items by selecting them and then clicking inside of them and dragging. You must use the Item tool (or Pseudo-Item tool) to drag items to new locations on a page. To move more than one item at once, you must use the Item tool, not the Pseudo-Item tool (see Chapter 8).

You move items by selecting them and then clicking inside of them and dragging. An outline of the item(s) being moved follows the cursor. When the outline is where you would like the item to be, release the mouse button, and the item moves from its previous location to the new one.

Sometimes, you can't get items to move exactly where you want them; they seem to jump to a different location whenever you get close. Before you rush off to a specialist to find out what could be causing uncontrollable nervous twitches in your right (mouse) hand, it isn't you causing these jumps. No, the problem is in QuarkXPress *guidelines*.

As long as any one edge of your object is near a guideline, it will try to align itself with that guideline perfectly, even if you aren't dragging near that edge. To fix this downright annoying problem, select **View→Snap to Guides**, which will turn off Snap to Guides. Now your objects will float around the screen as you direct, never falling prey to the seemingly uncontrollable magnetism of those evil guides.

TECHNO NERD TEACHES...

You can tell the exact location of the selected objects being moved if you look at the X (horizontal location) and Y (vertical location) in the Measurements palette. The values there change as the object is being dragged across your page.

Moving with the Measurements Palette

If you've been reading this book in order, you already know that you can use the Measurements palette to change the location of selected items. Come to think of it, if you just opened to this page for the first time, you know that now anyway.

However, I bet you didn't know (unless you've read ahead, of course) that you can move objects specified amounts from their current locations! Let's say you wanted to move an object 2 picas to the right and 3 picas, 6 points down. Well, you can do the addition, and then just change the amount, but that can be difficult, especially if you are using inches or centimeters as your measurement system. Besides, QuarkXPress can do the math for you. All you have to do is to click after the values in **X** and **Y** and enter **+2p** and **+3p6**.

So to move something to the right, type + *(distance)* after the number in the X field. To move something to the left, type – *(distance)* after the number in the X field. To move an item down, type + *(distance)* after the number in the Y field. To move an item up, type – *(distance)* after the number in the Y field.

You can use the Measurements palette to move items 1/2 as far from the left edge, or 3 times as far from the top by entering **/2** after the number in the X field or by entering ***3** after the number in the Y field.

Nimble Nudges

You can use the keyboard to carefully move selected items one point at a time by using the arrow keys on your keyboard. The only thing you must do is make sure you select the real Item tool (not that fake-out Pseudo-Item tool). Then press an arrow key, and the selected items will move exactly one point in the direction pressed.

At magnifications of less than 100%, the movement may not be visible on-screen, and the selected objects may not appear to move at all, or to move irregularly. Have no fear, they are moving along at the same pace as always.

Lock 'Em Up

You can lock items into place by using the Lock command when you select an item. To lock an item, select it, and select **Item→Lock** (**F6**). You can then no longer move or resize the item by using the Item, Pseudo-Item, or Content tools. When the cursor passes over the handles of locked items, they appear as little padlocks to indicate that you did, indeed, lock the item.

To unlock items, select them and select **Item→Unlock** (**F6**). You can then move unlocked items as always.

To move something just a weence (approximately 1/10 of a point), press **Option** (**Alt** for Windows) when moving items. Instead of moving an entire point, the selected object will move .1 of a point.

Even though you lock an item, you can move it and change its size by changing the values in the Measurements palette.

Flipping Text Boxes and Other Pointless Activities

When you select either a text or picture box with the Content tool, the middle of the Measurements palette displays the two boxes-with-arrows shown here.

Flip boxes

| X: 14p8 | W: 48p1 | ⊿ 0° | | ⇕ auto | | Caxton Book | 12 pt |
| Y: 7p1.5 | H: 48p1 | Cols: 1 | | | | F B I O S O U W K |

The Flip boxes on the Measurements palette.

Even though Boxes With Arrows sounds like a bad American Indian name (like Trips Over Shoelaces), you can use these boxes to "flip" the contents of items horizontally and vertically.

Why is this pointless, you ask? Well, flipping pictures inside picture boxes can be very useful, but flipping text? I'll tell you what, if you can come up with a realistic reason other than "great for Read-it-in-the-Mirror-code messages" let me know. And if it is a real use for flipping text, I'll try to get it into the next edition of this book. Deal?

The Least You Need to Know

This chapter was all about moving things. Let's hope you don't suffer from motion sickness.

- ☞ When you create objects, you place them on top of existing objects.

- ☞ No two objects can be on the same layer.

- ☞ To move objects forward and backward, select **Send to Back** or **Bring to Front** from the **Item** menu.

- ☞ You can move items in 1-point increments by pressing an arrow key while the Item tool is active.

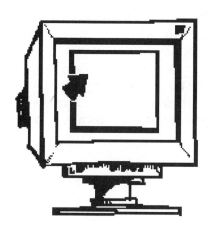

Chapter 27
Wacky Changes to Text Boxes

In This Chapter

- ☛ Vertically aligning text, whatever *that* means
- ☛ Framing your thoughts, not to mention your boxes
- ☛ Wrapping text around other objects

When I started this book, I knew I wanted a chapter on all the wacky things you can do with text boxes. But the more I thought about it, the less wacky those things became. It's not like you can change a text box into an albatross or use text boxes for bumper car pylons. Heck, even spelling "text boxes" backwards isn't that funny. *Sexob txet.* Hmm. Actually, that is kind of wacky, isn't it?

Vertical Alignment and Text

If you follow the soda-commercial hype, you know that when you drink Mountain Dew you "get vertical" and apparently become instantly cool. Unfortunately, the type of vertical I'll be talking about in this section has little to do with hip soft drink slogans. Nonetheless, it is important stuff. You'll learn how to move your text inside the text box, from the top where it usually resides to the center or bottom, or even to justify the text from top to bottom.

The following figure shows the different vertical alignment settings available to you. To change the vertical alignment, select the text box(es). Yes, you can change more than one, since this is an *item* activity, and select **Item→Modify**. The Text Box Specifications dialog box (shown in the figure) appears. In the middle of the right side there is a pop-up menu with four Vertical Alignment options available. Select the Vertical Alignment you would like to use, then click the **OK** button (or press **Return** or **Enter**).

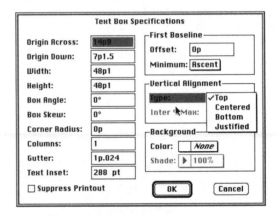

The four different Vertical Alignment options for a text box.

SPEAK LIKE A GEEK

Inter ¶ Max is the maximum amount of space allowed between paragraphs in vertically justified text. By having extra space between paragraphs, QuarkXPress will attempt to maintain the leading setting within text that you specify. By having no extra space between paragraphs, the text will have even spacing from one line to another, which is called *feathering*.

The first three settings (Top, Centered, and Bottom) work like they sound. Text inside text boxes with those settings will align at the top, center, or bottom of the text box. The last setting, Justified, is a little different, though.

For vertically justified type, there are several paragraphs in a text box, and a number of ways to control how you spread the lines of text from top to bottom. The ways you've learned already involve changing the leading and the paragraph spacing options, which are both found in the Paragraph Formats dialog box. (You can get there by selecting **Style→Format** or pressing ⌘-**Shift-F**. Press **Ctrl+Shift+F** in Windows.) The other way is by changing the amount in the Inter ¶ Max text field.

By increasing the number in the Inter ¶ Max text field, the paragraphs will have more and more space inserted between them. If you want the most distance between paragraphs without the leading of the text ever changing, enter a ridiculously high number (like 10") in the text field.

Bordering on Insanity

One of QuarkXPress' slickest features (that's right, I said "slickest") is its capability to put a border around each and every text and picture box. No, that doesn't mean you have to establish tariffs and rates of exchange in each document.

QuarkXPress calls these borders *frames*, and you can set them to surround a selected text or picture box. You can specify the color, thickness (weight, remember?), and shade of the frame, as well as the style, selected from choices similar to those for lines and paragraph rules.

I Was Framed!

To place a frame on a text or picture box, select it (with either the Content or Item tool) and select **Item→Frame** or press ⌘-**B** (**Ctrl+B** in Windows). The Frame Specifications dialog box appears, as shown here.

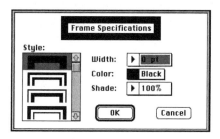

The Frame Specifications dialog box.

Most of the items in this box are self-explanatory. The only thing of importance here is that this frame goes around the entire box and has the same width, color, and so on, all the way around. When you change the shape of the box, the frame continues to be on the edge of the box. The weight of the frame won't change if you resize the box.

The frame normally appears on the inside of the text or picture box. By changing the preference to outside in the General Preferences dialog box, the frame will be outside the box. (To get to the General Preferences dialog box, select **Edit→Prefs→General Preferences**, or press ⌘-Y. Press **Ctrl+Y** in Windows).

The Frame Editor and PICT Frames

If you scroll down the list of frames, you'll begin to see some very "ornate" framing options. Be careful when using anything below the triple line style of frame. The ones below are bitmap frames, and not only are the designs hard on the eyes, they are also hard on the printer, often preventing entire documents from printing or causing it to take an extremely long time to print due to inadequate RAM in your printer.

You can select several picture and text boxes and apply the same frame to them as long as you have the Item tool selected. This can make a tedious procedure go by really quickly and easily.

As if this wasn't bad enough, along with QuarkXPress is a little file in your QuarkXPress folder called Frame Editor. Quark designed this program to enable you to create additional "ornate" PICT frames. They can be as tacky as your imagination. Save yourself time and energy; you're better off watching *Green Acres* reruns than creating frames with this toy of the devil.

(If you absolutely *must* use the Frame Editor, please refer to your QuarkXPress manual for instructions. I'm not including them here because there are more important things to talk about in this book.)

When a Text Box Is Bigger Than Its Text

Sometimes, it will be necessary to change the boundaries of your text box without changing the edges. For instance, if you had the definition of the word "Scrub" inside a text box with a hefty 12-point frame, you would want that definition centered within the text box, not huddled up in the corner where no one could see it. The following figure shows how I increased the Text Inset of the text box on the left until the text centered properly.

Scrub defined. On the left, the text as it would normally appear in a text box. On the right, the text showing the text inset increased.

Scrub: n. 1. A small furry creature. 2. Tumbleweed debri. v. 1. To clean thoroughly 2. to tousel hair of another.

Scrub: n. 1. A small furry creature. 2. Tumbleweed debri. v. 1. To clean thoroughly. 2. to tousel hair of another.

To change the text inset, select the text box, and select **Item→Modify** (**⌘-M, Ctrl+M** in Windows). In the dialog box, type in the new value in the Text Inset text field. The value you type is the amount of space from all four sides of the text box to the text.

TECHNO NERD TEACHES...

The text inset defaults at 1 point, which creates 1 point of nothingness around the inside edges of the text box. This can make things a little screwy, especially if "the boss" wants text set in a text box that is 15 picas wide. If the text inset is at 1 point, the text inside will only be 14p10 wide, 2 points too narrow. You can change the default by double-clicking on the Text Box tool with no documents open, and changing the Text Inset field to zero.

The Magical First Baseline Offset

Changing the setting at the very top right of the Text Box Specifications dialog box (shown in the first figure in this chapter) will change where the first baseline line of text will appear in a text box. There are three different options, but you can leave the setting at the default of Ascent, which makes sure that the tallest character in any font always fits in the text box. If you change this setting, characters may be cut off.

Ice-Text—Rapping Type

You no it ain't right; whatz happenin' ta night; gotta buncha type, and it's goin' right, thru da pictures in da doc-u-ment… or something like that.

Having your text wrap around objects is one of the most powerful features in a page layout program, and QuarkXPress excels at it. Here, once again, is a rule for wrapping type around objects.

The text box needs to be behind the object the text is wrapping around.

If you have a foot in your newsletter, and you want text to run around that foot, make sure that the picture box containing the foot is in front of the text.

To make text run around a picture or picture box, select the picture box and select **Item→Runaround** '(⌘-T, **Ctrl+T** in Windows). The Runaround dialog box appears, as shown in the following figure. To make text run around the outline of the picture, select **Auto Image**. To make the text run around the picture box, select **Item**. To turn off runaround, select **None**.

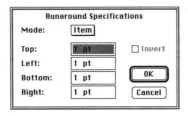

The Runaround dialog box.

The Manual Image option enables you to adjust the text wrapping boundary by dragging points around the object. The Invert check box enables you to flow text inside an image.

The amount of runaround you specify is how far the text must be from the edge of the item or picture. I've found that 6 points is a good amount to work with.

As a default, text wrap is "on" for text and picture boxes. This can cause text under objects to virtually disappear because it is trying to run around those objects, and there often isn't enough room. Close all your documents, double-click on each tool, and change the runaround to none to fix this.

The Least You Need to Know

Right about now I can imagine you jumping around like the Coco-puffs bird, having a wacky old time while using your text boxes. Of course, that isn't too much of an imaginative stretch for a person like me, who routinely can't sleep because he can't figure out if Adam had a belly button. (I'm currently leaning towards, "I don't think so, but maybe he did.")

- ☞ Adjusting Vertical Alignment in the Text Box Specifications dialog box affects the top/bottom position of text inside that box.

- ☞ You can create frames around any text or picture box by selecting **Item→Frame** and determining the style of the frame to surround the selected box(es).

- ☞ You can inset text a certain amount from the edges of the text box by increasing the text inset value.

- ☞ Text wraps around objects that have Runaround (⌘-T) activated.

Chapter 28

Stickin' Items Where They Belong

In This Chapter

- ☞ Groups and cliques
- ☞ Duplicating items precisely
- ☞ Aligning and spacing items

We know how to shuffle items around, but now we're going to learn how to organize them so that they go *exactly* where you want them. This chapter is sort of like military training. Except that I'm not a drill sergeant with bad breath and a really bad attitude. I just have a really bad attitude.

Focusing on Groups

There are times when you want certain items to always be together, such as a picture box with Ren, and one with Stimpy. To make sure that when you move one, the other moves with it, you can *group* these two items together.

How can you perform this amazing task? Simpler than you may expect. Just select the items you want to group (as many as you want) with the Item tool (remember, the Content tool only lets you work with the contents of one item at a time) and select **Item→Group** (**⌘-G, Ctrl+G** in

Windows). The selected items will have a dotted line surrounding them when you select one with the item tool, as shown in the following figure.

When selected, grouped items appear with a dotted line surrounding all the items.

Now, whenever you move one of the items in the group with the Item tool, the rest of the items in the group move as well. When you decide that you don't want the items grouped together anymore, select them, and select **Item→Ungroup** (⌘-U, **Ctrl+U** in Windows).

Level-Headed Groupies

After you create a group, you can add more items to the group by selecting both the group and the item and selecting **Item→Group**. In addition, you can group several groups together by selecting several groups and selecting **Item→Group**.

Each time you form another "level" of groups, QuarkXPress remembers the structure, so that ungrouping takes place in the reverse order of grouping. If that's all Group, er, Greek to you, then this might help: When you group two items, and then you group that new group with another group, selecting ungroup will only ungroup the last group to take place(?!?). In this case, there will still be two groups: one is composed of two items, and the other is the whole other group it was grouped to. Think of it this way:

Each ungroup only undoes the last *group done.*

Secret Movements Within Radical Groups

Although the purpose of grouping items is so they all move together, there may be a time when you need to move an item within a group without moving the rest of the items in the group. You *could* ungroup, select the item, and group again, but that's messy, and with a lot of other items on-screen, it's more than a little confusing.

To move an item within a group, use the **Pseudo-Item** tool. Remember, that's when you have the Content tool and press the ⌘ (**Ctrl** in Windows) key. Because the Content tool is active, you can only move one thing. The Pseudo-Item tool lets you move items, one at a time. Nifty, huh?

It is better to have grouped, ungrouped, and regrouped than to never have grouped at all.—Ted Alspach.

Send in the Clones

You can instantly duplicate any item in QuarkXPress. You can duplicate as many items as you can select, simply by selecting them and choosing the **Duplicate** command from the **Item** menu, or by pressing ⌘-**D** (**Ctrl+D** in Windows).

The first time you duplicate an item, the duplicated item appears 1/4" down and to the right of the original. If you keep pressing ⌘-**D**, additional duplicates appear 1/4" from the last duplicate. Why this strange measurement? Who knows. Why is QuarkXPress at version 3.3 instead of 5 or 6?

Step and Repeat

You can specify the distance a duplicate appears from the original as well as the number of duplicates by selecting **Item→Step and Repeat** (⌘-**Option-D**, **Ctrl+Alt+D** in Windows). Doing so displays the Step and Repeat dialog box, shown next.

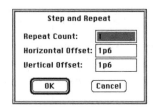

*The Step and Repeat
dialog box.*

If you enter a value of 0 in the Horizontal Offset and Vertical Offset text fields, the duplicate(s) appear directly on top of one another. You can create as many duplicates as will fit on the page with the different offset settings, up to a maximum of 99.

Once you have used Step and Repeat, the next time you use the Duplicate function, the duplicated objects appear in the direction specified in the Offset text fields.

Space and Align

What's the difference between Space and Align? Space is big and dark; a lion is big and hungry. (It's jokes like this that keep crippling my standup career.)

Use the Space and Align function to change the positioning of two or more items relative to each other. If you want six text boxes to have their tops aligned, you would select all six and then use Space and Align to align them. To use Space and Align, select the items (text boxes, picture boxes, or lines) and select **Item→Space and Align** (**⌘-comma, Ctrl+comma** in Windows). The Space/Align Items dialog box appears, as shown in the following figure.

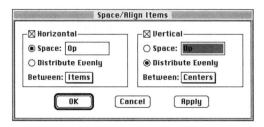

*The Space/Align Items
dialog box.*

If you check the Space option button, the items appear with the amount of space indicated in the text field either vertically or horizontally between them (or both, depending on which options you check). Those options let you determine whether the space is between the edges of items, the centers of items, or the items themselves. If the value is 0, the items will align directly on that edge, centered exactly, or butted up against each other.

To get items to align along their top edges, check the **Vertical** check box, select the **Space** option button, enter **0** as the value, and change the pop-up menu to Top Edges. The Distribute Evenly option distributes the items from side to side (horizontal) and top to bottom (Vertical), depending on the pop-up menu setting. (The best use for this—one most people can relate to—is the capability to fill a page with horizontal lines spaced exactly the same distance apart without doing math.) By using the Apply button, you can make several alignment changes at once from within the Space/Align Items dialog box.

The Least You Need to Know

Until this point in your life, you probably never realized the fascinating ways that text boxes could be grouped, duplicated, spaced out, and aligned. Well, now you know. In this chapter, you learned:

- ☞ Groups contain two or more items that remain in relative positions to each other.

- ☞ You can duplicate items precisely into position by using the **Step and Repeat** command (⌘-**Option-D**).

- ☞ Space and Align automatically aligns two or more items in several different ways.

Chapter 29
Page Juggling

In This Chapter

- ☛ Adding and deleting pages
- ☛ How to use the Document Layout palette
- ☛ Numbering all those wonderful pages
- ☛ Dividing a document into sections
- ☛ Creating and applying Master Pages

This is the chapter you've been waiting for. You'll learn all about the page layout options in QuarkXPress—from creating new pages in the same document to moving them around and deleting them.

I'll warn you now: This chapter isn't quite as amusing as some of the others in this book. Well, how can you make the Death and Birth of pages into an amusing anecdote? And what about the fascist regime of the Master Pages, whose rule (with a thickness of 3 points) has harbored over the innocent dwellers of every QuarkXPress document? If all this wasn't bad enough, most pages can't hold down a job *and* raise a family anywhere—they get moved around by you like you're Ming the Merciless. Oh, the horror of it all.

Adding and Deleting Pages

To add a page to your QuarkXPress document, select **Page→Insert**, which will display the Insert Pages dialog box, shown here. In this dialog box, you can specify how many pages you want to insert as well as where you want those pages inserted. In addition, you can tell QuarkXPress to link the text boxes on the new pages to a currently selected one.

The Insert Pages dialog box.

```
                    Insert Pages

Insert: [ 1 ] page(s)  ○ before page:
                       ● after page:    [ 1 ]
                       ○ at end of document

□ Link to Current Text Chain

Master Page: [ A-Master A ]

            [ OK ]    [ Cancel ]
```

If you select the **at end of document** option, QuarkXPress automatically places the new pages at the end of the document, keeping the order of the existing pages constant. If you choose After Page or Before Page, you need to enter the page number before or after which you want the pages inserted.

Deleting Pages

Let's set up a situation. You're at the office, and your mind has been wandering again. You've become distracted from the newsletter you're working on in QuarkXPress, and you've written a sonnet to a charming and lovely co-worker on page 5. Now you're lollygagging around on page 1, moving picture boxes a pica to the right, then a pica to the left. Suddenly, you hear your boss walk in the room behind you. You instantly panic. You've got to get rid of the incriminating evidence on page 5 before your boss wanders over to your desk and asks to see the newsletter. "What do you do, hotshot, what do you do?" (Say this like you're Dennis Hopper in *Speed*.)

Here's what you do: Delete the page. The easiest way to delete a page is to go to that page (⌘-J, **Ctrl+J** in Windows) and select **Page→Delete**. A dialog box appears, asking which pages to delete (see the following figure). The page you are on will be the current value in the text field. If you want to delete additional contiguous pages, type in the first page number, press **Tab**, and then type the last page to be deleted. You must go to this dialog box again if the pages you want to delete aren't next to each other.

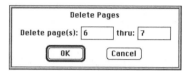

The Delete Pages dialog box.

Moving from Page to Page

The easiest way to go to another page in your document is to select **Page→Go To** or press ⌘-**J**, (**Ctrl +J** in Windows). Then in the dialog box that appears, type the page that you want to go to. The page you selected appears in the upper left corner of your screen at whatever view you are working in.

You can also move from page to page using the navigational keys on your keyboard. Pressing **Page Up** or **Page Down** takes you up or down the height of your window, while ⌘-**Page Up** and ⌘-**Page Down** takes you to the previous or next page, respectively. (Use **Ctrl+PgUp** and **Ctrl+PgDn** in Windows.) Pressing **Home** or **End** takes you to the top or bottom of your document respectively, regardless of your horizontal position on the page. Pressing ⌘-**Home** or ⌘-**End** takes you to the top of the first page or last page in the document, respectively. (Use **Ctrl+Home** and **Ctrl+End** in Windows.)

OOPS!

Deleting a page deletes *everything* on that page, including lines, text, and picture boxes and their contents. Make sure you are getting rid of the right page before you select OK. In addition, remember that when you delete a page early in the document, later pages are renumbered; so make sure the page you want to delete is really the right page.

The Document Layout Palette

All this moving around from page to page, inserting and deleting pages can get a little tiring, as you constantly change views and enter different dialog boxes. The Document Layout palette enables you to do these things and more.

To view the Document Layout palette, select **View→Document Layout**. It should appear and look something like the following figure. The information inside the Document Layout palette is relative to the number and organization of the pages in your document.

*The Document
Layout palette.*

The page in the lower section that has its page number outlined is the current page of the document. The pages appear as they do in your document, but in a reduced size. To move pages around, simply click on them, and then drag them into their new location. If you want to insert a page between two others, drag the page between the two pages until a double-sided arrow appears. When you release the mouse button, the page will snap into place between the other two.

You'll notice that as you move pages around, the page numbers change to reflect the new locations of the pages. This can get a little confusing, so it's a good idea to go to different pages in the document to see what is on those pages currently.

You might have noticed that, in documents that are made up of several pages, the Document Layout palette takes up a lot of room. Unless you have two monitors or a really big one, you probably don't want to have the Document Layout palette open all the time.

You can insert new pages by dragging down a page from the upper left onto the bottom section, and placing the page where you would like it. The only limitation in the Document Layout palette is that you can only add one page at a time, whereas in Insert Pages you can add as many as you need, all at once. To delete a page, select it by clicking on it once, and then clicking on the little page with an x going through it at the upper right of the palette.

Spread 'Em!

In this palette, you can also arrange several pages next to each other, side by side. This is called a *spread*. You can have up to five 8 1/2 × 11 pages next to each other in a spread. The only limitation is that the total width of all the pages must be 48" or less. This feature enables you to create brochures with several panels, or true fold-out gatefolds that appear in magazines.

Sets of two or more horizontally aligned pages are called **spreads**.

You can print spreads side by side (see Chapter 34) or separately at your discretion. The most beneficial thing about spreads is that they enable you to see on your screen what the printed document will look like.

Page Numbering

Automatic page numbering is one of the most powerful features of QuarkXPress. It may seem rather easy to just plop down a one, then a two, and then a three at the bottom of each of your pages, but what happens when you exchange pages two and three? They will be numbered incorrectly. Also, in a fifty-page document, this method is time-consuming.

To automatically number a page, press ⌘-3 or **Ctrl+3** in Windows (note the # sign above the 3). Doing so will actually put the number of the page right there in the text box. You can format that number anyway you want. Better than that, you can move this page anywhere in the document and the number will change to reflect the current page location! Amazing! (Special page numbering and automatic page numbering are discussed shortly in "The Sections Section" and "Mastering Master Pages.")

The Sections Section

Often you'll need to split a document into different *sections*. Why? Well, take a look at this book. The first part of the book consists of the title page, publishing info, contents, and introduction. Those pages are numbered with Roman numerals (i, ii, iii, iv, and so on). After those pages, the *real* chapters start with page 1, 2, 3, 4 and so on. If this book was created in one QuarkXPress document, it would have to be split into two different sections.

To split a document into sections, it is a good idea to first have several pages of the document created. Go to the first page of the first section (usually page one) and select **Page→Section**. The Section dialog box appears. Checking the **Section Start** check box tells QuarkXPress to start a new section here.

The Section dialog box.

Once you check the Section Start check box, the other options become available, such as which page number to start on, what prefix to put in front of the page number, and what type of number to use. In our example of this book, you would choose the **i, ii, iii, iv** option from the **Format** pop-up menu. Then you would go to the first page of Part 1, and once again select **Page→Section**. This time the Start page should be **1**, and the format would be standard (Arabic) numbers.

Sections are useful not only for introductory areas, appendices, and other such obvious applications, but also for when you're working on a manuscript you split into several pieces. The second, third, and other pieces have to start with a page number other than 1, and you can use the Section feature to begin numbering each section. This is especially good for formatting individual chapters of a book.

Mastering Master Pages

If there's one thing QuarkXPress doesn't handle as well as it possibly could, it's *master pages*. Until recently, they were awkward to get to—and they still are more than just a little confusing. This section will give you the important info on master pages and how to use them.

Mastering Master Page Page Numbers

The number one thing you can use master pages for is to automatically number all the pages in a document. Here is a step-by-step, no-fail method for doing just that.

1. In a document (a new one or an old one with lots of stuff in it), select **Page→Display→A-Master-A**. A-Master-A is the default name given to the original master page. A blank page appears. **A-Master-A** appears at the bottom of the document window instead of Page 1.

> **Master pages** are "hidden" pages of a document that contain the elements (text boxes, picture boxes, lines, and guidelines) that appear on every page in the document. With QuarkXPress, you can specify which pages have these master page elements and which ones don't.

2. Create a new text box in the upper right corner of the page that is about 5 picas wide and 2 picas high. Position this text box so that it doesn't overlap the automatic text box, if you have one. If you are in a facing pages document, you'll need to put a text box on each of the far upper corners of both pages.

3. Make sure you select the Content tool, click inside the text box, and then press ⌘-3 (**Ctrl+3** in Windows). Instead of a number, <#> will appear. This is because the master page doesn't really have a number.

4. Select **Page→Display→Document**. Look in the upper right corner of each page for the correct number.

5. If you don't want the page number to appear on one of the document pages (like page one), simply delete the text box from that document page.

And that's the long way. With some practice, you can set up page numbers in a matter of seconds.

Headers, Footers, and More on Master Pages

You can put headers and footers on your pages by creating them on the master page of the document. They will appear automatically on the document pages. You can also include lines, guidelines, or anything else that you think it would be helpful to have on every page in the document. You can't put text in the automatic text box that shows up on master pages. Instead, you must create a new text box and place text inside of it.

Master Guides

Remember those margin guides and the default settings for column and gutter width that you set up in the New Document dialog box? Well, the only place you can change them is in the Master Guides dialog box. And getting there is about as annoying as anything you'll run across in QuarkXPress.

First, display the master pages on your screen. Then select **Page→Master Guides**. In the dialog box that appears, change the margins and column/ gutter information. Click **OK**, and then redisplay the document. There is no other way to change master guides in QuarkXPress without going to master pages first.

Changing the Document Setup

Once you create the document, the only way to change page size of the document is by using the Document Setup option in the File menu (⌘- **Option-Shift-P**, **Ctrl+Alt+Shift+P** in Windows). The same text fields are in Document setup, allowing you to specify the exact size of the page. You must change Margin and Column Guides in the Master Guides dialog box.

The Least You Need to Know

QuarkXPress has a fairly good thing going with its master page setup and Document Layout palette. Here's what you learned in this chapter:

- ☛ You can add or delete pages by using the **Page→Insert** and **Page→Delete** commands, respectively.

- ☛ The easiest way to navigate through a document is by using the Document Layout palette.

- ☛ Master pages contain items that appear on every page in the document.

- ☛ You can number pages automatically by pressing ⌘-3 where you want a page number to appear.

Chapter 30
Whatever You Prefer

In This Chapter

- Document preferences versus application preferences
- A comprehensive list of changes you want to do *now!*
- Practical jokes I prefer

I would really prefer that you read this chapter, but you may prefer not to. If you prefer not to, let me tell you that preferences in QuarkXPress can solve many of the problems you would probably prefer to avoid. My preference is to change preferences before those preferably avoidable situations occur.

A Preference Primer

Preferences. We all have them, and being able to change preferences in a software program makes it just that much more user-friendly. The neat thing about preferences is that you can customize QuarkXPress to your style. You can change many, many things in QuarkXPress—from the measurement system to the font QuarkXPress starts with to the color of the Baseline Grid guides (normally a ghastly shade of pink).

Most of the preferences you can set are in the Edit menu in the Preferences submenu. Normally, you will have five different items in that submenu, but if you have any XTensions installed (such as EfiColor), you may have many more. Other preferences are in areas we have already talked about, such as colors, H&Js, and Style Sheets.

Preferences for Keeps

If you want to change a preference so that it's the default setting, change the preference when you have no documents open. If any documents are open, the preference change will affect only the frontmost document. When no documents are open, however, the change affects all documents created (via the New Document dialog box) after that change has been made. So, once again, a rule is in order:

Close all documents before you make "permanent" changes to documents.

Specific Document Preferences

To make changes to a specific document, open that document. As long as that document is in front of any other open documents, the preference changes will affect only that document.

There is one exception to the statement that changes to preferences affect only the current document if a document is open (or affect all future documents if there are no documents open). That exception occurs when the application preferences are changed. (To go to the Applications Preferences dialog box, use **Edit→Preferences→Application**, **⌘-Option-Shift-Y**, or **Ctrl+Alt+Shift+Y** in Windows.) These changes affect the way the entire application works, not the preferences for a specific document.

General Preferences, Major Changes, and Colonel Klink

The most dramatic of all the preference changes you can make are in the General Preferences dialog box. To get to it, select **Edit→Preferences→ General** or press **⌘-Y** (**Ctrl+Y** in Windows). The General Preferences dialog box appears, as shown in the following figure.

```
                 General Preferences for Document2
Horizontal Measure:  [Picas]      Points/Inch:    [72    ]
Vertical Measure:    [Picas]      Ciceros/cm:     [2.1967]
Auto Page Insertion: [Off]        Snap Distance:  [6     ]
Framing:             [Inside]     ☒ Greek Below:  [7 pt]
Guides:              [In Front]   ☐ Greek Pictures
Item Coordinates:    [Page]       ☒ Accurate Blends
Auto Picture Import: [Off]        ☐ Auto Constrain
Master Page Items:   [Keep Changes]
                ( OK )    ( Cancel )
```

The General Preferences dialog box.

Throughout this section (and the rest of the ones in this chapter), I focus on the important, relevant preferences that you can change. If it's just plain unnecessary, I'll pretend it doesn't exist.

Measure This!

The first things you can change are the horizontal and vertical measurement systems. You can customize both of them so that you don't have to view your document in centimeters, or whatever Uncle Fred changed it to last.

Does it seem strange that you can make the Horizontal and Vertical measurements different? Most QuarkXPress users outside the newspaper industry think so. Newspaper publishers think that this is the greatest thing to come along since the web press. They measure newspapers in columns that are so many picas wide and so many inches deep.

Stick Your Car Here—Auto Insertion

Auto insertion is the magical (though very annoying) way that QuarkXPress automatically creates pages for you when you run out of room in a text box. There are three places QuarkXPress can add these extra pages: at the end of the current story, section, or document. All of which are useful and all of which take into account that you don't know how long the document is going to be, or that it can be really any length that the text fits into.

However, the average publisher, printer, ad agency, or desktop publisher doesn't just have a faint idea of the size of the document, they have a budget. Therefore, they have an exact length. When creating a 32-page magazine, nothing is more annoying than having an extra page pop up every time a story runs too long (if you know writers the way I know writers, the stories always run long). Soon the document has 43 pages, 11 of which are blank or contain long-forgotten fragments of stories. Here is another rule for you:

> *Unless you are creating letters, reports, or book chapters exclusively, turn Auto Insertion off.*

Frames In and Out

The fourth option on the left controls how frames (all frames) appear on text and picture boxes. Your choices are rather simple: inside the text/picture box or outside (see the next figure). If the frame is outside the box, the box becomes wider and taller by twice the frame weight. Inside is the default and probably shouldn't be changed, since the outside setting is just plain confusing.

Frames can appear inside (left) or outside (right) of text and picture boxes, depending on the preference settings.

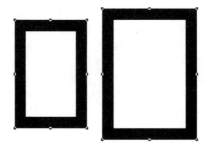

Under/Over Guides

This option controls whether guides appear in front of items on the screen or behind them. Having guides in front makes them easier to select and move, but they can get in the way of selecting and seeing items. Having guides behind items keeps them out of the way (snap to still works) but makes it hard for you to move them.

Greek Below!

Though it sounds like a battle cry warning that an army is about to pop up through the sewers, this option controls at what point size type is *greeked*. The default is 7 points, which means type smaller than 7 points will be greeked.

The weird thing about this setting is that it is totally dependent on the magnification level. For instance, 12-point type at 50% would be greeked at the default setting because it *looks* like 6-point type (which, mathematicians, is smaller than 7). This way you can view 3-point type as long as you set it at 234% or higher.

Greek Pictures (of Greeks, I'm Sure)

Checking this option will gray out any pictures in picture boxes that you have not selected. This is a big time-saver when the program slows to a crawl because you thought it would be fun to import pictures of each of your 300 friends. Keep it off unless the document you are working with is picture-happy.

SPEAK LIKE A GEEK

Greeked type is traditionally a series of Xxxx Xxxx xxxx, gray bars, or actual Greek words used instead of actual text so that the emphasis is on the design (or if the real copy isn't available). QuarkXPress substitutes gray bars for the Greeked type because it can redraw the gray bars much more quickly than it can render so many individual letters.

Typographic Prefs

Select **Edit→Preferences→Typographic** or press ⌘**-Option-Y,** (**Ctrl+Alt+Y** in Windows), and the Typographic Preferences dialog box appears, as shown in the following figure. Now, before you skip ahead to the next, not-as-intimidating section, let me assure you that it's really pretty simple—and that we won't go over more than half of it.

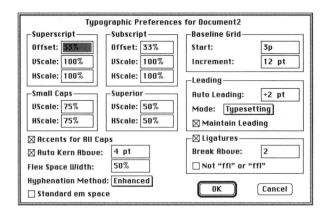

The Typographic Preferences dialog box.

As you might have already deduced, dear Watson, this dialog box enables you to change the way that type is used in QuarkXPress. Some of the options shouldn't even be changeable, and we'll just pretend they aren't, blowing them off with hardly a glance.

All Those Nasty %s Everywhere

The four boxes in the upper left corner of the Typographic Preferences dialog box take up about half of the box but do a rather simple task. They allow you to customize the way certain styles appear when chosen from the Measurements palette. The nasty codes next to the numbers are also quite simple.

HScale is the horizontal scale, where 100% is the normal width, 200% is twice as wide, 50% is half as wide, and so on.

VScale is the vertical scale, where 100% is the normal height, 200% is twice as tall, 50% is half as tall, and so on.

Offset is how far up (Superscript) or down (Subscript) the text is to move.

Just one piece of advice: I wouldn't change these until I felt comfortable about what those styles normally do.

Adjusting the Baseline Grid

Only read this if you've read the section on baseline grid, back in Chapter 18. Now you're probably wondering how to get the baseline grid to match the leading of most of the text in your document, right? Well, this is the place.

Change the Baseline Grid Increment to match the smallest common leading value you use in your document. Then go back to your document, and make sure that **Lock to Baseline Grid** is checked in the Paragraph Formats dialog box for all of your text. (To get to the Paragraph Formats dialog box, press ⌘-**Shift-F**. Use **Ctrl+Shift+F** in Windows.)

Auto Leading and You

Don't read any more until you have changed this value to +2 from 20% (the default). Done? Whew. The setting here controls how much leading QuarkXPress inserts between lines when you type **auto** into the leading field. At 20%, enormous amounts of space appear between lines, especially at large point sizes. When you set the field to +2 points, the leading is always 2 points greater than the point size, allowing for an eye-pleasing distance between the lines.

Some people prefer only one point between the lines (+1) while others prefer no extra space, sometimes referred to as "set solid" (+0).

Tool Preferences

You can access the tool preferences options by either selecting **Edit→ Preferences→Tools** or by double-clicking on any of the tools for which the preferences can be changed.

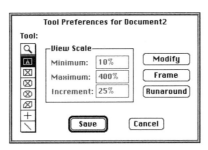

The Tool Preferences dialog box.

The buttons on the left will be gray when you select the Zoom tool, and the zoom preferences in the middle will be gray when you select any of the other tools.

Zoom Tool Prefs

The minimum and maximum settings are the minimum and maximum zoom levels when using the Zoom tool. You can still change magnification to greater or less than these values by entering the value in the Custom view box, in the lower left of the document window. The limits, however, are still 10% and 400%.

The increment is the amount of magnification or reduction when you click the **Zoom** tool or **Option-clicked** on the screen (or **Alt-clicked** if you're using Windows).

Tool Prefs

These preferences control what you create with each of the tools, and the particular attributes of those items. Clicking the **Modify** button brings up the Box Specifications dialog box for either picture boxes or text boxes; you can adjust most of the options within there, just as if you had chosen Item→Modify with an actual box selected. About the only things you *can't* change are the location and size of the boxes, as well as information about the pictures inside picture boxes.

In addition, you can specify the type of frame and runaround on each of the boxes you create with the **Frame** and **Runaround** buttons.

Application Preferences

The Application Preferences dialog box affects the way that QuarkXPress works, not the way you deal with a particular document. It doesn't matter if documents are open or not when you change these preferences. To access this dialog box, select **Edit→Preferences→Application** or press ⌘**-Option-Shift-Y** (**Ctrl+Alt+Shift+Y** in Windows).

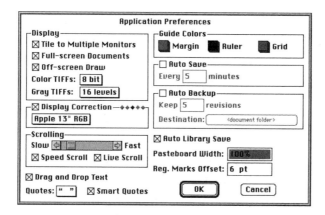

The Application Preferences dialog box.

This dialog box looks as nasty as (or possibly even nastier than) the Typographic Preferences dialog box. But it is actually quite simple—and a heckuva lot more fun.

Changing Guide Colors for Fun

Use the three squares at the upper right to change the guide colors (margin, ruler, and grid) from ocean blue, pea soup green, and tacky magenta to other equally horrendous colors, if you want. This preference, like many of the application preferences, is solely a personal thing. If you like these colors, don't change them (but have your eyes checked).

Quotes and Dragon Droppings

The two options in the lower left corner of the Application preferences dialog box are more important than any others in the whole dialog box. If you check the Drag and Drop Text option, text suddenly becomes hard to select. But you can get used to it easy enough. Drag and Drop Text enables you to move text by selecting it, clicking on the selection, and dragging it to its new location. QuarkXPress' incorporation of this feature is nowhere near as smooth as Microsoft Word's, but it works okay and is invaluable if you are, shall we say, a Dragon Dropper.

The Smart Quotes is not a listing of Einstein's sayings, but rather a mechanism that automatically changes standard inch and foot marks to curved typesetting quotes as you type. Check this, it is invaluable.

AutoSave and Backup

Use both of these or neither.

This may be a strict-sounding rule, but it's one to live by. Auto save automatically saves your document at specified time increments. Autobackup makes a certain number of backups of previously saved versions of your document.

AutoSave used by itself is a big problem. Let's say you bump the Spacebar when you have selected all your text. The text disappears and is replaced by a space. Of course, ⌘-Z (**Ctrl+Z** in Windows) will fix this, right? Suddenly the File menu becomes highlighted. AutoSave has kicked in to save your document, *without* your crucial text. Revert to Saved won't save you here, either. However, auto backup would. You could open up the previous version of the document, which actually has the missing text in it.

Preferences That Aren't Preferences

There are other things that fall into the category of preferences but aren't in the Edit menu's Preferences submenu. These are all things that you can change when no document is open and that will show up in future documents. All the changes you can make in the H&Js, Colors, Style Sheets, and the Hyphenation dictionary are examples of these preferences.

Changing the Normal Style

Whenever you create a new document with the Textbox tool, the text in the text box is the Normal style, which is (by default) 12-point Helvetica. However, what if you always use Times 10-point?

You can change this by selecting **Edit→Style Sheets** with no documents open. Double-click on the **Normal** style, and edit the style just as you would any other style. Now whenever you create a text box in a new document, it will be your typeface and size, as well as any other settings you've changed to the character/paragraph preferences.

Changing the Auxiliary Spelling Dictionary

This is one of those annoying things that you don't find written in many places. When you work with documents and perform spell checks (see the next chapter), there will be words, such as Alspach, that normally don't appear in the standard dictionary. However, since those words will appear again and again in your documents, you don't want QuarkXPress to flag the word as misspelled each time it runs across it.

So you add the word to an auxiliary dictionary. The problem is, there is no default auxiliary dictionary. If you create one while a document is open, it'll only be open when you're using that document; when you perform spelling checks on other documents, you'll have to open the auxiliary dictionary each time.

To prevent this, create an auxiliary dictionary with no documents open by selecting **Utilities→Auxiliary Dictionary**. Click **New**, type a name, and save your dictionary. Your newly created dictionary will then appear for all your new documents, solving your spelling problems forever.

Preferences Practical Jokes

Danger, Will Robinson! These jokes could get you fired or shunned (for the Amish in the audience) if used on the wrong people. However, they sure are a lot of fun. These are things that you can do to other's systems to have a little fun, or do to your own system to prevent others from using or abusing it.

The Blank Document

This is my personal favorite, and it is sure to cause even the most weathered QuarkXPress veteran a tumultuous time figuring out what is going on. With no documents open, go to the toolbox preferences. For each of the creation tools, click the **Modify** button and check the **Suppress Printout** boxes. Now, when your boss creates his weekly 10-page newsletter, every text box, picture box, and line he creates won't print. He gets a blank sheet from the friendly neighborhood laser printer, which he proceeds to kick, shove, or push off its perch shortly thereafter.

Changing this back to printable status is quite a pain; the boss will have to change each text box, picture box, and line back to printable status one at a time.

The Grayed-Out Type

This is a good one for new QuarkXPress users. With no documents open, open the General preferences and change the Greek Below field to 720 points (its maximum). Now in all new documents, text will always be grayed out—unless it is 720 points or 180 points at 400%. Heh-heh-heh. Of course, this is easily fixed by just changing the number in the Greek Below field back to 7.

The Invisible Type

Keep everything in the Normal style (no documents open) the same except for one thing: In the Character Attributes dialog box, change the color to white. White text + white background = invisible type.

No Little Text Boxes

With no documents open, change the text inset of the Text box creation tool to 288 (its maximum). In order for the text box to have an inset of 288 points on each side, it needs to be about 8" on each side. This can drive unsuspecting co-workers bonkers.

The Unclickable Zoom Tool

With no documents open, change the Zoom tool preferences to minimum 100%, maximum 100%, and increment 400%. Unless they drag, the viewing scale just won't change.

No Guides

In the Application Preferences dialog box, change the guide colors for each of the three types of guides to white. In the General Preferences dialog box, change the guides pop-up to behind. The guides will work, but they can't be seen!

Change These Prefs NOW!

You should change the following preferences immediately, with no documents open. Not all of them may apply to you, but overall they should make your life easier.

General Preferences   Picas/Picas, Auto Insertion Off, Guides in Front.

Typographic Preferences   Leading to +2.

Tool Preferences   Change the text box and the first three picture box tools to a runaround of none. Change the text box (modify) to a text inset of 0.

Application Preferences   Turn on the Smart Quotes option.

Auxiliary Dictionary   Create a new one.

Now you are ready, as they say, to rock-n-roll.

The Least You Need to Know

Changing your preferences *before* you start working is key to avoiding sessions where your temper runs rampant. Remember this stuff:

- ☞ Typographic preferences control the way QuarkXPress works with type.

- ☞ Preferences control the way you interact with QuarkXPress, and you can customize them in several ways.

- ☞ Change preferences with no documents open to make the preference changes effective for all future documents.

- ☞ Only play QuarkXPress practical jokes on those who can't hurt you financially or physically.

- ☞ Application preferences affect the way the program runs, not how you deal with documents.

Chapter 31
Stuff That Just Didn't Fit Anywhere Else

In This Chapter

- ☞ How to use the spell checker
- ☞ What libraries are, and why QuarkXPress doesn't fine you for being overdue
- ☞ How to place picture boxes (and text boxes) in the midst of your text
- ☞ Finding and replacing type and fonts

This itsy-bitsy chapter is crammed full of QuarkXPress information about features that really don't fit in other places, such as the spell checker, Libraries, Anchored text and picture boxes, and finding and changing text and fonts.

In fact, I tried to add even more stuff that wouldn't fit anywhere else, like my recipe for Chicken Simon & Garfunkel (you add parsley, sage, rosemary and thyme to mozzarella cheese covered chicken—yummy!), a compilation of David Letterman Top Ten lists (like The Top Ten Words You Can't Print In A Book From Alpha Books), or the shoe sizes of the world's leaders (Clinton wears a size 11). But my editor said no.

Trieen tu Yuz tha Spelchek fe Chure

The QuarkXPress spell checker is above average as spell checkers go, though it contains a smaller dictionary than I would have included. You won't find common terms, such as *displume* (to remove plumes, of course), *nystacin* (who doesn't have a bottle of that yellow powder), or even *zizith* (you know, those tassels worn on the outer fringes of your tallith). Those few exceptions aside, the dictionary is rather complete.

You can check the spelling of a word (selected or if the insertion point is in the midst of it), the entire story that the insertion point is in, or the entire document. I like checking the entire document, because all too often I have created a headline in one text box and a story in another. This way I can check everything at once, without feeling like I might have missed something.

To make any of these spelling checks, select **Utilities→Spelling** and select the item (word, story, document) that you want to check. QuarkXPress does the rest, and in a second or two, the Word Count dialog box (as shown below) appears, telling you how many words were checked, how many were unique (different from any other word checked), and how many are *suspect*. Suspect? Like a word that has committed a heinous crime? Well... no, not really. Instead, words that QuarkXPress calls *suspect* are really words that aren't in the main or auxiliary dictionary. QuarkXPress suspects that they are misspelled.

The Word Count dialog box.

You have no option at this point but to click the **OK** button, which brings up another bigger dialog box, called **Check Document** or **Check Story** depending on which option you chose from the menu. Here is the Check Document dialog box in all its splendor.

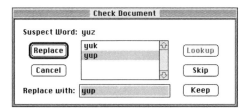

*The Check Document
dialog box.*

This dialog box will slowly plow through word after word that is suspect until they have all been replaced, skipped, or kept in the auxiliary dictionary. If a word similar to the one you typed is in the user or main dictionary, it appears in the box below the word you typed. The document will move around behind the box so you can see the context of the word, in case you aren't sure what it was you typed there. You can then select an alternative, keep the word in the user dictionary as is (QuarkXPress won't flag that spelling again), or skip that word and go to the next. Whatever you choose, the next suspect word will appear, with choices.

There's no limit to the size of your auxiliary dictionary (within reason) so feel free to keep names or places—anything at all that wasn't in the main dictionary.

Modifying the Auxiliary Dictionary

Instead of going directly to spell checking, select **Edit Auxiliary** from the **Utilities** menu, and a list of all the words you've ever kept appears. You can weed out words put there accidentally, or add words so the spell checker won't flag them in the future.

You can use your word processing dictionary in QuarkXPress if you know how to save it as a text file. The QuarkXPress dictionary is a text file with one word per paragraph, so simply open any standard text file and copy the contents of your word processing dictionary into it. Nifty.

Libraries

Libraries are special QuarkXPress documents where you can store elements you've created in QuarkXPress with the formatting and positioning intact. To create a new library, select **New→Library**. QuarkXPress asks you to name and save the library, after which an empty library palette appears. When you drag entries—any item, multiple item, or group(s)—into the library, they will appear in a much smaller form. By double-clicking on a library entry, you can name that entry so that you can access it later by name.

If you turn on the Auto Library Save feature (in the Application Preferences dialog box), QuarkXPress saves the library every time you add or remove an entry . If not, it'll be saved only when the library is closed. When you finish using a library, close it by clicking the white box in the upper left corner. The library disappears, but you can open it again with the **Open** command.

You can reshape the library to take up as much space as necessary on your desktop. When you do, the entries are realigned to better fit the current library shape.

A Picture That Thinks It's a Letter

One of the niftiest features in QuarkXPress is that it enables you to insert pictures right in with the text. "But wait," you cry, "That goes against everything you've told us. If this is true, the rest of the book is no good at all!" Well, that may be overdoing it a bit, but we're not really breaking any rules here.

You see, we're not going to put just a *picture* inside of a text box. We're going to put a *picture box* inside a text box. See? Isn't that more logical? And if a picture is inside that picture box, more power to it, right?

This is a fairly simple procedure. Select a picture box with a picture in it that isn't bigger than the destination text box (go for a 1" box or smaller). Select the **Item** tool and select **Edit→Copy** (⌘-C, or **Ctrl+C** in Windows). Select the **Content** tool and click on a text box. Select **Edit→Paste** (⌘-V, **Ctrl+V** in Windows). The picture box appears inside the text box.

Furthermore, the picture box acts like any other dumb letter, even though it may be a little big. If you put a return before it, it will move down a line. To select it, drag the insertion point over it. If you change the alignment to Centered, it moves to the center of the line. While it is inside the text box, you can change the size of the picture box (a few handles are available) or manipulate the picture inside the picture box.

The only problem that ever comes up with these "anchored" picture boxes is that it seems they are hard to delete. The problem is that you still think it's a picture box, when QuarkXPress thinks it is just another character. Place the insertion point to the right of the picture box and press the **Delete** (Backspace) key. QuarkXPress deletes the picture box as it would any other character. This technique also works for putting text boxes inside other text boxes.

Finding and Replacing

You can perform two major types of find and replace operations in QuarkXPress. You can find and replace text, or you can find and replace fonts. For this reason, QuarkXPress provides two similar, yet rather different dialog boxes. You access the Find/Change dialog box through the Edit menu, and you access the Font Usage dialog box through the Utilities menu.

Finding and Replacing Text

To find and replace a word or series of letters, select **Edit→Find/Change** (**⌘-F**, **Ctrl+F** in Windows). The Find/Change dialog box appears (see the following picture). The Find/Change dialog box may only show the top half on your screen if you checked the Ignore Attributes button. When you uncheck this option, the rest of the dialog box comes into view.

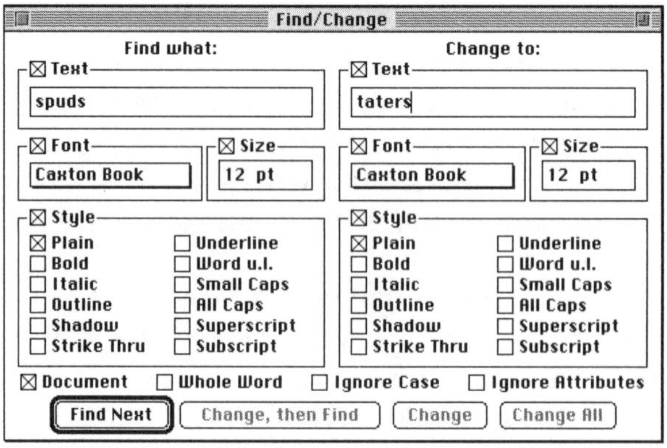

The Find/Change dialog box.

Under Find What, check the **Text** check box and enter the word or words you want to find. Under Change To, check the **Text** check box and enter the word (if any) you want to use in place of the word you are looking for. Click the **Find Next** button to find the next occurrence of this word. If you aren't searching in just one text box, be sure to check the **Document** check box.

If QuarkXPress finds the word you are looking for, the document behind the text box scrolls to the word. Click the **Change** button to change that occurrence. Click **Change All** to change all occurrences of that word to the word in the Change To text field.

Changing Fonts

You can access the Font Usage dialog box (shown below) by selecting **Utilities→Font Usage**. This dialog box enables you to change from one font to another, document-wide.

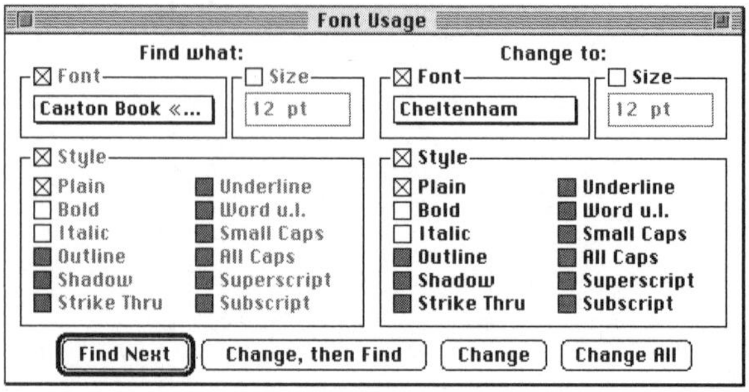

The Font Usage dialog box.

You might need to change a font throughout an entire document if, for example, your boss tells you that Cheltenham is the ugliest font he has ever seen, and you've just finished a newsletter in which you used almost twenty different weights of Cheltenham. To make the change (and keep the big guy happy), select **Utilities→Font Usage**, and then go one at a time through the fonts in the pop-up menu on the left, changing each one to your choice on the right. In a matter of minutes, you can change all the fonts in even the largest document.

The Least You Need to Know

Well, this chapter certainly has been a catch-all of topics, covering the magnificent spell checker and how to put the word "Shouting" in a text box and then put that text box into a library (just to prove that old wizened librarian wrong—there *can* be shouting in a library!). It even covered the process of putting pictures in text boxes and how to find and replace both words and fonts. Whew!

- ☛ Check spelling throughout an entire document by pressing ⌘-**Option-Shift-L** (**Ctrl+Alt+Shift+L** in Windows).

- ☛ Libraries are handy places to store formatted QuarkXPress items and their contents or graphics.

- ☛ You can place a picture box or another text box in a text box by copying the picture box with the Item tool and pasting it in a text box with the Content tool.

- ☛ Use the **Edit→Find/Change** command to replace occurrences of words with other words.

Part V
XPressing Yourself on Paper

Without printing capabilities, QuarkXPress would simply be a piece of software that costs $895 and takes up a lot of space on your hard drive. What would be the purpose of using it if you couldn't print out your work?

In the next few chapters, you'll learn about setting up the document to print, as well as printing it. I've also added a chapter that contains some of the darker aspects of QuarkXPress, specifically trapping, service bureaus, and color separations.

Chapter 32
Setting Up Your Pages Before You Print Them

In This Chapter

- ☞ Why you need to go to Page Setup before you print

- ☞ How to change your orientation

- ☞ How to ensure that you'll only have to change Page Setup once per document

- ☞ The mystery of the uncheckable boxes

So you think you're ready to print your document, eh? Well, it's my sworn duty to tell you that you just shouldn't print until you have checked (*unchecked*, technically) the Page Setup dialog box (Print Setup for Windows).

What Is This Silly Page Setup Box?

I know, I know. You have Document Setup and Blind Date Setup, and now there's Page Setup? When will it all end? Actually, this is one of the simpler dialog boxes in QuarkXPress, even though it seems rather imposing. And you usually only have to do one or two things inside this dialog box. I'll tell you about that in a little while.

To get to the Page Setup dialog box, select **File→Page Setup** or press ⌘**-Option-P** (**Ctrl+Alt+P** in Windows). My Page Setup dialog box is shown in the following figure. Yours may look a little different, depending on which printer you selected.

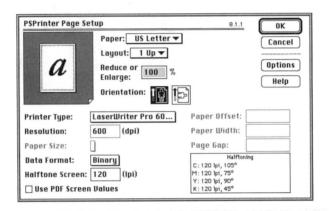

The Page Setup dialog box.

Choosing the Right Printer

If the wrong printer is selected in your Page Setup dialog box, mayhem may ensue. Documents may appear disoriented, graphics may not print, and the document may appear shrunken or enlarged. Other times, it just won't print at all. Make doubly sure that you select the right printer in the pop-up menu before continuing.

If your printer isn't in the list, you can contact your printer manufacturer and ask if there is a good substitute to choose or if there is a printer driver available for your printer. Usually one of the many printers in the pop-up menu list is a compatible substitute for another printer.

Unchecking the Evil Check Boxes

There are certain check boxes in the Page Setup dialog box that should always be unchecked. Of course, to keep things interesting, they are always checked, and there is no way to turn them off permanently (unless you are using Laserswriter 8.1.1 or later).

TECHNO NERD TEACHES...

While it seems strange that boxes are always checked and you have to always uncheck them, this is a system software problem and not a QuarkXPress problem. The engineers at Apple, in their ever-present wisdom, thought that those boxes should always be on, so they are.

Never ever let the four printer effects remain checked when you print. More trouble comes from leaving these boxes checked (usually the default) than from anything else. The four check boxes to uncheck are:

1. **Font Substitution.** When this is checked, QuarkXPress replaces any fonts that you don't have the printer font version of with a comparable font in the laser printer, which usually means Courier. If you don't have the font, you shouldn't be using it.

2. **Text Smoothing.** Use this setting to smooth out blocky text that's generated when there is no printer font available for the font you've chosen. See above.

3. **Graphics Smoothing.** This smooths out blocky graphics, for example, if you were going to print out the pixels in an icon at 500%.

4. **Precision bitmap alignment (4% reduction).** Don't do it. This reduces bitmap graphics so they print better on dot matrix printers, which usually have a resolution of 144 dpi (dots per inch).

If you don't have a laser printer, this entire chapter doesn't really apply to you. Instead, just make sure the settings are what your printer's manual recommends.

If you don't see your printer listed, try the Laserwriter and the General printer drivers first. Believe it or not, more printers work with the Laserwriter option than with the General option.

In addition to all these options being unnecessary, they also use up valuable printer RAM, which directly affects how fast a document is printed. All of these printer effects take up memory in your printer and then don't do anything, making your life potentially miserable.

If you are using PSPrinter or LaserWriter 8, these options only appear in the Options section of the Page Setup dialog box.

What's Your Orientation?

I'm facing due west as I type this. But the orientation I'm talking about is *page orientation*. If your document is taller than it is wide, the orientation is *portrait*, and you should have the left page icon highlighted. If your document is wider than it is tall, you should have the *landscape* (right) icon selected.

Normally, you set up the orientation correctly when you create a new document, but if you change the page size (via Document Setup), the page orientation may be off. If you don't have the correct page orientation selected, QuarkXPress crops off either the sides of the page or the top or bottom of the page.

Saving Your Page Setup

Here's a typical scenario. You finish with your document, save it, change the page setup effects, print, and then close your document. But the next time you open that document, you will have to change the page setup again. This gets old pretty fast.

Oddly enough, QuarkXPress doesn't automatically remind you to save the changes in the Page Setup dialog box. You can save them with the document, but QuarkXPress doesn't remind you to do it when you close the document. However, you can save yourself some trouble if you remember this rule:

Always save after changing Page Setup effects.

If you do, the next time you open your document, the Page Setup will be correct—and you can just pretend it isn't there.

Choosing a Printer (Mac Only)

Macintosh users have one reason to be jealous of Windows users, and that's that Windows users don't have the silly Chooser program to deal with. The Chooser on a Mac is used to tell the computer which printer to print to, as well as a host of other things, including file sharing.

To change printers, select the Laserwriter icon on the left of the Chooser dialog box. The available printers (usually one) appear in the box to the right. Click on the appropriate printer, and that's where your documents will print.

The neat thing about the Chooser is that you don't have to select that printer ever again. From now until eternity, you will be printing to that printer, even if you turn the computer and the printer off in the meantime. The only way to stop printing to that printer is by selecting another printer in the Chooser.

The Least You Need to Know

Setting up pages in QuarkXPress is much easier than you'd think. Keep the following in mind though:

☞ Access the Page Setup Dialog box by selecting **File→Page Setup**, or by pressing **Command-Option-P** (**Ctrl+Alt+P** for Windows).

☞ Always check the printer setting in the Page Setup dialog box before you print.

☞ Uncheck the four Printer Effects check boxes in the Page Setup dialog box.

☞ Save immediately after making Page Setup changes.

Chapter 33
Printing Primer 101

In This Chapter

☞ Printing documents as quickly as possible

☞ Fixing those documents you printed quickly so that they look right

☞ Everything you'd ever want to know about the Print dialog box—and then some

Nothing is more satisfying after a hard day of Quarking than to get a nice, bright, crisp printout of all that hard work you've done (except maybe indulging yourself in a bit of gluttony by eating several chocolate cheese-cakes in one sitting).

However, as with all jobs in QuarkXPress, printing requires that you check and uncheck boxes, set settings, and fill text fields that are just aching for the numbers of your choosing. This chapter is your guide to the basics of printing.

Printing on the Fly...

...stepping on the spider. You would've said it if I didn't.

In theory, you should be able to print by simply selecting **File→Print** or pressing ⌘-**P** (**Ctrl+P** in Windows) and then clicking the **Print** button (or whacking the **Return** or **Enter** key). That should print out a perfect page with all your stuff on it, right? Well, theories can be silly things.

A few things can go wrong here. The pages may come out misaligned. Depending on the resolution of the printer and the line screen setting, the grays may appear as a solid mass or as gigantic dots. Fonts may not print correctly, if at all. In fact, the document may not print at all, but the lights on your printer will just keep blinking, and blinking, and blinking.

I'd like nothing better than to go through as few steps as possible when printing in order to do it as quickly as possible. However, there are a few things that you must take care of in order for your printer to happily spew out page after page of usable QuarkXPress documents.

- ☞ First, set up the Page Setup dialog box correctly, as explained in Chapter 32.

- ☞ Second, decide which pages you want to print. More often than not, you'll want to print all of the pages in the document, but sometimes it is less than that.

- ☞ Third, decide which of the many options for printing you want to incorporate, and select them. (Read about some of the more advanced options in Chapter 34).

The Mystical Print Dialog Box

The Print dialog box, shown in the following figure, looks really nasty at first glance. Fortunately, it contains rather simple and basic options; QuarkXPress just arranged them in the most confusing manner possible. To display the Print dialog box, select **File→Print** or press ⌘-**P** (**Ctrl+P** for Windows).

```
┌─────────────────────────────────────────────────────────────┐
│ Printer: "6 Million Dollar Spooler"          8.1.1   ┌─Print─┐│
│ Copies: 1      Pages: ⦿ All   ○ From:    To:          └───────┘│
│                                                      ┌Cancel─┐│
│ ┌Paper Source──────────────┐  ┌Destination┐          └───────┘│
│ │⦿ All ○ First from: Auto Select ▼│ ⦿ Printer │    ┌Options┐  │
│ │   Remaining from: Auto Select ▼│ ○ File    │    └───────┘  │
│ │                          │  └───────────┘    ┌─Help──┐    │
│ └──────────────────────────┘                   └───────┘    │
│ Page Sequence: All          ☐ Collate      ☐ Back to Front  │
│ Output:  Normal             ☐ Spreads      ☐ Thumbnails     │
│ Tiling:  Off                Overlap: 3"                      │
│ Separation: Off             Plate: All Plates               │
│ Registration: Off           OPI: Include Images             │
│ Options: ☒ Calibrated Output  ☐ Print Colors as Grays       │
│          ☒ Include Blank Pages                              │
└─────────────────────────────────────────────────────────────┘
```

The Print dialog box.

The first thing to consider is the printer that you will be using. The top line of the Print dialog box shows you which printer you will be printing to. If you only have one printer, you can set this the first time you ever print from QuarkXPress, and that will suffice. If you have more than one printer, you may often be switching between printers; consequently, you may choose the wrong printer.

If the top line of the dialog box shows the wrong printer, click the **Cancel** button or press ⌘-**Period** (**Ctrl+Period** for Windows) to cancel printing and to exit the dialog box. Choose the correct printer in the Chooser, and then return to the Print dialog box. Don't forget to stop by Page Setup.

Printing Copies

Usually, you will want to print one copy of your document, which just so happens to be the default (1). If you want to print more than one copy, change the number in the Copies text field.

To print just one page, type the same page number in both text fields. To print a certain series of pages, type the first page in the first text field and the last page in the second text field. For example, if you want to print pages 4–8, type 4 in the first box and 8 in the second.

Printing a Range of Pages

To the right of the number of copies option is the option that enables you to print all the pages in the document or only a specific set of pages (such as from page 3 to page 5). Once you enter a number in one of the fields, the From option button activates.

Printing from Different Paper Sources

When you send your letter to your boss telling him you don't need his @#$@! company and that now that you know QuarkXPress really well you are going to work for a competitor, you'll want to use that competitor's stationery to really make an impact. However, only the first page of your fancy shmancy letter should go on letterhead, the rest should go on plain white paper.

You can do this right from QuarkXPress, providing you have more than one paper tray or have a manual feed tray in addition to a regular paper tray. Insert the letterhead in the Manual feed tray, check the **First from** option button, and select **Manual feed**. In the second (Remaining from) pop-up menu, select **Paper Tray**. Note: This only works with PSPrinter and LaserWriter 8 or newer model.

Printing to Your Printer

In the destination box, always make sure you choose **Printer** (the default) and not File. Checking File will create a file that you can send to the printer or a service bureau at a later time. You would only want to do this if you wanted to send your files to someone else who didn't have your fonts and pictures, but was going to print your document.

Changing the Way Pages Come Out

There are several options that control the order of the pages as they come out from the printer. Checking the Collate check box will print several copies of the document in order (1, 2, 3, 4 then 1, 2, 3, 4 then 1, 2, 3, 4) instead of together (1, 1, 1 then 2, 2, 2 then 3, 3, 3 then 4, 4, 4).

Checking the Back to Front check box will print the pages out in reverse order. This is useful for printers that print pages face up, where the first page ends up on the bottom of the pile.

You can change the Page Sequence pop-up menu to print out odd or even pages instead of all the pages, which is the default. This option is useful when you want to print double-sided pages; you can print the odd pages, flip the stack of printed pages, reinsert them into the printer, and print the even pages on the backs of them. This takes quite a bit of foresight and planning; therefore, I encourage you to experiment with the proper alignment in the paper tray before you do double-sided pages on a deadline.

Printing Blank Pages

This has to be one of the silliest options available. But what's sillier than its existence is the fact that I understand why it's an option. If you check this box, QuarkXPress prints out a blank sheet of paper where there is a blank page in the document. Why? Well, it might be helpful if you were creating a multiple-page publication and wanted to glance through it to see where ad pages or unintentionally blank pages appeared. It is also useful when the page before a chapter is blank, but counts as a page in the book.

Printing Master Pages

If you want to print out just what is on your master pages, display your master pages in the document, and then select the **Print** command from the **File** menu.

The Least You Need to Know

That was it. The basics of printing. Not too bad, was it? In fact, it's so much fun that you might find yourself getting a call from your local environmental faction, demanding that you cease and desist your excessive printing, lest the Pacific Northwest become as barren as southern Arizona.

- ☛ To access the Print dialog box, select **File→Print**, or press ⌘-**P** (**Ctrl+P** for Windows).

- ☛ Check the Page Setup dialog box and the destination printer before printing.

continues

continued

☛ A quick way to print page 1 only is to press **Tab**, **1**, **Tab**, **1** within the Print dialog box.

☛ You don't need to change most of the other options in the Print dialog box.

Chapter 34
Evil, Nasty, Rotten Printing Concepts

In This Chapter

- ☛ The lowdown on service bureaus, those bastions of mediocrity
- ☛ How to print color separations
- ☛ A primer on trapping issues

There are some things in QuarkXPress that are better left alone, like trapping, color separations, and having to deal with service bureaus. If you're a risk taker, heart breaker, etc., then dive right into this chapter, but don't say I didn't warn you.

Service Bureaus

When your laser printer isn't spitting out high enough quality pages, and you need something a little or a lot better, it is time to find a service bureau. Finding the best service bureau for your needs is really important, so this section tells you all about them, and what to look for in a good one.

What *Is* a Service Bureau, Anyway?

A *service bureau* is a business (or part of a business) that provides high-end output services for individuals or companies that don't have access to high-end output equipment. They provide this service at a fee, usually charged per output page.

High-end output usually refers to printing to *imagesetters*, Scitex or Crosfield drum imagers, or high-quality proofing devices. Many top notch service bureaus have all three output capabilities.

In addition to output services, service bureaus may also provide additional services such as typesetting, drum scanning (high-end image input), disk conversion, and other miscellaneous desktop publishing services.

Prices May Vary Significantly

Depending on the location, equipment, technical prowess of the staff, and quality control, prices for output and other services may vary dramatically. Usually, you get what you pay for, but it doesn't hurt to compare prices. Where I live, $7 per page is a fair price for 1693 dpi 8.5 × 11 output.

Imagesetters are laser printers, but they have resolutions ranging from 1200 dpi to 4800 dpi, and can etch images on photographic paper or film that must be processed and developed much like camera film. The cheapest imagesetters run less than $25,000. The largest ones with all the bells and whistles run more than $150,000.

When outputting documents that are a single color, you can often go with the cheapest outfit you can find. Even if it has equipment less than 25K, the output should be good enough for most single color jobs. It's the multiple color situation where people start running into problems.

Color jobs need the utmost care because individual color separations need to line up perfectly. They often won't, even with good equipment. It is a mix of quality control, equipment, and talented workers that will provide the best color separated output.

What to Look for in a Service Bureau

The following are requirements for a quality service bureau:

- ☛ They use QuarkXPress. If they don't, they aren't technical enough to be running a service bureau.

- ☛ The operators can tell you the brand of imagesetter and dpi settings that are available.

- ☛ They should change the chemicals in their processor *at least* once a week. Twice is better, and every day is a requirement for color work.

- ☛ They have a reasonable selection of fonts. You don't want to get in the illegal situation of supplying them with fonts, or the equally bad situation of having to save your files as POSTSCRIPT files.

- ☛ They can accept Syquest 44MB cartridges, which are the industry standard. Of course, if you don't have a Syquest drive, this won't matter. Better is the service bureau that takes all Syquest sizes as well as both optical cartridge sizes.

- ☛ They are helpful and friendly. These are people you have to talk to, and that can be difficult if they have an attitude.

Preparing Files for a Service Bureau

Before you up and go to a service bureau, there are a few things that you should do. First, within the document, select the **Prepare for Service Bureau** option in the **File** menu. This will send all the picture files from your hard drive that are in your document to the floppy, Syquest, or whatever medium you are using to transport your QuarkXPress file to the service bureau.

Check the fonts you are using and check with the service bureau to make sure they have those fonts. If not, they will have to purchase those fonts, or you will have to save your file as a POSTSCRIPT file (print to file in the Print dialog box).

Always, always, always print out a proof and take it with you to the service bureau. This will help them to determine right off the bat if the file they print does not look the way it should.

Color Separation

This section refers to printing out each color on its own page. Using color separations, your local printer can use different colored ink for each printed page, combining the colors on the final page.

Color separation doesn't just happen. Normal printing produces a combination of all the colors in a document—whether they are Pantone colors, process colors, or custom spot colors. A black and white printer will not differentiate the various colors unless the **Print Colors as Grays** check box is checked.

To print the colors in a document on separate sheets, the Separation pop-up menu must read **On**. When this is on, each color prints on its own sheet of paper. If any one color isn't used in the document, the page for that color won't print. Often, just choosing On will print all four separations (CMYK), even if they aren't used.

Process Colors

Process colors are cyan, magenta, yellow, and black. By combining different percentages of these colors, you can create most of the printable colors. When you use process colors, four output pages print for each document page, one for each of the process colors. The powers that be cleverly nicknamed this four-color-process printing.

Spot Colors

Spot colors are colors that appear on their own page. You can create as many spot colors as you want. A separate page prints for each spot color on a page in the document.

Combining Process and Spot Colors

You can combine two types of colors. A document can be five-color, meaning that it has the four process colors and one spot color. The spot color is used because it will be clearer than its process-color combination.

Other spot colors are used for colors that can't be produced with four-color printing, such as metallics and fluorescents.

For more information on colors in QuarkXPress, turn to Chapter 22.

Trapping in Season

Trapping is one of those things that will most definitely make you feel like an idiot if you are new to the subject. This section is just a primer.

Printing presses move along such great volumes of paper at such great speeds that they don't always align different color separations correctly. What happens then is a gap of white space between two adjoining colors. Trapping is a way of anticipating that error and protecting against it.

Trapping is the process of specifying that lighter colors overprint darker colors where two different colors butt up against one another. Actually, it's a little more technical than that, but that's what it boils down to.

The best rule of thumb is to leave trapping up to the experts. If they don't have the capability to do your trapping, find an expert to look at your particular document and tell you how to trap it. Another rule of thumb is that you can overprint the edges of darker colors with the edges of lighter colors by *spreading* the lighter color into the darker color. And the final rule (I'm out of thumbs) is that you can set black to *overprint* most other colors to prevent white space gaps.

How to Trap

QuarkXPress has automatic built-in trapping, which you can learn a great deal from. Place an object of one color on top of an object of another color, and then select **View→Show Trap Info**. The Trap Information palette appears, telling you which object is spreading, choking, or overprinting. If you click on the little question mark that appears, QuarkXPress explains why that particular trapping is taking place.

Should you want to change the automatic trapping, you may do so by choosing a pop-up menu, changing the overprint to spread or choke, and specifying how much.

Better to Trap After the Fact

There are two excellent products on the market that enable you to trap after you complete the document but before it zips out of the imagesetter. Island Trapper and TrapWise each cost several thousand dollars, but they trap better than QuarkXPress—and provide options that make the professionals drool.

If your service bureau has one of these software packages (many do), they can do the trapping on your document for you. Of course, they will undoubtedly charge you an arm and a leg for the service, but the software will trap your document perfectly!

The Least You Need to Know

A good thing to keep in mind when reviewing the stuff in this chapter is that *everyone else knows more than you.* Even if that isn't the case, you are much better off nodding quietly as your printer reads off what he says is the best trapping amount, and your service bureau tells you why they think QuarkXPress is not as good as FrameMaker (don't ask, just keep nodding quietly).

- ☞ Service bureaus are companies that provide high-resolution output and other computer-related services.

- ☞ Color separations are individual pages printed for each color in a document page.

- ☞ Trapping is the practice of anticipating and preventing white gaps from appearing in printed color documents.

Part VI
XTra Goodies

I can't end the book on that last chapter, leaving you muttering and spitting about nasty printing concepts. So I've thrown in these last few chapters, as well as a complete listing of Geek-like terms.

The chapter on XTensions tells you about some of the great add-ons for QuarkXPress, and the troubleshooting chapter tells you about how to avoid some of the great disasters common with QuarkXPress.

Chapter 35
Terrific XTensions

In This Chapter

- ☞ All about XTensions
- ☞ How to get XTensions
- ☞ A look at that there Thing-a-ma-bob XTension
- ☞ The Cool Blends XTension
- ☞ The Stars and Stripes XTension

The entire concept of XTensions is quite humorous, when you think about it. It's like Quark is saying to the world, "Our product is okay, but it's much better with this file that has extras in it, and we'll charge our customers for that file, on top of the $700+ they've paid for the main product." Ha! Unfortunately, when it comes to spending lots of money, most people lose their sense of humor.

An XTended XPlanation of XTensions

In QuarkXPress, XTensions are files found in either the QuarkXPress folder or the XTension folder that give QuarkXPress additional capabilities. (Whatever you do, don't forget to capitalize that T in XTension.)

XTensions enable QuarkXPress to do something it currently does not do. There are over one hundred XTensions currently available from one major source. You can add and remove XTensions at any time, and the next time you start QuarkXPress, it will reflect your changes. So if you add an XTension to QuarkXPress while it is running, you will have to quit QuarkXPress and then start it again.

Some XTensions come with QuarkXPress. There are others you can download from online services, purchase from various vendors, or find on this book's CD-ROM.

Xtensions Installed in QuarkXPress

To find out which XTensions you currently have installed, press **Option**, click on the **Apple** menu (press **Ctrl** and click on the **Help** menu in Windows), and pull down to **About QuarkXPress**. On the right is a list of the currently installed XTensions.

Where to Get XTensions

One company, XChange out of Fort Collins, Colorado, has a virtual monopoly on XTensions. Call them at 1-800-788-7557 for a catalog and ordering and price information. XChange, an XTension warehouse of sorts, is a supplier of third party XTensions.

The CD-ROM with this book contains more than eighty demo XTensions from XChange, so you can get some idea of what they do before you purchase them. You can also get XTensions by downloading them from various online services.

XTension XAmples

You already have several XTensions in your XTension folder from when you installed QuarkXPress. These are mostly filters for importing and exporting different text file formats. Some of the other XTensions that come with QuarkXPress include Cool Blends (discussed shortly) and the EfiColor XTension.

The remainder of this chapter discusses three XTensions and how to use them. Two of the XTensions are on the enclosed CD-ROM; the other—Cool Blends—comes with QuarkXPress.

The Cool Blends XTension

The Cool Blends XTension has one purpose: to create different color blends than you can create with the standard linear gradients option in the Colors palette. If you install the Cool Blends XTension, five more blends are available.

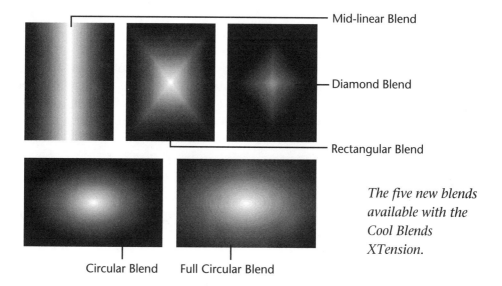

Mid-linear Blend

Diamond Blend

Rectangular Blend

Circular Blend   Full Circular Blend

The five new blends available with the Cool Blends XTension.

To create one of the Cool Blends, select an item with the Item tool, and select the blend from the pop-up menu on the Colors palette. Click on the name of the color you want to use as the first blend color. Select the #2 option button on the palette and pick a second color to which the first color will blend. Once you have two colors for a blend set, you can select a different blend from the pop-up menu to see how that blend looks with those colors.

Instead of blending from two different colors, blend from a tint of one color to another tint of that color. For instance, blend from 10% black to 50% black.

Banding is the appearance of stripes of solid color within a gradient. Banding usually happens when there isn't enough of a color change from one color to another, or when the two colors are very far apart.

When blending across a large area, it may be beneficial to create two custom colors, each with slight percentages of the other color. This can help hide potential *banding,* the scourge of the desktop publisher.

Use the Angle field to rotate your blends from the standard 0°. Nothing is more boring than a blend from left to right. Stay away from the common 90° and 45° as well. Try 15° or 70° for a more realistic looking blend.

Thing-a-ma-bob

QuarkXPress created the latest in the long line of Bob filters, Thing-a-ma-bob, expressly for version 3.3. Previous incarnations of this XTension were XTensions called Bob, Son of Bob, and Bobzilla. Most of the features in the earlier Bobs are in version 3.3 of QuarkXPress, but there are a few extra capabilities that you will need Thing-a-ma-bob for.

Make Price/Fraction

Under the TypeStyle submenu in the Style menu, two new items will appear called Make Price and Make Fraction. These automate creating prices and fractions.

You cannot undo a Make Price/Fraction command. Be sure that you want to do this before you choose it.

To create a price, select a dollar amount in dollars and cents (like 10.95) and select **Style→Type Style→Make Price**. The decimal (typesetting nerds call it a "radix") and the cents will shrink in size. To create a fraction, select a typed fraction (such as 3/4) and select **Style→Type Style→Make Fraction**. The 3 shrinks and is tucked above the slash, and the 4 shrinks and is tucked under the slash.

The Value Converter Palette

Thing-a-ma-bob adds the Value Converter palette to your already cluttered screen. To display this palette, select **View→Show Value Converter**.

The Value Converter shows measurements in six different measurements systems. You enter a value into the Value box and press **Enter** or **Return**. The Value Converter instantly displays that value's corresponding values in other measurement systems.

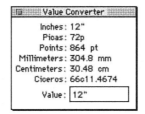

The Value Converter at work.

Remove Manual Kerning

With the Thing-a-ma-bob XTension, you can remove kerning from selected characters (it's a bear to get rid of otherwise). You must select the characters to be unkerned with the Content tool. The best way to do this is to click in the text box and press ⌘-A, (**Ctrl+A** for Windows), which will select all the characters in the text box. You can then select **Utilities→Remove Manual Kerning**, and QuarkXPress removes all the kerning in the range of text. All kerning changes to zero.

Stars and Stripes

This is one of the coolest XTensions there is. It does two amazing things. First, it enables you to create starburst-shape picture boxes (stars). Second, it enables you to modify the underlines for characters (stripes).

To create a starburst shape, double-click on the **Starburst** tool (which now occupies a new slot in the toolbox). Enter the number of spikes you would like and the depth of those spikes. Checking the **Random** check box makes the spikes vary in length. Click and draw with the Starburst tool in the document, and you can create a starburst!

To create a custom underline, select **Style→Type Style→Underline Styles→Custom**. Enter the color, shade, and thickness of the underline.

The Least You Need to Know

Adding XTensions is somewhat of an experimental procedure. Unless you read the accompanying documentation (yeah, right), you'll have to hunt for the location of an XTension's features like you'd hunt for a parking space at the mall on Christmas Eve. Here are a few things to keep in mind:

☞ XTensions are stored in the XTension folder in the QuarkXPress folder.

☞ QuarkXPress powers up XTensions the next time you start QuarkXPress after putting them in the XTension folder.

☞ There are free(!) XTensions on the enclosed CD-ROM.

Chapter 36

Troubleshooting Common Problems

In This Chapter

- ☞ The best places to get technical support
- ☞ Some common troubleshooting steps
- ☞ Answers to common problems

You probably didn't even know that it was trouble season (me, I thought it was still Elmer season). In this chapter, I will give you some hints and insights for solving some of the most common problems that can happen with QuarkXPress.

Getting Help from Others

Maybe this is a guy thing, but I really hate having to ask someone for help. It follows the same principle as guys (not that I am one or know any) who won't ask for directions when they've run out of interstate, paved roads, and dirt roads and are approaching the edge of a cornfield. So when it comes to getting technical support, I used to figure that if I didn't know the answer, I just didn't *want* help.

However, QuarkXPress is a monster of a program, and without help (you did, after all, buy this book), you can't get too far. When problems occur, the thing to do is ask somebody for help. If you work with others who use

QuarkXPress, that might be a good place to start. If that doesn't work, you might be able to get answers from a QuarkXPress user group. But if you don't find answers right away, don't panic. You can always fall back on the people who make the product.

Getting Help Directly from Quark

Quark actually encourages QuarkXPress users to call with questions. And technical support at QuarkXPress has become much more efficient, polite, and truly helpful in the last year, making it (in my opinion) one of the best places to call for technical support.

Calling Quark technical support (303) 894-3398 is something that you should not fear doing; average response time is well below five minutes from connection to technician. The best time to call is between 7 a.m. and 5 p.m. Mountain time Monday through Friday. The worst times to call are during lunches (11 a.m.–1 p.m. MST) and on Mondays—the angst of users suffering through a weekend of printing duress clogs the lines, and the wait can be much longer than usual. The best time to call is in the afternoon.

If you aren't in a rush (although you always are, I'm sure), you can fax your question to Quark at (303) 894-3398, and they will fax you back an answer, usually the same day. If you have access to an online service, such as America Online, CompuServe, or AppleLink, Quark has forums on each that are staffed with technicians who routinely answer questions, sometimes within the hour (if you get lucky).

Technical support by phone is free for 90 days after you purchase QuarkXPress. After that, you have a choice of two plans: $25/month of unlimited calls or $150/year unlimited calls. The yearly fee covers all sorts of incidentals, such as replacement disks and the "Expressions" newsletter.

You must have a valid serial number to use Quark's technical support lines. The person answering the phone won't even give you the time of day (I tried... no dice) if you don't have a real serial number.

Technical Support from Others

Computer dealers are not the best sources of support unless a desktop publishing or graphics specialist supplied your equipment/software.

User groups may be a great source of help, providing they are desktop publishing focused. Many user groups have question and answer sessions that graphics professionals attend. Also, many online services, in addition to having officially represented Quark forums, have user forums that contain some useful information.

One of the best places for help is your service bureau. Technicians at quality service bureaus know QuarkXPress inside and out, and more likely than not, have already run across the same problems you are experiencing now.

Trouble in QuarkXPress

All sorts of nasty things can happen when you are using your computer. Most of these problems are relatively harmless because they usually don't hurt the computer equipment. For example, QuarkXPress quits unexpectedly, the cursor freezes up, or you see a big box with a bomb in it in the center of the screen. The worst thing that happens during one of these "system errors" is that you lose everything that you have been working on since the last time you saved your work.

System errors very rarely damage the data on a computer. Such damage is most likely to occur when you are accessing the hard disk, especially when you are opening or saving a file. If a system error occurs when you are saving a file, chances are that the file is toast.

The issue here is not whether you remember to save or not; saving should be a reflex any time you pause in your work. I base the interval of time between saves on how long a program takes to save something. In a word processor, you can save after every sentence and never miss a beat. In QuarkXPress, saving takes a little longer, but not enough to really annoy me, so I save about every five minutes or so. When I am working with a multiple-page document, saving may take up to a full minute. A minute doesn't sound like much, but when you are humming along in QuarkXPress, 60 seconds of waiting can seem like an eternity.

Troubleshooting

Troubleshooting is the process you go through to determine where the problems are, and it is one of the most scientific things that you can do with your computer. You hypothesize what the problem could be, develop a theory, and test it. The test results prove or disprove the theory.

To begin troubleshooting QuarkXPress problems, you first determine whether the problem is related to hardware or software. If the problem is hardware related, your problems have just begun, because correcting the problem could cost a great deal of money in repairs, upgrades, or replacements. If the problem is software related, your task is to determine whether the problem is system software related or application software (QuarkXPress) related. If the problem is system software related, you may need to reload, reorganize, or delete parts of the system software.

If the problem is application related, you need to determine whether the problem is specific to a document or to the program in general. If the problem is related to QuarkXPress, the software may contain a bug. If the problem is related to a document, you can do a number of things to try to correct it.

Finding the Source of the Problem

The hardest part of troubleshooting is determining what the source of the problem is. Fixing the problem can be the most frustrating part, especially if you have misidentified the source of the problem. Be sure that you know the origin of the problem before you seek a solution to it.

After you discover the source of the problem, many times the solution is all too obvious, especially if the problem is hardware related. Application problems are the toughest problems to resolve because not only do you have to do extensive testing to be sure that the application is the cause of the problem, but tech support people are notorious for claiming that the problem just can't be the fault of their perfect software.

Most of the Quark technicians to whom I have spoken have been very helpful and haven't shooed me off the line immediately because "their software wasn't at fault." Instead, they have often gone out of their way to help me determine what I was doing wrong (and I was at fault ninety percent of the time) without making me feel stupid.

Hardware Related or Software Related?

The process of deciding whether a problem is hardware related or software related mainly involves eliminating the possibility that it is a hardware problem. Any time you are investigating an unexplained problem, no matter how insignificant it is, check all cabling before you do anything else. The most common cause of hardware-related problems is cable connections. Power cables become loose, printer cables are plugged into modem ports, video cables are plugged into on-board video instead of video cards, and so on. SCSI (pronounced "SCUZ-zy") cables on Macintosh computers are another constant source of problems. Sometimes the 50-pin end of a SCSI cable is attached to a SCSI port but not attached securely enough. Always make sure that the clips on the SCSI cables are connected correctly. At a quick glance, they often look fine; but further study can show you that the cable is not snug.

Loose SCSI cables can cause problems that seem to be software related. I wasted two hours reloading system software, getting a fresh copy of software by modem, and uttering words that would have garnered the afternoon an NC-17 rating, before I realized that my scanner's SCSI cable was slightly loose.

The following general tips and guidelines may help when you are troubleshooting hardware problems. However, it is not the final word on anything. If you aren't sure whether a particular device is causing a problem, I recommend that you have a Mac specialist (not a retail store) look over your system.

☛ If you have trouble saving a file, see whether you can save it to another hard drive or a floppy disk. If you are successful, try putting other software on the drive. If you can't load the software either, the problem is surely related to the drive.

☛ If you have display problems, try hooking up the monitor to a different computer or a different video card. If the problems persist on a different computer or card, the monitor (or monitor cable) is probably at fault.

☛ If you have printing problems, see the "It Just Won't Print!" section later in the chapter.

☛ Hardware problems may be the result of incorrectly configured software.

☛ If you can swap the questionable piece of equipment with an identical piece of equipment, try swapping it. If everything works fine with the alternative equipment, the original equipment is probably at fault.

☛ Memory and logic-board problems are common, but they are hard for the average user to fix. If you suspect that you are dealing with this type of problem, call in a Mac specialist.

If all the hardware seems to be fine (that is, no matter which hardware you hook up to the system, you experience the same problems), the problem is probably software related.

System Specific or Application Software Specific?

Solving this puzzle is easier than it sounds. Try to do the same task that you are having trouble with, but use different software. If you are successful, the application is causing the problem.

The following examples describe some possible methods for determining whether you have system problems or application problems:

☛ If choosing a certain font causes the system to crash, try choosing that font in another program. If the system crashes again, you know that the font is bad.

☛ If a job acts as if it is printing but never emerges from the printer, try printing a file from a different but similar computer. If the file prints, the problem is in your version of the original program.

☞ If choosing a certain color results in strange color patterns or the wrong color on the screen, try choosing the same color in another program. If the color is fine in the second program, the problem is in the original program.

If the system software is causing the problem, try to narrow down the problem by checking out any related files in the System Folder.

The quickest, most surefire way to tell whether the system software on the hard drive is causing problems is to start up with the Disk Tools disk that came with your System Software disks. If the problem doesn't occur when you are running off the floppy disk, the problem is almost definitely related to the system software on the hard drive.

Application or Document Trouble?

After you have determined that a problem is related to the application (QuarkXPress) and not to the system software or hardware, a fairly simple way to determine whether the problem is related to an application or to a document is to create another document and try to do the same thing in the new document. If you can perform the same task in the second document, the problem is related to the original document. If you can't, the problem is related to the application.

Techniques for Quality Troubleshooting

You can do many things to make your troubleshooting more effective so that you can get to the root of the problem and solve it in record time.

Before You Call Tech Support

When you call for technical support, the tech people will ask whether you did this, that, and the other thing. If you haven't done this, that, and the other thing, they may ask you to call back after you have done them. If you have been on hold for 15 minutes at your own expense and you don't want to let this tech person go, you may say, "Yes, now that I think about it, I did the other thing first, and I just got done doing this and that."

At this point in a tech-help conversation, the information you get is probably useless unless you really did do this, that, and the other thing. The tech person will ask what happened after you did that, and if this produced anything. Then you will be forced to lie again.

To avoid this scenario (whether you choose to lie and waste the tech person's time or hang up and try this, that, and the other thing), make a habit of doing several things before you call.

☞ Always try to determine that the problem is specific to either the application or to a particular document. If you can't identify the problem within a reasonable iota, the tech person may not be able to help you anyway.

☞ Narrow down the problem to a specific document if you can. If a document is the culprit, copy everything from that document to a new document and close the original. See whether the problem duplicates itself in the copy. Sometimes, individual files become corrupt, but the objects in them are fine.

☞ Always see whether you can duplicate the problem with extensions off (to do so, press the **Shift** key when you start up your computer).

☞ Restart the computer and run QuarkXPress. Immediately check to see whether the problem exists. If not, it may not be related to QuarkXPress.

☞ If you think that the problem is with QuarkXPress in general and not with a specific document, quit the program and delete the Preferences file that is located in the Preferences folder of the System Folder. Then run QuarkXPress again. If the problem still exists, reload QuarkXPress from the original disks.

☞ Increase the amount of RAM to QuarkXPress as much as you can. "Too much RAM is never enough." Please quote me on that.

☞ Always keep system information handy so that when the tech person asks for it, you don't spend valuable long-distance phone time trying to figure out how much RAM you have in the system and how much is allocated to QuarkXPress.

When You Talk to Tech Support

Listen to everything that the tech support person says and take notes. The tech support people are trained to answer questions; the more information you absorb, the better. If you don't take notes, you may miss out on important information.

In order to get a live tech person to talk to you, you must have a serial number and be the registered owner of the software. Don't try to pull a fast one on the Tech people, because they are probably tracing your call and sending a red flag to the Software Publishers Association as you speak.

Beating Common QuarkXPress Problems

There are two major problems you will encounter when using QuarkXPress: printing and printing. The former is no more difficult to troubleshoot than the latter, if that makes it seem a little easier. If I had a nickel for every possible thing that could go wrong with printing documents from QuarkXPress, I would have... well, a lot of nickels. Other things can go wrong, but most of them have to do with printing.

It Just Won't Print!

If your document never emerges from your printer's out tray, several things may be happening. First, check to see if you are connected by printing a document from software that you know prints to that printer.

Then create a new document within QuarkXPress and print it to the printer. If that doesn't work, it probably has something to do with the document you are working in.

Usually the problem is that you have checked some or all of the printer effects check boxes in the Page Setup dialog box. Uncheck them. Make sure you aren't printing pages that are blank or just don't exist. Click on a text box with text in it and select **Item→Modify**. Make sure that you didn't check the Suppress Printout box.

To narrow the problem down further, try to get different pages of the document to print. Change the Color separation settings. Change the fonts. Remember, if you go really overboard, just select **File→Revert to Saved** to get an unaltered version of the file back.

Sometimes documents are just bad. In that case, you can copy all the items from one document to another simply by putting two document windows next to each other and dragging items from one page to the other. You can even copy entire pages by viewing in Thumbnail view and dragging pages from one document to another, providing each document has the same size pages.

Fonts Are Wrong or Pictures Don't Print

Your printer may not have enough memory to print out the complex document you are pushing through it. If there are several graphics or even one really complex graphic on the page, lowering the line screen in the Page Setup dialog box will reduce printing time and problems.

If fonts are being replaced by a font that looks like typewriter type, you may be out of printer memory or may not have the correct printer fonts for that font.

Everything Disappears

This is one of the scariest things that can happen when using QuarkXPress. It usually happens when you accidentally click the Automatic Text box with the Content tool. The Automatic Text box will obscure anything else in the area it takes up, making everything else appear to have been deleted. The best thing to do is to press the **Tab** key, which will deselect everything on the page, showing your document as it was before your heart fell into your stomach.

The Least You Need to Know

The whole troubleshooting process is not for the weak-hearted, whether you bag it in early and call tech support, or work to find the cause yourself. It's frustrating, aggravating, annoying, and can be used as a defense in a court of law, "I'm pleading temporary troubleshooting, your honor." Here's what you've learned:

☞ Troublesome things often happen when using QuarkXPress, but you can overcome them.

☞ Learning the source of the problem is most of the battle.

☞ When calling for tech support, make sure you have tried the obvious first.

☞ Uncheck those Printer Effects check boxes!

Chapter 37
About the CD-ROM

In This Chapter

- What's on the CD-ROM
- Watching the tutorials
- Troubleshooting tutorial problems

If you haven't gone outside after buying this book and played football frisbee with the silver disc in the back of this book, read this chapter. If you just got in from a rousing match, remember to back-pivot for position next time.

That Seedy Thing

First, take out the CD-ROM in the back of this book. If it isn't there, you've already taken it out, and now you'll have to search for it in what is undoubtably a cluttered computer area. (The way I see it, if your computer area isn't cluttered most of the time, your computer just doesn't work.)

This is not an audio CD. Truth is, it won't even make that much noise if you break it in half (I don't suggest this course of action, however). This CD is a *CD-ROM*, which all drawn out and non-acronymized means

"Compact Disc Read-Only Memory." The important thing here is "read-only," which means you can't put anything on it, just get things from it.

Using the CD-ROM

This CD-ROM is Mac-compatible only. If you don't have a CD-ROM drive, run out to the computer-mart and get one. Good. Now, insert the CD-ROM into the CD caddy or tray and push it into the machine in the appointed slot. A little CD-like icon will appear on your desktop. Double-click on the icon and a window will appear with a bunch of folders.

The first folder, Tutorial, is explained in the next section. The second folder, Fonts, contains shareware fonts for your enjoyment. The third folder contains free shareware and demos of QuarkXPress XTensions. The Template folder contains a template for printing Rolodex cards with QuarkXPress. The QuickTime folder contains the latest version of QuickTime.

Kicking Back and Watching the Tutorials

After reading a few chapters in this book, watching related tutorials on what you just read is fun and really helps burn that information directly into your brain. So I've included more than seventy-five tutorials ranging on subjects from creating a text box to understanding trapping.

To watch the tutorials, open the Tutorial folder and double-click on the "Tutorial Program" file. After the program loads, just click once on what you would like to see, and it will be shown to you. The tutorials are organized into the same sections that the book is, so that you can easily find what you're looking for.

If you don't feel like watching a tutorial anymore, just press the Esc key.

What You Need

I tried to make this tutorial as painless as possible. In order to watch it you must have a minimum 4MB of application RAM (RAM not being used by the System or any other programs), a 68020 or better Mac, a 13" or bigger color monitor, and a double-speed CD-ROM player. You must also have QuickTime version 1.6.1 or better installed (1.6.2 for PowerMacs).

That's what you *must* have for it to work. I would also recommend that you quit all other programs, disable any unnecessary extensions and control panels, and have 8MB of RAM available. A triple or quadruple speed hard drive would be nice as well.

Troubleshooting Tutorial Trouble

If you run into trouble, disable the extensions and control panels you aren't using, make sure virtual memory is turned off, that QuickTime is installed, and that the computer is plugged in.

The biggest problem you will likely run into is audio trouble—sound skipping or sound not available at all. This is usually a low memory problem, and can be fixed by shelling out cash for more RAM SIMMS (single inline memory modules).

Speak Like a Geek: The Complete Archive

QuarkXPress is full of terms, concepts, and other things that are plainly stranger than fiction. This glossary serves as a guide to the language of typesetters, desktop publishers, and Quark-heads.

alignment   Vertical alignment of text controls whether text is flush against the top or bottom, centered from top to bottom, or justified (distributed evenly) from top to bottom of a text box. Horizontal alignment of text controls whether text is flush left, flush right, centered, or justified (distributed evenly) from left to right.

Apply button   Found in some dialog boxes, the Apply button enables you to see the result of the settings in the dialog box before you apply those settings by clicking the OK button. You select this button by pressing ⌘-A within a dialog box. If you press Option when you click the button or when you press ⌘-A, the Apply button is turned on and shows changes as you make them within the dialog box.

ascender   That part of a character that extends above the x-height of the lowercase letters b, d, f, h, h, k, l, and t.

auto leading   An automatic setting to provide a percentage or a specific amount of additional leading between lines of type. The default is 20%, but I like +2 points. Also how much space should be between cars on the freeway.

automatic text box   A text box that will appear on every page in a document if the Automatic Text Box check box in the New Document dialog box is checked when you create a document.

background color   The color of a text or picture box, which is behind the text or picture in that box. You change the background color in the Colors palette or by selecting Item→Modify (⌘-M).

banding   The appearance of stripes within a gradient. Banding usually occurs when there isn't enough of a color change from one color to another in a gradient, or when the two colors within a gradient are very far apart.

baseline grid   An imaginary series of horizontal lines used to align lines of text in multiple columns across a page or spread. You can view the baseline grid by selecting View→Show Baseline Grid.

baseline shift   The vertical position of a character on a line. A positive number moves the selected character(s) up; a negative number moves the selected character(s) down.

black   One of the four process colors. The "K" in CMYK.

bleed   What happens when you fall off your scooter racing down a steep hill as a child. Also the term used for objects that run off the edges of a document page in QuarkXPress.

bold   A heavier, darker version of a typeface. Select the type to be bolded, and click the "B" in the Measurements palette or press ⌘-Shift-B or choose Bold from the Style→Type Style menu.

borders   The frames that go around text and picture boxes. You create borders by selecting Item→Frame or by pressing ⌘-B.

bullet   A round dot used to indicate an item in a list. You create a bullet by pressing Option-8.

byte   The smallest useful piece of computer information. One character equals one byte.

caps Capital letters. You can force selected letters to capitals by clicking the "K" in the Measurements palette or by pressing ⌘-Shift-K.

CD-ROM Compact disc for computers, one of which is included with this book.

character Any single letter, number, or symbol that you type in QuarkXPress is called a character. Every time you press a key while working in a text box, a character is generated. Characters also include spaces, tabs, and returns.

check box A little box next to an option. When selected, check boxes have an "x" inside of them. Within a group of check boxes, any number of check boxes can be selected or deselected.

CMYK Short for Cyan, Magenta, Yellow, and Black. I know, Black starts with a B, not a K, but the people who came up with this thought that really stupid people might think that CMYB's last letter was for blue, brown, or Bugs Bunny.

color separation The process of printing each color on a separate sheet so the people at the print shop can make a plate for each color, apply ink to that plate, and print the finished job with each color applied independently.

columns Vertical divisions for text flow on a QuarkXPress page.

copyright symbol (©) Created by pressing Option-G.

crashing Sleeping really hard. Also when letters are kerned or tracked too tightly and overlap each other.

crop When a picture does not entirely fit within a picture box, it is cropped by the edges of that picture box.

cross-platform Refers to being able to take a file generated on one system (such as a Macintosh) and open it on a PC running Windows, and vice versa.

cyan One of the four colors in process color printing. A light blue.

default settings Settings that are set at the factory, which you can usually change. For instance, the QuarkXPress measurement system defaults to inches. If you prefer to work in picas all the time, you can change the default setting to picas instead of inches. Most of the default settings that can be changed appear in the Preferences submenu, located at the bottom of the Edit menu.

descenders All the letters in the word "gjpqy" have *descenders*, or letter parts that fall below the baseline of the word. These descenders smash right into underline characters when they are used together.

dialog box A box that demands your immediate attention. You must click OK, Cancel, or some other option for dismissing the dialog box before you can do anything else.

dot leader The person in charge of the dots. Also a tab that consists of periods spread between two other characters.

DPI The number of dots per inch used to draw an image. Laser printers are typically 300 dpi. Imagesetters range from 900 to 4800 dpi.

ellipsis (…) Three dots used to indicate a pause. Create an ellipsis by pressing Option-semicolon.

em dash (—) A long dash the width of two numbers (00) in the current point size. Create an em dash by pressing Shift-Option-hyphen.

em space A space that is the width of two numbers (00) in the current point size.

en dash (–) A shorter dash the width of one number (0) in the current point size; one half of an em dash. Create an en dash by pressing Option-hyphen.

Encapsulated PostScript A graphics file format or language that consists of PostScript code and can be placed in most desktop publishing software.

EPS Encapsulated PostScript. See above.

export   To save text contained in a QuarkXPress document in a file that can be read by a particular word processor. See *import*.

fill character   A character (you can have up to two) in the space created by a tab stop. Dot leaders consist of a "period" fill character.

flip   To reverse the horizontal or vertical appearance of a text or picture box. Also the first name of a comedian.

flush left   Text that is aligned on the left.

flush right   Text that is aligned on the right.

font   There is usually some confusion as to exactly what a font is, versus a typeface, typestyle, or font family. The terms font and typeface are both the most basic of terms, and apply to "Times Roman," "Helvetica Bold," and "Palatino Italic." Typestyle is simply a confusing term that can mean a hundred different things; consequently, you shouldn't use that term at all. Font families are groups of fonts with the same first name, such as "Helvetica," "Times," and "Palatino." A font is a set of characters that look similar in style and design.

formatting   The wide variety of changes that can be made to text, including making it bold, italic, a different font, a different point size, flush left, and so on. If it changes the text, it's a formatting change.

four-color process   A term used by printers, publishers, and designers that means that a print job will consist of four runs through a printing press (once each for magenta, cyan, yellow, and black) or one run through a four-color press. These four colors combine to create a whole spectrum of colors, creating photorealistic photos in full color. See *color separation*.

GB   See *gigabytes*.

gigabytes   1,024 megabytes. See *megabytes*.

greeked type   Traditionally a series of Xxxx Xxxx xxxx, gray bars, or actual Greek words of a particular font and size so that the emphasis is on the design (or that can be used if the real copy isn't available). In QuarkXPress, gray bars are substituted because it requires more memory to draw the letters, which therefore slows down scrolling and other functions.

groups   When several objects need to retain their proportionate locations to each other, you can group them together by selecting them and selecting Item→Group or pressing ⌘-G. Groups can be grouped together, and groups can be grouped with items. You ungroup objects by selecting Item→Ungroup or by pressing ⌘-U.

guides   Dotted or colored lines that are visual cues for alignment.

H&Js   Hyphenation and justification tables. Preset hyphenation and justification rules that you can create and modify by selecting Edit→H&Js. H&Js are applied to paragraphs using the Paragraph Format dialog box (select Style→Formats or press ⌘-Shift-F).

halftone screen   See *line screen.*

handles   Little squares on each corner, on the middle of each side, on each end of the lines of picture and text boxes, and at polygon intersections. Handles are only visible when objects are selected.

hanging indent   What happens to an indent when it commits a capital offense like treason. Also, when all the text lines in a paragraph except the first line indent to the right; the first line "hangs" to the left.

imagesetter   Film output (such as negatives) are created by a laser printer called an *imagesetter.* Using a photographic process, a laser burns images (teeny tiny little dots in various patterns and shapes) onto film. The film is then processed by running it through various chemicals (all of which smell terrible) until an image appears.

import   To bring text that was originally typed in another program into QuarkXPress and put it directly into a QuarkXPress text box. See *export.*

insertion point   When you are working with text in a text box or in a text field, a blinking insertion point (just a slim vertical line) appears to indicate where new characters that you type will appear. You can place the insertion point anywhere within a block of text, between any two characters that are side by side.

inter ¶ max   The maximum amount of space allowed between paragraphs in vertically justified text. If you leave extra space between paragraphs, the text will maintain the leading setting that has been specified. If you leave no extra space between paragraphs, the text will have even spacing from one line to another (called feathering).

italic   A text style in which letters are skewed to the right a bit. Make type italic by selecting it and clicking on the I in the Measurements palette or pressing ⌘-Shift-I.

JPEG   Joint Photographic Experts Group. A format for saving bitmapped images that significantly reduces the amount of disk space an image needs.

K   See *kilobytes*.

kern   To add or remove space between two characters. To kern, place the insertion point between two characters and select Style→Kern. A negative number removes space, and a positive number adds space. Kerning values are measured in 1/200ths of an em space. To kern 10/200ths of an em space at a time, place the cursor between two characters and press ⌘+Shift+[to reduce space or ⌘+Shift+] to add space. To kern at 1/200th of an em space, press Option in conjunction with the preceding keyboard equivalents. See *em space*.

keyboard equivalent   A shortcut to a QuarkXPress task that uses only the keyboard. Pressing ⌘-M is a keyboard equivalent for selecting Item→Modify.

kilobytes   1,024 bytes, commonly referred to as a K. There are 1,024K in a megabyte. See *megabytes*.

kissing   When letters just barely touch each other, they are *kissing* (awwww). When letters downright run into each other, they are *crashing*.

laser printer   A printer that uses the precision placement from a laser to place several dots on a page (841,500 on an 8 1/2 × 11 page at 300 dpi).

lazy printer   A commercial printer that never gets jobs printed on time.

leading   The space between lines of text, measured from baseline to baseline. Increasing leading is the process of adding more space between lines, while decreasing leading is the process of removing space between lines. The term leading was coined from the old typesetting machines in which actual lead strips were used to separate lines of type blocks. Very few hot lead typesetters are in use anymore since the advent of phototypesetting and then desktop publishing.

least common angle   The least common angle is the smallest angle that all of the selected items are rotated. If one of the items was not rotated, the value reads 0. If the first item was rotated 10°, the second 25°, and the third item 15°, the angle displayed would be 10°, which is the lowest of all the angles.

ligature   A pair or trio of characters that are joined together to make a more eye-pleasing result than if the two separate letters were just smashed together normally as a result of character spacing.

line screen   When a printer asks you what *line screen* or *halftone screen* you are using, he is talking about the screens used for determining the fineness of a gradient. Tell him the answer in lines per inch.

lines   What you draw with the line tools.

magenta   One of the four process colors. The M in CMYK.

margin guides   Visual guides positioned a certain distance (specified in the New Document dialog box when a document is created) from the edges of the document page.

marquee   A line that appears around an area that you want to select. To draw a marquee, you click in an empty area with the Item tool and drag at an angle. QuarkXPress creates a rectangular box, called a *marquee*, from the point you first clicked to where you release the mouse button. If any part of an item falls within the marquee, the item becomes selected.

master pages   "Hidden" pages of a document, in which the elements on them (text boxes, picture boxes, lines, guides) appear on every page in the document to which that master page has been applied. You can edit or delete master page items from QuarkXPress document pages.

MB   See *megabytes*.

Measurements palette   The palette that tells both item (left side) and content (right side) information about the selected object(s). Display the Measurements palette by selecting View→Measurements or by pressing ⌘-Option-M.

megabytes   Both RAM and hard disk space are measured in megabytes and are commonly referred to in print as MB. (Don't ever say "em-bee" though, always say megabytes, or if you want to sound like you're really on the cutting edge, call MBs "megs."). Most hard drives on Macintosh systems are at least 80MB, and some are as large as 1,024MB (called a "gigabyte," or GB).

option buttons   Little circles next to options in dialog boxes. You know an option button is selected when there is a black dot in the middle of it. Option buttons are grouped together; you can only select one option button in a group.

orphan   An orphan is the first line in a paragraph that stands all by itself at the bottom of a column or page. See *widow*.

page numbers   Press ⌘-3 to create an automatic page number that will show the current page. Very useful for placing on master pages.

PageMaker   A lesser page layout program that got to the market first.

Pantone colors   The industry standard for specific spot colors. Most printers can easily duplicate any Pantone color. Printers use this standard to ensure uniformity in color of inks from one shop to the next, or from coast to coast.

PCX   A common graphics file format. The PC equivalent of the PICT format on Macs.

pica   A measurement used in typesetting and page layout. There are six picas in one inch.

PICT   A common graphics file format. The Mac equivalent of the PCX format on PCs.

picture box   Pictures can only exist in QuarkXPress inside of *picture boxes*, which are created with any of the four Picture Box creation tools.

pixelization   Because scanned images are made up of thousands of little pixels, those pixels blend together to form photographs and pictures. When those pictures are enlarged, each of the tiny pixels becomes larger, which eventually distorts the image.

point   When you want to show someone something, you extend your index finger in the direction of that thing. Also a common typesetting measurement. Type size is measured in points. There are 72 points in one inch. There are 12 points in one pica. There are 4,561,920 points in a mile.

PostScript   An imaging system used as a page description language developed by Adobe Systems to create images by defining the outlines of those images, instead of specifying each individual dot that is printed.

preferences   Things that you can change about how QuarkXPress and your document work. Found in the Edit menu.

Pseudo-Item tool   An Item tool that you access if you press the ⌘ key when another tool has been selected in the toolbox (usually the Content tool). The main difference between it and the Item tool is that the Pseudo-Item tool cannot select more than one item at a time, whereas the Item tool can select any number of items.

QuarkXPress (spelling of)   The *real* QuarkXPress users always spell the software the way you will see it throughout this book: QuarkXPress. Note the capital X and P in the middle of the word. Note also that QuarkXPress is one word, and not two. To spell it "Quark Express" is a mortal sin.

radio button   See *option button*.

ragged right   When text is set flush left, the right edge of each line is allowed to stop wherever it's necessary, making it quite uneven.

RAM (Random Access Memory)   Memory that your computer uses for running applications (programs) and files (documents). The more RAM in your system, the more programs and documents, and the bigger the programs and documents, you can open at one time.

RGB   An acronym which stands for Red, Green, and Blue. This is a color system that is very good for creating and editing colors on a computer screen, where colors are created with red, green, and blue pixels. It is a color system that is not very good for creating and editing colors that will be printed using traditional CMYK process printing.

register mark (®)   Created by pressing Option-R.

rounded corner radius   In rounded corner picture boxes, the rounded corner radius is a measurement that states that the curve at such a corner would belong to a circle with that value as a radius.

rulers   Measurement bars that appear on the top and left edges of the document window. Show and hide rulers by pressing ⌘-R or by choosing them from the View menu.

rules   Use rules to separate paragraphs using the Paragraph Rules command (⌘-Shift-N).

section   A portion of a document that can have different page numbering than the rest of the document. You create numbering for sections by going to the first page of the section, selecting Page→Section, and clicking the Section Start check box.

spot color   A color that is printed separately on its own page.

spread   Two or more horizontally aligned pages.

style sheets   Macros that contain preset character and paragraph information, such as fonts, style attributes (bold, italic, underline), tracking settings, indents, space between paragraphs, tabs, paragraph rules, and anything else that can be applied to characters or text.

text wrap   Text can be set to flow around objects that are in front of the text box. Select the item in front of the text box and select Item→Runaround or press ⌘-T.

TIFF   Tagged Image File Format. A graphics file format commonly used on both Macintosh and Windows platforms.

toolbox   The set of tools available in QuarkXPress. If the toolbox is not visible, select View→Show toolbox to display it.

Toulouse   The brown kitten in Disney's *The Aristocats*.

tracking   A way of changing the amount of spacing to loosen or tighten a whole block of text at once. Kerning changes the amount of space between one specific pair of letters.

typesetting quotes   Called a number of names, including Curvy Quotes, Curly Quotes, Real Quotes, Smart Quotes, and strangely enough, Cool-looking Quotes. Inch and foot marks (" and ') are commonly referred to as Straight Quotes and Typewriter Quotes.

widow   A widow is a line on the top of a page or column that is separated from the rest of its paragraph on the preceding page or column. See *orphan*.

WYSIWYG   What You See Is What You Get. A typically overstated acronym describing how page-layout software displays documents. Nobody who is cool will ever say "wizzy wig," which is its pronunciation. Dweebs will spell it out. Better is WTHIT, short for What The [Heck] Is This?

X   All this X and Y stuff is annoying, isn't it? Well, remember that in everything except that science-fiction series on Fox, X means horizontal. Y (because we *like* you) means vertical. And you thought you'd never use all that silly stuff you learned in Mrs. Dull's geometry class.

XTensions   Files that reside in the QuarkXPress folder (inside the XTensions folder if you're using version 3.3), which QuarkXPress uses to be able to do additional things that weren't part of the original program.

Yellow   One of the four process colors. The "Y" in CMYK.

Index

Symbols

, (register mark), 339
130% document views, 52
200% document views, 52-53
386 PCs, 16
3D (moving items), 231-238
486 PCs, 16

A

About QuarkXPress command (Apple menu), 308
active document, 51
Advanced Apple Events Scripting option (Installation dialog box), 18
Aldus PageMaker compared to QuarkXPress, 11
Align On: tab, 148
alignment (paragraph formatting), 134, 138-140, 160, 329
  centering text, 139
  flush alignment, 139
  justifying text, 139-140
  numbers with decimal tabs, 147
  vertically aligning text, 239-241

all caps style, 120
Apple Events Preview option (Installation dialog box), 18
Apple menu commands
  About QuarkXPress, 308
  Control Panels, 105
Application Preferences dialog box, 270-272
application software problems (troubleshooting), 316, 318-319
Apply button, 148-149, 329
applying style sheets, 169
arrow heads (lines), 223
arrows (leading), 137-138
ascenders (type), 113, 329
auto hyphenation, 162
auto insertion (preferences), 265-266
auto kerning, 128-129
auto leading, 138, 269, 329
Auto Library Save feature (Application Preferences dialog box), 280
AutoBackup (preferences), 272
automatic flush right tab, 148
automatic text box, 330
  hidden page objects, 234
  troubleshooting problems, 322

AutoSave (preferences), 272
auxiliary dictionary, 273, 278-279
Auxiliary Dictionary command (Utilities menu), 273

B

background color, 330
  picture boxes, 208
  text boxes, 87, 208
  white as default, 208
Backspace key, 92
backtracking (dragging), 101
Balloon Help option (QuarkXPress 3.2 installation), 20
banding (colors), 310, 330
baseline grid, 330
  paragraph formatting, 157-159
  preferences, 269
  showing and hiding, 54-55
baseline line, changing, 243
baseline shift, 124, 330
Baseline Shift command (Style menu), 124
black (process color), 330

Who cares what you think? WE DO!

We take our customers' opinions very personally. After all, you're the reason we publish these books. If you're not happy, we're doing something wrong.

We'd appreciate it if you would take the time to drop us a note or fax us a fax. A real person—not a computer—reads every letter we get, and makes sure that your comments get relayed to the appropriate people.

Not sure what to say? Here are some details we'd like to know:

- ☞ Who you are (age, occupation, hobbies, etc.)
- ☞ Where you bought the book
- ☞ Why you picked this book instead of a different one
- ☞ What you liked best about the book
- ☞ What could have been done better
- ☞ Your overall opinion of the book
- ☞ What other topics you would purchase a book on

Mail, e-mail, or fax it to:

Faithe Wempen
Product Development Manager
Alpha Books
201 West 103rd Street
Indianapolis, IN 46290

FAX: (317) 581-4669
CIS: 75430,174

Special Offer!

Alpha Books needs people like you to give opinions about new and existing books. Product testers receive free books in exchange for providing their opinions about them. If you would like to be a product tester, please mention it in your letter, and make sure you include your full name, address, and daytime phone.